ZIONISM, MILITARISM, AND THE DECLINE OF US POWER

ZIONISM, MILITARISM, AND THE DECLINE OF US POWER

JAMES PETRAS

CLARITY PRESS, INC.

ISBN: 0-932863-60-4
       978-0-932863-60-7

In-house editor: Diana G. Collier
Cover: R. Jordan P. Santos

Library of Congress Cataloging-in-Publication Data
Petras, James F., 1937-
Zionism, militarism and the decline of US power / James Petras.
     p. cm.
 Includes index.
 ISBN-13: 978-0-932863-60-7
 ISBN-10: 0-932863-60-4
 1. United States—Foreign relations—Israel. 2. Israel—Foreign relations—
United States. 3. United States—Foreign relations—Middle East. 4.
Middle East—Foreign relations—United States. 5. Lobbying—United
States. 6. Zionists—United States—Political activity. 7. Militarism—United
States. I. Title.
E183.8.I7P48 2008
327.7305694—dc22

                      2008028103

Clarity Press, Inc.
Ste. 469, 3277 Roswell Rd. NE
Atlanta, GA. 30305
USA
http://www.claritypress.com

To Xana and Liam

ACKNOWLEDGMENTS

I would like to acknowledge the great editorial and substantive support of Robin Eastman Abaya and Diana Collier.

TABLE OF CONTENTS

PART I. ZIONISM AND US MILITARISM

II. EMBRACING THE ISRAELI MODUS OPERANDI OF ENDLESS WAR

III: MILITARISM AND THE DECLINE OF US POWER

"[A] passionate attachment of one nation for another produces a variety of evils. Sympathy for the favorite nation, facilitating the illusion of an imaginary common interest in cases where no real common interest exists, and infusing into one the enmities of the other, betrays the former into a participation in the quarrels and wars of the latter without adequate inducement or justification. It leads also to concessions to the favorite nation of privileges denied to others which is apt doubly to injure the nation making the concessions; by unnecessarily parting with what ought to have been retained, and by exciting jealousy, ill-will, and a disposition to retaliate, in the parties from whom equal privileges are withheld. And it gives to ambitious, corrupted, or deluded citizens (who devote themselves to the favorite nation), facility to betray or sacrifice the interests of their own country, without odium, sometimes even with popularity; gilding, with the appearances of a virtuous sense of obligation, a commendable deference for public opinion, or a laudable zeal for public good, the base or foolish compliances of ambition, corruption, or infatuation.

George Washington
Farewell Address

"A US House of Representatives Resolution effectively requiring a naval blockade on Iran seems fast tracked for passage, gaining co-sponsors at a remarkable speed, but experts say the measures called for in the resolutions amount to an act of war. H.CON.RES 362 calls on the president to stop all shipments of refined petroleum products from reaching Iran. It also "demands" that the President impose "stringent inspection requirements on all persons, vehicles, ships, planes, trains and cargo entering or departing Iran...

Congressional insiders credit America's powerful pro-Israel lobby for the rapid endorsement of the bills....The Resolutions put forward in the House and the Senate bear a resounding similarity to AIPAC analysis and Issue Memos in both its analysis and proposals even down to its individual components."

Andrew W. Cheetham
"House Resolution Calls for Naval Blockade Against Iran"
Global Research.ca
June 18, 2008

Part I

ZIONISM AND US MILITARISM

CHAPTER 1

HOW ZIONIST POWER IN THE U.S. PROMOTES U.S. WARS IN THE MIDDLE EAST

The True Cause of the War on Iraq: From Pretexts to Cover-ups

Explanations for the US attack on Iraq range from military-political pretexts to accounts focusing on geopolitical and economic interests.

The original official explanation was the now discredited claim that Saddam Hussein possessed chemical, biological and other weapons of mass destruction (WMD), which threatened the US, Israel and the Middle East. Subsequent to the US military occupation, when no WMD were discovered, Washington justified the invasion and occupation by citing the removal of a dictator and the establishment of a prosperous democracy in the Arab world. The imposition of a colonial puppet regime, propped up by an imperial occupation force of over 200,000 troops and irregular death squads, which have killed close to a million Iraqi civilians, forced over 4 million into exile and impoverished over 95% of the population, puts the lie to that line of argument.

The latest line of justification revolves around the notion that the US occupation is necessary to 'prevent a civil war'. Most Iraqis and military experts think the presence of the US colonial occupation army is the cause of violent conflict,[1] particularly the US military's devastating attacks on civilians, their financing of rival tribal leaders and Kurdish mercenaries, and their contracting of local police-military to repress the population. Since most Americans (not to speak of the rest of the world) are not convinced by these specious arguments, the Washington regime rationalizes its continued war and occupation by citing the need for a colonial military victory to maintain its world and regional status as a superpower, and to assure its Middle East client regimes that Washington can defend their ruling cliques and its hegemonic ally, Israel. The Bush White House and pro-Israel Congressional leaders claim a victory in Iraq will bolster Washington's image as a successful global 'anti-terrorist' (anti-insurgent) regime. These post-facto justifications have lost credibility as the war drags on, and popular resistance grows in Iraq, Afghanistan, Palestine, Lebanon, Somalia, Thailand, Philippines, Pakistan and elsewhere. The longer the war continues, the greater the economic cost and demoralization and depletion of military personnel, and hence the more difficult the task of sustaining the capacity of the United States to intervene in defense of its empire.

If the official political and military justifications[3] for the US colonial wars in Iraq and Afghanistan ring hollow and convince few, what of the commonly accepted alternative explanations for the war put forth *mostly but not exclusively* by critics of the Bush administration?

The War for Oil Argument

The major focus of the economic determinists of the war centers on the issue of oil, as in 'war for oil'.[2] These explanations in turn break down into several variants: The first and most popular is that the big US oil companies were behind the war, that Bush and Cheney were pressured by their Big Oil handlers into launching the war so that US oil companies could seize the nationally-owned Iraqi oil fields and refineries. A second, slightly modified, version argued that the White House was not pressured by Big Oil but acted on their behalf as a reflex action. (This is put forth to explain why the spokesmen for Big Oil multinationals were so conspicuously absent from the media and halls of Congress in the lead-up to the war.)

A third version argued that the US went to war to secure oil for US national security interests threatened by Saddam Hussein. This explanation cites the danger of Saddam Hussein closing down the Strait of Hormuz, invading the Gulf States, inciting revolts in Saudi Arabia and/or reducing the flow of Middle East oil to the US and its allies. In other words, the 'geopolitics' of the Middle East dictated that a non-client regime was a threat to US, European and Japanese access to oil. This is apparently the latest argument put forth by Alan Greenspan, a former proponent of the WMD propaganda.

The major advocates of the 'war for oil' (WFO) argument fail several empirical tests:

1. The oil companies were *not* actively supporting the war via propaganda, congressional lobbying or through any other policy vehicle.

2. The proponents of WFO fail to explain the efforts by major oil companies to develop economic ties with Iraq prior to the invasion. The oil companies, in particular Haliburton,[3] were in fact working

through clandestine third parties to trade in Iraqi oil, their access to the Iraqi oil market having been thwarted due to the US-promoted UN imposition of economic sanctions on Iraq.

3. All the major oil companies operating in the Middle East were mainly concerned with political stability, the liberalization of the economic policies of the region and the opening of oil services for foreign investors. The big oil companies' strategies were to advance their global interests through the ongoing liberalization process in the Middle East and conquering new markets and oil resources through their formidable market power—investments and technology. The onset of the US invasion of Iraq was viewed with anxiety and concern as a military action that would destabilize the region, increase hostility to their interests throughout the Gulf, and slow down the liberalization process. Not a single CEO from the entire petroleum industry viewed the US invasion as a positive 'national security' measure, because they understood that Saddam Hussein, after over a decade of economic and military sanctions and frequent bombing of his military installations and infrastructure throughout the Clinton years, was not in a position to launch any acts of aggression against Gulf oil companies or states. Moreover the oil companies had several real prospects of developing lucrative service and commercial oil contracts with Saddam Hussein's regime in the lead-up to the war. It was the US government, pressured by the Zionist Power Configuration (ZPC), which pushed legislation blocking (through sanctions) Big Oil from consummating these economic agreements with Iraq.

4. The "windfall profit" argument was then put forward by Greg Palast, who now argued that the war in Iraq was intended to generate huge windfall profits for oil companies due to a resultant oil scarcity. This argument—now that it is clear that American oil companies have not profited directly from Iraqi oil, not just because of the Iraqi parliament's staunch refusal to pass the oil law, but because of the drastically reduced production now coming out of Iraq—is round two of Pallast's insistence that the war is for oil, retooled to fit later developments. Now we are to believe—not that the oil companies are to reap massive profit from direct control of Iraqi oil—but that it's the very *scarcity* of that oil, which has contributed to rising global prices, which the oil producers anticipated, despite the fact that they, like all Americans, were assured by DoD neo-cons that American forces would be met with flowers.

The argument that Big Oil promoted the war for its own benefit fails the empirical test. A corollary to that is that Big Oil has failed to benefit from the US occupation because of the heightened conflict, continuous sabotage, the predictable resistance to privatization of the Iraqi oil workers and even of an Iraqi parliament elected under the supervision of its occupiers, and the general insecurity, instability and hostility of the Iraqi people.

The American Left jumped on Alan Greenspan's declaration that the Iraq war was about oil, as if word from the now increasingly discredited "maestro" represented a confirmation in the absence of any evidence. Yet every day that has transpired since the beginning of the war in 2003 demonstrates that 'Big Oil' not only did not promote the invasion, but has failed to secure a single oil field, despite the presence of 160,000 US troops, 127,000 Pentagon/State Department paid mercenaries[4] and a corrupt puppet regime. On September 19, 2007, the *Financial Times* of London featured an article, "Big Oil Plays a Waiting Game over Iraq's Reserves', on the conspicuous absence to date of the 'Oil Majors' in Iraq. Only a few small companies ('oil minnows') have contracts in Northern Iraq ('Kurdistan'), which has only 3% of Iraq's reserves. 'Big Oil' did not start the Iraq war, nor has Big Oil benefited from the war. The reason why 'Big Oil' did not support the war, the article noted, is the same reason they haven't invested after the occupation: "The level of violence is still unacceptably high…if anything the prospect of agreement appears to be receding as tensions between parties grow." Big Oil's worst nightmares leading up to the Zionist-influenced war have all been utterly confirmed. Whereas Big Oil's negotiations and third party deals with pre-war Iraq provided a stable and consistent flow of oil and revenue, the war has not only reduced these revenues to zero, but has all but eliminated any new options for the next decade.

Despite the war, liberalization elsewhere in the region has proceeded, and US oil and financial interests have advanced despite the increased obstacles and hostilities, which have grown out of the ongoing US slaughter of Muslims.

Big Oil, Texas billionaires, even big contributors to the Bush family political campaigns were no match for the power and influence of the severally-termed Zionist, Pro-Israel, or Jewish Lobby (which has been elaborated in earlier works,[5] and here is henceforth referred to as the Zionist Power Configuration [ZPC] when it came to Middle East war policy. They lacked the domestic and external influence of the disciplined grassroots organizing enjoyed by Jewish community organizations to overcome the ZPC's warmongering power over Congress, its position in strategic executive offices and its army of academic scribes from Harvard, Yale and Johns Hopkins churning out bellicose propaganda in the US media.

What is striking about the position papers and op-ed reprints in the *Daily Alert* is the total absence of any deviation from official Israeli pro-war positions. Whether it is killing children in Jenin, bombing population centers in Lebanon, or shelling Arab families relaxing at the beach in Gaza, the *Daily Alert* simply echoes the official Israeli line and blatant lies about human shields, accidents, gunmen among school children, and self-induced atrocities. Never in the entire period analyzed is there a single critical article questioning Israel's massive displacement of hundreds of thousands of Palestinians. No crime against humanity is too great for the Conference of Presidents of Major American Jewish Organizations to refuse to defend.

It is this slavish obedience to official Israeli policy that marks out the Zionist Power Configuration as something much more than just another lobby, as its 'left' apologists and even Walt and Mearsheimer claim. The ZPC is much more sinister, both as a transmission belt for the policies and interests of a colonial power hell-bent on domination in the Middle East, and as the most serious authoritarian threat to the democratic freedoms of Americans. No single individual who dares criticize Israeli policy can escape the long hand of the pro-Israel authoritarians. As will be discussed in greater detail below, booksellers are picketed, editors are intimidated, university presses and distributors are threatened, university presidents are blackmailed, local and national candidates are browbeaten and smeared, meetings are cancelled and venues are pressured, faculty are fired or denied promotion, corporations are blacklisted, union pension funds are raided, and theater performances and concerts are cancelled. And the list of repressive actions taken by these authoritarian Zionist organizations at the national and local levels runs on, arousing fear among some, anger among many more and a slowly burning resentment and growing awareness among the silent majority.

The National Security Argument

The second geo-political alternative argument for the war on Iraq focuses on national security issues. But after the First Gulf War in 1991 and eleven years of economic sanctions and military disarmament, Iraq was an impoverished, weak nation partially dismembered by the US-backed Kurdish enclave in the north and constant US bombing and over flights. Iraq was severely bombed several times during the Clinton regime and over 1 million of its citizens, including an estimated 500,000 children, died prematurely from conditions related to the US-imposed sanctions, which were so extensively applied as to result in the deprivation of food and essential medical and water treatment supplies.

Before the invasion in 2003, Iraq did not even control its shorelines, airspace, or even a third of its national territory. As the US invasion demonstrated, Saddam's military lacked the most elementary capacity to mount any defense in a conventional war; not even a single fighter plane presented a threat to any offshore US client or to the Strait of Hormuz. The stiff resistance to the US came only post-invasion in the form of irregular forces engaged in guerrilla warfare, not from any organized force established by the Ba'athist regime. In other words, no matter how far the concept of 'national security' is stretched to include US military bases, oil installations, client rulers and transport and shipping lanes in the Middle East, Saddam Hussein was clearly not a threat.

If, however, the concept of 'national security' is re-defined to mean the physical elimination of any potential opponent of US and Israeli domination in the region, then Saddam Hussein could be labeled a national security threat. But that takes the discussion of the explanation for the US war against Iraq to another terrain, to a discussion of the political forces that manipulated the phony WMD, regime change, and 'bringing democracy' pretexts, and as backup in the event of critical opposition, the 'War for Oil' propaganda, to justify and cloak a war for US and Israeli hegemony in the Middle East.

From Iraq War Cover-up to Iran War Propaganda

Even more importantly, the disinformation campaign about who was responsible for the US invasion and occupation of Iraq is highly relevant to the current propaganda blitz driving us toward a war with Iran. Despite the quagmire in Iraq, the pro-Israel power configuration beats the war drums for an assault on Iran with even greater insistency and successfully induces the Democratic Congress and Presidential hopefuls as well as the Republican White House to "put the military option on the table", even as Democratic candidates run on a commitment to withdraw American troops from Iraq.

Similar to the Democratic hopefuls, and without the slightest embarrassment at the contradiction, a number of liberal critics of the Iraq war have published articles arguing that Israel "really opposed the Iraq war". Writers as diverse as Gareth Porter, ex-CIA analyst Ray McGovern, Colonel Wilkerson (Colin Powell's Aide), ultra Zion-Con Michael Ledeen and others claim that in fact Israel had opposed the war against Iraq because it wanted the US to target Iran—entwining Iraq and Iran in such a manner as to kill two birds with one stone. Others argue that Israel had advised the US that an invasion of Iraq would have dire consequences for the Middle East, tipping the balance toward Iran and which they now claim to have predicted. These Israel exonerators point to other culprits, namely Bush-Cheney-Rumsfeld or the American Neo-Cons (who should better be known as the Zion-Cons) who, they insist, have acted independently of Israel or ignored Israeli priorities in the region.

There is an alternative view, which argues that Israel promoted the US attack on Iraq, and did all in its power through its US pro-Israel followers to design, propagandize and plan the war. This alternative view asserts that at no point did the Zion-Cons act contrary to Israeli state interests. In fact, Israeli officials worked on a daily basis with Israel's US agents inside the government, particularly the Pentagon's Office of Special Plans, to provide disinformation to justify the military attack. If, as we will show, Israel was deeply involved in pushing the US to attack Iraq and is behind the current disinformation campaign to provoke a US war against Iran, then anti-war forces and US public opinion must openly confront the 'Israel factor'.

We will argue that the effort to exonerate Israel is mainly an attempt to deflect US public hostility away from those American Israel Firsters who manipulated us into this costly, bloody unending war on Iraq. Exoneration of Israeli responsibility for the US invasion of Iraq not only allows the Jewish state and its US agents to escape any blame for the degradation of US forces in Iraq; it also seeks to provide them with a 'clean moral slate' for launching a new bloody US attack against Iran. Rather than seeing Israel as giving us a double dose of an incurable colonial disease, exoneration allows Israel and its agents to follow the same Iraq invasion pattern of manipulation and duplicity in leading us to war with Iran. Here, too, the White House and Democratic Congress, echoing Israel, are using inflated threats of nuclear attack, demonizing Iran's leaders, financing low intensity warfare through the training and funding of violent Iranian exile-based clients, pressing for economic sanctions and trumpeting 'failed' diplomatic maneuvers ... to lead up to a new war.

Taking advantage of the liberal-led (Zion-lib) exoneration for their role in the invasion of Iraq, the Zionist Power Configuration, through such loyal mouthpieces as Senator Joseph Lieberman, blames the Iranians for the deaths of US soldiers in Iraq. However, it is not the Zionist pro-war officials in and out of the government who sent young American soldiers to die in Iraq at the behest of the Israeli state to whom the US public should direct its anger, but rather the Iranians who are accused of arming and training Iraqi resistance fighters. Leaving Israel out and bringing Iran into the debacle in Iraq serves the Israeli purpose of covering its backside while inciting Americans into a new military adventure against the much larger and better-armed Iranians.

The exonerators of Israel are not homogeneous in their political background or goals. Some liberals, fearful of arousing a powerful Zionist backlash, seek to whitewash Israel's lobby operatives in the US as a way of gaining sympathy among pro-Israel Congressional Democrats and financial backing from wealthy Jewish liberals critical of the Iraq war. Democratic Party Chairman Howard Dean, following the new Israeli script, declared during a visit to Tel Aviv in 2006 that the 'the US invaded the wrong country!'

The price of the 'exonerate Israel' strategy is to overlook the powerful role that the Israel First lobby is playing in bringing us to a new war with Iran as part of a sequence of invasions promoted by Israeli strategists. These clever ploys are backfiring—at least as it relates to any efforts to promote peace. Playing to the prejudices of the liberal pro-Israel crowd in the Democratic Party has led to the current absence of any significant anti-war movement against the Zionist-led propaganda and war-mongering blitz against Iran.

There is no question that some anti-war Zion-Libs are trying to put some distance between themselves and the Zion-Con/Israeli policymakers who promoted the invasion of Iraq. But this does not come from any opposition to another new and more dangerous military commitment. On the contrary, the Zion-Libs criticize the discredited Bush-Cheney Iraq policy in favor of a new more aggressive war policy toward Iran. By exonerating Israel and its transmission belt of organized local and national Jewish and fundamentalist Christian organizations, the liberals have not found allies for peace—they have revived the powerful influence of Israel and its US apparatus which was being increasingly rejected by the US public and elements in the US military. By putting the blame for the debacle in Iraq exclusively on Bush/Cheney and their allies in 'Big Oil' and excluding the role of Israel, the ZPC and their toadies among the Democrats in Congress, the liberal exonerators, open the way for a new cycle of war in the Middle East. To prevent a future Zionist and Israeli-orchestrated US attack against Iran, we must be perfectly clear about who maneuvered the US into attacking Iraq.

Israel, the ZPC, and the Run-up to the Invasion of Iraq

Analytically, the differences between Israeli state policy and the leading US Zionist organizations are, with very rare exceptions, indistinguishable. The run-up to the US attack on Iraq is a case in point. From the late 1980s through the first Gulf War, the Clinton Administration's sanctions, daily bombings and territorial separation of northern Iraq, 'Kurdistan', from the rest of the country, to the 2003 US invasion of Iraq, the Israeli government pressured US Congress-people and senior policymakers toward bellicose policies toward Israel's 'enemies'. Israeli state policy urging further US degradation of Iraq was transmitted through the major Zionist organizations and key Zionist officials in the Clinton and later Bush administrations. Dennis Ross, Martin Indyk, Madeleine Albright, Richard Holbrook, Sandy Berger, William Cohen and others were the most important foreign policymakers toward the Middle East in the Clinton Administration and they produced and implemented the sanctions, bombings and territorial dismemberment of Iraq. Following their term of office, key Clinton Zionists went to work at pro-Israeli think tanks in Washington. Following the attacks of September 11, 2001, the Zion-Cons in top level positions in the Bush Administration and others—Ari Fleischer, Paul Wolfowitz, David Frum, Richard Perle, Douglas Feith, Eliott Abrams, Irving (Scooter) Libby, David Wurmser,

Eliot A. Cohen (State Department Counselor to Condoleeza Rice) Randy Scheuneman, (former director of PNAC, drafter of 1998 Iraqi Liberation Act, Chair of Committee for the Liberation of Iraq), Philip Zelikow (principal author of the 2002 National Security Strategy which outlined the Bush doctrine of pre-emptive war) —and key Zionist Congress-members like Senator Joseph Lieberman, called for the US to attack Iraq, as part of a series of sequential wars, to include Syria and Iran. They echoed the policies of the Israeli state and in particular, Prime Minister Ariel Sharon.

Israeli state officials at no point expressed any reservations or differences with the bellicose efforts of its highly placed liaison agents in the Bush Government, nor with its servile lobby, AIPAC, nor with the pro-Israel Op-Ed writers of the major newspapers and broadcast media. Zionist ideologues prevailed everywhere, berating the US military officials for their timid caution. Israel, consistent with its policies since the late 1980s, encouraged the Bush Administration toward an invasion and occupation of Iraq in all of its top level meetings with Rumsfeld, Powell, Rice and Bush. The Israeli media, with rare exceptions, demonized Saddam, played up his 'threat' to the Middle East and Israel's security, conflated Palestinian suicide bombings with Iraqi support for the Palestinian people's national aspirations, and energized their fundamentalist Christian allies in the US to follow suit in calling for an invasion of Iraq.

An analysis of the relationship between the Israeli state and highly placed Zionist officials in the Bush Administration reveals first and foremost that Tel Aviv laid out the strategic policies of eliminating Middle East regimes opposed to its ethnic cleansing of the occupied territories, its unlimited expansion of colonial settlements in Occupied Palestine, and the consolidation of Israeli hegemony in the Middle East. The Zionist elite in the Bush regime invented the pretext and the propaganda for war and most important, successfully designed and operationalized the US invasion of Iraq. This 'division of labor' included the Zion-Cons in the executive branch, backed by the Conference of Presidents of Major Jewish American Organizations (including AIPAC), and the regional, state and local Jewish federations through their influence over Congress.

Testimony by former Pentagon analyst, retired U.S. Air Force Lt. Colonel Karen Kwiatkowski, confirms that throughout the period leading to the Iraq war, Israeli military officials, intelligence officers and other high ranking functionaries had daily access to top Zionist Pentagon officials like Under Secretary of Defense, Douglas Feith. Frequent consultation, intelligence coordination and joint planning between top Zion-Cons in the Pentagon and top Israeli military operatives in the US indicates that there was close agreement in directing the US to invade Iraq. There was Zion-Con/Israeli agreement, confirmed in the immediate aftermath of the initial 'successful' occupation, that Iraq was the first of a series of invasions in the Middle East, to be followed by attacks against Iran and Syria. The Israeli joke current at the time was: 'Anyone can take Baghdad, real men go for Tehran.' In November 2002, Ariel Sharon, in an interview with *The Times* of London, called for the bombing of Iran 'the day after the US invades Iraq'.

The Zion-Con/Israeli blueprint for sequential wars was explicitly stated in the policy paper, "Project for a New American Century", a kind of American-Israeli *Mein Kampf* of US world domination in which Israel would be a co-benefactor of American military might and treasure. Most of the Zion-Con designers and executers of US war policy in the Middle East were listed as authors or sponsors of the 'New American Project'. Many were also contributors to the policy paper for Likud leader, Benjamin Netanyahu, which specifically called for the dismemberment of Iraq into manageable ethnic enclaves.[6]

Israeli intelligence 'disinformation' about Saddam Hussein's 'threat' to the region was embellished and adapted to the propaganda needs of the White House. While Israeli propaganda pounded away at 'Saddam Hussein as the modern Hitler', Zionist propagandist and Bush speechwriter, David Frum, repeated the same theme in the infamous 'Axis of Evil' speech in which Bush pronounced to the world his intention to attack other nations preemptively. Given the Israeli regime's pro-war propaganda, it is understandable that Israeli public opinion was overwhelmingly in favor of the war as were all the leaders of the major American Jewish organizations—but not the majority of American Jews, especially young Jews and those who were not members of any of the Zionist (Israel First) front organizations.

Israeli advisers and Zion-Cons in the US government were highly influential in the dismantling of the entire civilian and military administrative structures in Iraq implemented by Paul Bremer III—the so-called De-Ba'athification campaign and the dissolution of the entire Iraqi army—in order to decisively weaken any attempt to reconstruct Iraq as a modern secular republic serving as a focus for an Arab nationalism opposed to Israeli regional hegemony. The Israeli policy, pursued by the Zion-Cons, was to fragment the Iraqi state and society into pre-modern ethno-religious entities run by pro-Israeli Iraqi exiles (like Ahmed Chalabi who had business ties with Douglas Feith) incapable of ever challenging Israeli policy in the Middle East.

Israeli Zion-Con policy succeeded insofar as it secured the US destruction of the Iraqi state but it failed to secure a rapid victory on the road to the second phase of invading Iran because of the massive armed resistance by the Iraqis. In their blind racism against Arabs, the Israeli officials and their American agents discounted any possibility of Iraqis mounting a people's war against the destruction of their society. As the Iraqi resistance gained momentum and US military and economic losses multiplied, US public opinion turned against the war and began to ask who was responsible for the military debacle. In the face of this potentially dangerous question, Zionist propaganda shifted gears in order to cover their tracks. Top Zionist officials who framed the war quickly left the scene, beginning with the most obvious war perpetrators: Paul Wolfowitz, Douglas Feith and Abram Shulsky in the Pentagon, and David Frum and Ari Fleischer in the White House. The hardliners with less overt profiles in the State Department stayed on for a while longer—Elliot Abrams, Scooter Libby, David Wurmser. Libby later was convicted of a felony for his role in exposing the CIA operative married to Ambassador Joseph Wilson in retaliation for his exposing Libby's Zionist cohorts' fabrication of 'intelligence' in the lead up to the war.

War with Iran: The Highest Priority for the ZPC (and Israel)

Israel's campaign for the destruction of Iran has already led to two acts of war. In June 2006 Israel assaulted Lebanon, aiming, unsuccessfully, to destroy the Shiite political-military organization Hezbollah, an ally of Iran. A little more than a year later (Sept 6, 2007) Israel engaged in an even greater incitement, an unprovoked bombing mission over Syrian territory, purportedly destroying a military installation. Since Syria and Iran have a mutual defense pact, the Israeli action was designed to test the willingness of Iran and Syria to respond to a surprise (sneak) military attack.

The propaganda arm of the Israeli intelligence services prepared a piece of disinformation comparable to their earlier weapons of mass destruction lie: they claimed that they had bombed a nuclear site which North Korea was constructing and supplying with nuclear material. Israeli disinformation was immediately reproduced verbatim in the leading US newspapers, *Los Angeles Times*, *Washington Post*, *Wall Street Journal* and *The New York Times*, and all the major television networks. Pro-Israeli propaganda experts justified the attack and were in turn quoted in the *Washington Post*.[7] The *Post* quoted Bruce Riedel, formerly an intelligence 'expert' at the pro-Israel Saban Center for Middle East Policy (housed in the now discredited Brookings Institute):

> There is no question it was a major raid. It was an extremely important target. It came at a time the Israelis were very concerned about war with Syria and wanted to dampen down the prospects of war [*sic*]. The decision was taken despite their concerns it could produce a war [*sic*]. The decision reflects how important this target was to Israeli military planners.

In other words, Israel was "concerned about war" so it engaged in an unprovoked act of war in which its propagandists didn't even know the nature of the target!

On September 21, 2007, the *Daily Alert*, the house organ and principle propaganda sheet of the Conference of Presidents of Major American

Jewish Organizations (PMAJO) then reproduced the Riedel pro-war propaganda which had been cycled through the *Washington Post* and sent it out to all top officials and Congresspeople in Washington and across the country citing that newspaper as the source, activating its lobbyists in AIPAC to ensure US support for the blatant Israeli act of war. True to its deceptive propaganda function, the *Daily Alert* also published a highly misleading excerpt from an article in the *Financial Times*[8] which combined the Israeli propaganda line of a *'potential'* Syria-North Korea nuclear tie *without including* several paragraphs debunking the Israeli-Zionist disinformation campaign. The *Financial Times* article quotes Joseph Circcione, Director of Nuclear Policy at the Center for American Progress, as saying:

> It is highly unlikely that the Israeli attack had anything to do with significant Syrian-North Korean nuclear cooperation. The basic, well-documented fact is that the 40-year-old Syrian nuclear research program is too basic to support any weapons capability. Universities have larger nuclear facilities than Syria.[9]

A former senior Asian adviser to President Bush and expert on North Korea, now at the Center for Strategic and International Studies, also debunked the Israeli-Zionist nuclear weapon ploy: "I would be very, very surprised if the North Koreans were dumb enough to transfer fissile material to Syria or were trying to do work outside of North Korea in a place like Syria".[10] Equally damaging to the Israeli-Zionist war propaganda, the Bush Administration never even raised North Korea's supposed involvement with Syria during the entire series of meetings with that country during 2007, despite the fact that it was greatly hostile to Syria and looking for any excuse to attack it. In contrast to previous Israeli provocations in which the Bush Administration rushed to vouch for Israel's pretexts, Bush declined to comment on the Israeli attacks against Syria, likely advised by his intelligence chiefs that it was an Israeli act of provocation hoping to draw in the United States.

The issue did resurface much later, however, but more likely in relation to a US effort to impede its own negotiations with North Korea. As *The New York Times* wrote on April 24, 2008:

> When *The New York Times* published a lengthy account of the Syria attack on Oct. 14, revealing that Israeli and American analysts judged that the target was a partly constructed nuclear reactor, Mr. Bush and the White House refused to answer questions about it. Later, officials said they feared that the Syrians would retaliate against Israel if they felt publicly humiliated…

Mr. Hill has argued in private that the Syrian episode and the uranium enrichment are side shows, and that the critical issue is stopping North Korea from producing more plutonium and giving up what it has. But his State Department colleagues say that he has been told not to defend the deal, or even explain it.[11]

Clearly, the speculation that the US feared *Syrian reaction against Israel* is a canard, as Syria has long scrambled to avoid giving Israel any pretext to attack it.

The Israeli act of war against Syria and its defense and promotion by the US Zionist Power Configuration is but one of the latest steps in bringing the US into a joint war against Iran and Syria. A survey of the *Daily Alert* from January to September 2007 (180 issues)[12] reveals that there is an average of three articles in each issue calling on the US to engage in acts of war, impose strict economic sanctions and a naval blockade, and prepare for a widespread confrontation with Iran. There is not a single voice or article that questions Israel's pro-war posture. Every issue of the *Daily Alert* parrots the Israeli line, even when it involves supporting the brutal cutting of electricity, gas and drinking water to over a million trapped civilians in Gaza—a war crime under international law. In the words of the *Daily Alert*, Israeli-murdered unarmed teenage Palestinian boys and girls are labeled 'militants' or 'gunmen'. And the *Daily Alert* describes Israeli 'peace negotiations' as being carried out in 'good faith'—despite continued land grabs and assassinations of scores of Palestinians, including young kids even in the days immediately preceding the Annapolis Peace Conference. As the *Financial Post* pointed out, "In the time between George W. Bush, US President announcing the (Annapolis) peace meeting on July 16, 2007 and October 15, 2007, the Israeli military had killed 104 Palestinians including 12 children." [13]

After the November 2006 Democratic Party Congressional victory thanks to the increasingly angry anti-Iraq War voters, Israeli Foreign Minister Tzipi Livni attended the AIPAC meeting in Washington to urge the thousands of Zionist activists and a large contingent of US Democratic and Republican congressmen to continue to support the Bush Administration's occupation of Iraq, and incited them toward another war against Iran. In a highly charged screed, she ejaculated on the non-existent "existential threat" of Iranian nuclear capability. The entire Jewish Lobby picked up the line and went into action.

Zionist Power in the United States

The scope, depth and centralized structure of the Zionist Power Configuration far exceed anything which can be properly conceived of as a 'lobby'. In that sense, Mearsheimer and Walt, in their study of the Israel

Lobby, underestimate the power and political influence of the pro-Israeli forces. The measure of the ZPC power must take account of several factors, including its *direct* and *indirect* power. ZPC power is exercised directly on political, academic, and cultural decision makers to make sure their policies back pro-Israel, pro-Zionist interests. An even more *direct* expression of power is when Zionists occupy top decision-making positions and make policies on behalf of Israeli military and economic interests. Elliot Abrams, President Bush's key Middle East advisor on the National Security Council, is one of many examples, as is the Director of Homeland Security, Michael Chertoff, who allocates over three-quarters of available funds for the 'security' of private Jewish organizations, and Eliot A. Cohen who now serves as State Department Counselor to Condoleezza Rice.

Equally formidable is the ZPC exercise of indirect power through several mechanisms:

1. *Parleying influence* over a small group of Congressmen into a large majority. For example, AIPAC wrote up the bill, presented by Senator Lieberman and co-signed by Senator Kyl, labeling the Iranian Revolutionary Guards as 'terrorists', which paved the way for Bush to launch an attack. It was passed by 80 percent of Congress.

2. *Cumulative power* is the convergence of different sectors of the ZPC on a single issue. For example, pro-Israel writers and Jewish leaders from all major organizations and spheres of its media from Left to far Right joined to denounce Mearsheimer and Walt's essay and subsequent book, most resorting to either ad hominem attacks ('anti-Semites') or illogical and convoluted arguments ignoring the empirical data.

3. *Propaganda of the deed* is a favorite power tool of the ZPC. This involves *publicizing* the successful punishment of critics of Israel and the ZPC in order to intimidate current or future policymakers. An example is how Ziono-fascist Professor Alan Dershowitz of the Harvard Law School successfully campaigned, with backing from the ZPC, to deny Professor Norman Finkelstein tenure at his university post, thus serving as 'exemplary punishment' to any future academic critics of Israel. Dershowitz' campaign went so far as to slander Professor Finkelstein's deceased mother, a survivor of the Nazi death camps, as a Jewish 'kapo' or Nazi collaborator.

4. The ZPC has *multiple resources* that are *mutually re-enforcing* in both the private and public spheres. Large-scale, long-term party

and electoral financing buy Congressional influence. This in turn increases the power of the large minority of Zionist Congressmen in gaining control over party nominations and committee assignments in Congress. This in turn feeds back into greater influence for the ZPC in shaping US-Middle East foreign policy and facilitating access of pro-Israeli writers to the Op-Ed pages of the major dailies, weeklies and other branches of the corporate media.

5. *Longstanding, pervasive and totally one-sided propaganda* which demonizes Israel's Arab, especially Palestinian, critics, and paints Israel (the world's fourth largest and Middle East's only nuclear power) as a democratic fortress, surrounded by hostile authoritarian governments, has been invaluable in augmenting Zionist power. Through its access and partial control over most of the major media, the Zionist Power Configuration provides heavily biased reports on events such as the Israeli terror bombings of population centers in Lebanon, Gaza and elsewhere. The reputational power projected by the ZPC in the US counteracts reality in the Middle East to the extent that Palestinian victims of all ages and genders, suffering 40 years of Israeli military rule, land expropriation and constant violent assaults, have come to be viewed by the American public at large as aggressors while their Israeli executioners are viewed, in line with their portrayals, as virtuous, peaceful victims.

'Jewish Vote', 'Israel Lobby' or 'Zionist Power Configuration'?

Mearsheimer and Walt describe the pro-Israel power configuration as a 'lobby, just like any other US lobby', a 'loose collection of individuals and groups' outside of government, acting on behalf of Israel. Nothing could be further from the truth. The power of Israel in the United States is manifested through a multiplicity of highly organized, well-financed and centrally-directed structures throughout the United States. The ZPC include several score political action committees, many with innocuous names which disguise their pro-Israel agenda, at least a dozen propaganda mills ('think tanks') employing scores of former highly connected top policymakers mostly in Washington and on the East Coast, and the 52 major American Jewish organizations grouped under the umbrella listing 'Conference of Presidents of Major American Jewish Organizations' (CPMAJO). AIPAC and other national organizations (the Anti-Defamation League [ADL], and the American Jewish Committee [AJC], etc) are important influences at the national Executive-Congressional lobbying levels. But equally or even more important in censoring and purging critics, controlling local media and shaping opinion throughout cities, towns and villages are the local Jewish community federations and organizations which browbeat local cultural programmers, editors, bookstores, universities, churches and civic groups to deny public platforms to speakers, writers, artists, religious spokespeople, and other public figures critical of Israel and its Zionist disciples.

The power base of the ZPC is found in the local activist doctors, dentists, lawyers, real estate brokers and landlords who preside over the local confederations and their several hundred thousand affiliates. It is they who harass, badger, browbeat, raise money and organize propaganda junkets for elected officials, and ensure their support for Israeli wars and increases in the US multi-billion dollar aid packages to Israel. The local Zionist power structure organizes successful campaigns forcing state pension funds to purchase billions of dollars in under-performing Israel state bonds and to disinvest in companies engaged in economic transactions with Israel's self-described 'state terrorist' adversaries. Jewish-based pro-Israel student organizations spy on US professors who may or may not be critical of Israel, smear them in local and national newsletters, and pressure administrations to fire them. Even where fewer than one percent of the local population is Jewish, Zionist zealots were able to pressure the University of St. Thomas, a small private Christian college in St. Paul, Minnesota, to ban a Nobel Peace Prize-winning theologian like Bishop Desmond Tutu from speaking on its campus. The Zionist octopus has extended its tentacles far beyond the traditional centers of big city power and national politics, reaching into remote towns and cultural spheres. Not even the American small town obituary pages are exempt: When a Connecticut newspaper published a memorial in May, 2003, for a prominent Palestinian grandmother and community leader from Hebron, 61 year old Shadeen abu Hijleh, who was shot in her home by Israelis soldiers, members of the local Jewish confederation expressed outrage at the exposure of Israeli military crimes—thus censoring a moving obituary page tribute written by her American friends and relatives.

Centralized structures—coordinated policy, targets, quotas, fund-raising, large-scale special campaigns, the generation of fear of antipathetic labeling ('anti-Semites' and 'self-hating Jews'), black lists, and networks—all are integral parts of the ZPC. Mearsheimer and Walt have failed to analyze the organizational relations between the head office, regional staff and local organizations of the major pro-Israel Jewish organizations and how quickly they can be mobilized to stigmatize, censor or support a given speaker, activity or fundraiser in favor of Israeli interests.

Throughout the country, the newsletters of local Jewish Community Relations Councils have parroted the line or reprinted libelous canards of their national offices denouncing Mearsheimer and Walt's book *The Israel*

Lobby—and from their rather ill-informed caricatures of M and W's discussion, it is clear they have barely even read the book's cover.

One thing is clear from the largely emotional ejaculations from the predominantly Jewish intellectuals' attacks against the Mearsheimer/Walt book, the intellectual level of contemporary Jewish intellectuals has seriously deteriorated to the point that envy, communal spite and partisan vitriol has gotten the better of a reasoned review of data and logic. The literary efforts by Abraham Foxman of the ADL to answer M and W are reminiscent of the Stalinist diatribes featured during the Moscow show trials of the 1930s (our Jewish version of Andrei Vishinsky). What accounts for the influence of these intellectual mediocrities is neither the evil vapors emanating from their venomous writing, nor their appeal to reason—though some pretense to reasoned debate is made by Zionist progressives, if such exist—but the fact that their repetitious messages circulate throughout their mass media outlets uncontested.

Having organized the war through falsified data via the top two officials in the Pentagon (Wolfowitz and Douglas Feith), the Vice President's office (Wurmser and Irving Scooter Libby) and the National Security Council (Elliot Abrams) and the President's office (Ari Fleischer) and written Bush's pre-emptive war speech (David Frum), the ZPC are now fearful they will face the anger of the American people who have suffered the loss of thousands of soldiers—to an extent not experienced by the authors and implementers of this war for Israel. To avoid identification with this disastrous war, Zionist Power Configuration war planners and propagandists have resorted to lies (denial of the crucial role of Israel in bringing the US to war) and the somewhat more clever operators like Alan Greenspan have joined the mindless American left to drag out the old canard of 'War for Oil'. Indeed, one can't help but wonder how this relates to *The New York Times* exposure of the "75 generals"[14] mobilized by the Pentagon to push its views through the media. The message there is again: it was the Pentagon who wanted this war, who set the media up for it. Are we to believe that the media suspected nothing and was taken in…?

War for Oil or for Israel: What the Public Record Reveals

Zionist Power Configuration support for the Iraq War was an open, relentless, propaganda campaign by well-known writers, publicists, and community leaders as well as by the 52 leading Jewish organizations. There was no 'conspiracy' or 'cabal'—the Zionist campaign was brazenly public, aggressive and reiterative.

A systematic review of the major propaganda organ of the Presidents of the Major American Jewish Organization's newsletter, *Daily Alert*, from 2002 to September 2007—1,760 issues—provides us with a scientific sample of ZPC opinion. On average, each issue contained 5 articles in favor of the war or moves toward war with Iraq and/or Iran. The *Daily Alert* featured op-ed articles by the major liberal, conservative and Zion-fascist writers and academics which regularly appeared in the *Washington Post, Wall Street Journal*, the *New York Sun, The New York Times, Los Angeles Times, Daily Telegraph* and *Times of London*, YNet and others. In other words, in the crucial pre-war to post-invasion period, the leading pro-Israel Jewish organizations produced approximately 8,800 pieces of pro-Iraq war propaganda and circulated it to all its member organizations, every Congress-person, and every leading member of the executive branch , with follow-ups by local activists and an army of Washington lobbyists (150 from AIPAC alone) plus several hundred full-time activists from local and regional offices.

In a comparable survey of the leading Anglo-American business and financial newspaper, the *Financial Times*, between 2002 and September 2007, regarding Big Oil's policy toward war with Iraq and now Iran, is just as revealing. I reviewed the opinion, editorial and letter pages of 1,872 issues of the *Financial Times* and there is not a single article or letter by any spokesperson or representative of a major (or minor) oil company calling for the invasion and occupation of Iraq or the bombing of Iran. There was no oil lobby or grass roots organization demanding that Congress or the Bush Administration go to war in defense of US oil interests. But the fact that the ZPC had been active was visible in the wealth of *FT* pages promoting the lie that disarmed and embargoed Iraq represented an 'existential threat' to nuclear-armed Israel, whose army ranks fourth in the world.

A similar comparison of Zionist and Big Oil regarding propaganda for a US military confrontation with Iran reinforces the argument of the centrality of the major Jewish organizations in promoting United States involvement in Middle East wars for Israel. Between 2004 and September 2007 (3 years and 9 months) the Zionist propaganda sheet, the *Daily Alert*, published 960 issues in which an average of 6 articles argued for an immediate or near-future US or Israeli preemptive military attack on Iran, tougher economic sanctions than the Security Council was willing to support, and organized disinvestment and boycotts of Iran. A survey of 1053 issues of the *Financial Times* during the same period (the *FT* prints 6 times a week, the *Daily Alert* 5 times) fails to produce a single letter or op-ed article by any representative or spokesperson of Big Oil supporting war against Iran. On the contrary, as was the case with Iraq, major oil leaders expressed anxiety and fear that an Israeli-instigated war would destabilize the entire area and lead to the destruction of vital oil installations, undermine transport routes and shipping lanes, and cancel lucrative service contracts.

In fact, the ZPC has orchestrated legislation to ba US financial institutions, pension funds and major oil and gas companies from lucrative investments in Arab and Persian markets. Not a single oil company has favored or benefited from the restrictive legislation on Iran authored by AIPAC, sponsored by Zionist Congressman Tom Lantos and approved by a Congress dominated by the Zionist 'lobbies'—the alphabet soup of organizations— whose prime reason for existence is to promote Israeli state power. Every big oil company in Europe and Asia opposes the US confrontational posture to Iran. As the *Financial Times* states, "Europe's oil majors have plans to invest billions (in Iran) but US sanctions mean they are reluctant to go ahead."[15]

Contrary to Zionist propaganda, Big Oil wants the US to lift its sanctions against investment in Iran, since it has lost lucrative deals to competitors. Clearly, the lessons Big Oil must have drawn from Iraq— drastically reduced access to Iraqi oil, plus an oil privatization bill that can't even get past an Iraqi parliament installed under US occupation—would hardly be conducive to their seeking a repeat performance in Iran. While indeed, they might have inadvertently profited from the rise in oil prices, they have on the other hand reaped wave after wave of public antipathy and a Congressional inquiry which might lead to the even more dreaded anti-capitalist menace of regulation.

In complete contradiction to the 'leftist' Trotskyist-Zionist finger pointing at Big Oil as the main push for war, big Texas oil was working profitably with Saddam Hussein's Iraq, signing hundreds of millions of dollars in illegal contracts with the now executed ruler. Oscar Wyatt, a Texas oil billionaire recently convicted for paying bribes to Saddam Hussein, was one of many Big Oil dealers involved in the lucrative pre-war oil trade with Iraq.[16]

As far as Iran is concerned, take, for example, the writings of Michael Klare, author of a number of books on the oil issue, who raises the issue of Iran's oil as an underlying reason for an attack on that country, further enlarging upon that claim by writing:

> Because Iran occupies a strategic location on the north side of the Persian Gulf, it is in a position to threaten oil fields in Saudi Arabia, Kuwait, Iraq, and the United Arab Emirates, which together possess more than half of the world's known oil reserves. Iran also sits athwart the Strait of Hormuz... It is these *geopolitical* dimensions of energy, as much as Iran's potential to export significant quantities of oil to the United States, that undoubtedly govern the administration's strategic calculations.

However, Klare then goes on to note, in the same article:

> No doubt the major U.S. energy companies would love to be working with Iran today in developing these vast oil and gas supplies. At present, however, they are prohibited from

doing so by Executive Order (EO) 12959, signed by
President Clinton in 1995 and renewed by President Bush
in March 2004.

Surely these questions might have dawned on the average reader: why not
lift the sanctions and solve the problem? Who is it that wants sanctions,
and indeed war, against Iran, since they appear to be bad for Big Oil?
Nonetheless, Klare's 2005 article was widely circulated on leftist internet
sites promoting the notion of Big Oil culpability.[17]

Zionist Warmongering: Fear and Venom

As the pressure from Israel for a US-backed military attack on Iran
mounts, and as top US military officials and the general public grow
increasingly hostile to Zionist arm twisting and gross manipulation of policymakers, the ZPC turns aggressively authoritarian in its effort to silence
opposition which exposes its role as a disloyal actor for a foreign power. In
the past, agents for a foreign power, once detected, usually received severe
sanction or worse. Today, numerous Zionist insiders know they are playing
an increasingly risky game as the perceived costs of a new war with Iran rise
and their Israeli 'handlers' press them to place promoting an attack on Iran at
the top of their agenda.

Ultimately, the Zionist Power Configuration, despite its wealth and current
dominance over US Middle East policy, knows that it represents less than 1%
of the population: Its membership is an elite without a mass base. They have
power only as long as the other 99% of the population is inactive, manipulated
or intimidated to serve Israel's interests. But as the growing flow of books,
articles and speeches begin to call attention to the Israeli-directed ZPC and
their destructive warmongering activities, their self-promoted images of their
members as brilliant professionals, successful leaders in the world of business
and finance, and compassionate politicians serving the best interests of the
USA, begins to erode. The ugly side of their servile loyalty to Israel—an arrogant,
racist colonial power provoking wars via the US to establish itself as an
unchallenged regional power—has at last entered into the American public
debate.

The ZPC is at or near the peak of its political power—in Congress,
the Executive, the Office of Homeland Security and the Attorney General, in
'culture' and in the mass media propaganda. But paradoxically, as the ZPC
peaks, it also exposes more of itself—much more than it wants to be seen
by the American public.

Even the brash and impudent Zionist polemicists who hole up in the
prestigious universities and 'think tank-propaganda mills' are beginning to
feel public anxiety, even perhaps private worries. As they do so, they

backtrack, trying to cover their fingerprints on all the war plans and propaganda leading to the now massively unpopular invasion of Iraq. They resort to outright lies in the form of denials of complicity or 'war-mongering'. Outrageous denials abound! For the more aggressive die-hard Zion-Cons, exposure of the disloyal role of the ZPC and its complicity evokes savage rejoinders, academic screeds in the gutter language of ad hominem abuse, which reflects poorly on their vaunted elite academic positions. The ZPC, its scribes, operatives and power brokers *are* vulnerable—they have committed great crimes against the interests of the American people. Their actions have led to the death and maiming of tens of thousands of US soldiers, 99.9% of whom have no 'loyalties' to the interest of greater Israel or its US agents who have their own children pursuing lucrative civilian careers. Recent estimates found less than 0.2% of US soldiers serving on the ground in Iraq are American Jews, some of whom were Jewish immigrants from the former Soviet Union—this despite the strong Zionist pressure to invade and destroy Iraq and Iran. The manipulations of the ZPC in pushing the Bush Administration into invading and occupying Iraq has led the US military into an unprecedented state of disgrace and demoralization, with thousands of officers tendering their early retirement, thousands of troops going AWOL and facing court-martial, and an increasing number of retired senior officers expressing outrage. It is no surprise that Secretary of Defense Robert Gates was able to secure the support of top military officers in the Middle East in opposing an immediate invasion of Iran.

Zionist vituperation against their critics expresses fears of exposure and unmasking of their double discourse, their false amalgamation of Israeli colonial policies with the democratic values of the American people. Nothing else can explain the shrill verbal personal assaults—aimed at killing the messenger rather than facing unpleasant realities, and working to rectify a disastrous situation. While the state of Israel has placed its American promoters in an uncomfortable position as the occupation of Iraq crumbles and Americans resist shrill calls for attacking Iran, nevertheless Israel has turned out to be the real winner in the short term, having achieved the destruction of the unified, secular republic of Iraq.

From a Scratch to Gangrene:
The Transition from Zionism to Zion-Fascism

The 'mainstream' Zionist conservatives early on demonstrated their authoritarian politics through their whole-hearted and un-problematical support for Israel's brutal campaigns driving hundreds of thousands of Palestinians from their homes and lands. Subsequently, the Zion-Cons fully and unquestioningly endorsed the killing and jailing of thousands of Palestinian civilians protesting the Israeli military occupation and conversion of the occupied West Bank and Gaza into 'open air' concentration camps, with over 500 military outposts and roads blocks. More recently, the entire leadership of the major Jewish organizations, comprising both Zion-Cons and Zion-Libs, defended Israel's building of a massive 30 meter wall, effectively corralling the entire Palestinian population in ghettos resembling the walls constructed around the huge Jewish population in Warsaw by the Nazis. The wall and the military outposts strangle trade, movement of food and people from the occupied territories to markets, schools and hospitals, and prevent farmers from even tilling their lands.

On October 10, 2007, the *Jerusalem Post* quoted Aron Soffer, head of research and lecturer at the Israeli Defense Forces (IDF) National Defense College. The 71-year old father of 4 and grandfather of 8 had said on May 21, 2004: "*When 2.5 million people live in a closed off Gaza, it's going to be a human catastrophe. Those people will become even bigger animals than they are today, with the aid of an insane fundamentalist Islam. The pressure at the border will be awful. It's going to be a terrible war. So if we want to remain alive, we will have to kill and kill and kill. All day...every day.*"

This is the literal message of murder taught to Israeli officers at their most advanced military school by eminent Zion-Fascist lecturers. This helps us understand the naked brutality and homicidal behavior of Israeli soldiers in the occupied territories—and indeed, the fear-mongering to which the Jewish Israeli masses themselves fall victim.

A recent Israeli study by two prominent psychologists further illustrates the deep strain of sadism and racism inculcated by Israel's military academies and backed by Israel's top politicians, including the Prime Minister's Office. According to *Haaretz* on September 21, 2007, two Israeli psychologists interviewed 21 Israeli soldiers, who expressed "their innermost emotions about the horrendous crimes, in which they took part: murder, breaking the bones of Palestinian children, acts of humiliation, destruction of property, robbery and theft." One of the Israeli psychologists was "shocked to find that the soldiers enjoyed the 'intoxication of power' and had pleasure from using violence." She said, "Most of my interviewees enjoyed their own instigated violence during the occupation."[18] Absolute colonial domination brings out the psychopathic tendencies in an occupation army, particularly towards a dehumanized enemy. Soldier C testified, "If I didn't enter Rafah (Palestinian City in Gaza) to put down some rebellion—at least once a week I'd go beserk." Like previous colonial occupiers, the Israeli soldiers adopt a totalitarian 'super-race complex'. Soldier D testified, "What is great is that you don't follow any law or rule. You feel that YOU ARE THE LAW. Once you go into the Occupied Territory YOU ARE GOD!" The soldiers' internalization of the powerful Zion-fascist ideology provides a self-justification in the eyes of the interviewees for castrating a man, bashing in the face of a woman protester, shooting an innocuous pedestrian, breaking the arm of a 4-year old child and other 'gratuitous' acts of random violence.

The Conference of Presidents of Major American Jewish Organizations never ever mentions, let alone criticizes, the daily psychopathic behavior of the IDF. Major Jewish billionaire philanthropists contribute hundreds of millions in support of the IDF's violent occupation and repression of Palestinian civilians, described with cruel pleasure by the soldier-subjects of the Israeli study. In fact, the biggest Zionist contributor to the Democratic Party, Haim Saban ($12.3 million dollars in 2002), has a 'soft spot for Israeli combat soldiers.' According to *Haaretz,* Saban declared, *"I can't handle combat soldiers, whenever I have any interaction with them...I cry."*[19] There is a powerful emotional bond that links Israeli Zion-fascism to its US counterparts. Saban arrogantly points to the primacy of his loyalty to Israel, *"I strut around like a peacock in America and say I am an Israeli-American. What you hear ... an Israeli-American."*[20] The formerly respectable Brookings Institute now houses the 'Saban Center', financed by Haim Saban, turning Brookings into just another of a dozen propaganda mills churning out apologetics for the totalitarian practices of the IDF—their leading research directors and their prime minister.

The deadly 'sentimentality' of the Israeli-American billionaires toward the psychopaths in the IDF does not extend to the young Americans serving Israel's interests as US soldiers in Iraq who are suffering the burdens of a war to extend Israel's regional power. Saban, like the great majority of the top leaders of the most influential Zionist organization are pushing for another war—this time with Iran. According to Saban, *"I would try other things first, but if they don't work, then attack ... In Iran you go in and wipe out their infrastructure completely. Plunge them into darkness. Cut off their water."*[21] These are not the homicidal rantings of a fanatical Jewish settler beating a pre-adolescent Palestinian shepherd. Saban is a major leader in AIPAC, family friend and political broker of the Clintons and the entire current Israeli leadership. His $2.8 billion dollars buys the fawning attention of all major US presidential "candidates courting Jewish support".[22]

While at first one might be struck by the frankness of the *Haaretz* coverage and inclined to congratulate the paper for providing more truth in media than would be published in the United States, second thoughts lead one to wonder how such inflammatory words could responsibly even be published, and why there is no negative (or indeed, horrified) rejoinder from the educated Israeli public to the notion of "going in and wiping out the infrastructure" of another state—which is clearly a war crime, if not a crime against humanity. Has this level of expression found a wide acceptance and tolerance within the Israeli public?

Deflecting Peace Initiatives

The Zionist Power Configuration has buried three recent top-level political initiatives designed to reach a settlement of the Israeli colonial occupation of Palestine.

1. A statement to President Bush and Secretary of State Rice sent by former top political officials of both political parties, including Brzezinski, Lee Hamilton, Brent Scowcroft and others, calling for Israel to abide by UN Security Council Resolutions 242 and 338 and other initiatives, was totally dismissed by the Democratic Congress and the Republican White House—after the ZPC intervened and labeled Brzezinski as 'hostile to Israel', following the Israeli state's complete dismissal of the statement.

2. Tony Blair's effort as head of the 'Quartet Peace-Making Mission' has been a total failure in resolving even the humanitarian plight of the Palestinians, in the face of Israeli intransigence and rejection of any but the most banal conversations with the now subdued (formerly so frenetic) ex-British prime minister.[23]

3. Secretary Rice's efforts to organize a Middle East peace conference for late November 2007 in Annapolis, Maryland were diluted to pointlessness by Israeli pronouncements. Israel rejected any substantive agreements on borders, timetables, Jerusalem, settlements, territory, etc. They insisted the conference focus on meaningless general agreements that committed them to nothing. In action designed to further humiliate US Secretary of State Rice, the Israeli government illegally seized several hundred acres of Palestinian lands—a clear example of extending the settlements.[24] While trying to appear stylish in a dunce cap, Secretary Rice responded that the new Israeli confiscation of Palestinian land might 'erode confidence in the parties' commitment to a two state solution'.[25] Recognizing that the ZPC has completely tied up her negotiation position, that she cannot demand anything substantive from Israel, Secretary Rice signaled the futility of the Annapolis meeting by calling for 'lower expectations', that is, no agreements of substance. And so it came to pass. Israel and its Fifth Column effectively scuttled Bush's own Annapolis initiative.

What is more ominous, the Israel/ZPC successful sabotage of the White House Annapolis Peace Conference is likely to encourage them to press ahead with further violent seizures in the Occupied Territories, new more deadly incursions into Lebanon and Syria, and heightened pressure for war with Iran. Zion-fascism feeds on the sense of irresistible power over US Middle East policy and the ability to subdue any major US institutional force that fails to follow the Israeli line.

Along with the right-wing radicalization of Zion-Con ideology with regard to Israel's push toward totalitarian solutions, came overt manifestations of racist anti-Islamic, anti-Arab and anti-Persian practices and speeches from leading Zion-Con spokespeople and especially academic propagandists in the United States.

War propaganda and military solutions dominate Zion-Con rhetoric: first against Palestine, then Afghanistan, Iraq, Lebanon, Syria, Somalia and Sudan. A growing number of repressive acts within US society accompany the radicfalization of Zion-Con rhetoric.

The ZPC and Armenian Holocaust Denial: At the Service of Israel

For many years the state of Israel and its academic specialists both in Israel as well as in the US have denied Turkish-led genocide against the Armenians in their ancient homeland between 1915-1917 despite the voluminous documentary record complied by scholars throughout the world. One reason is that the Jewish Holocaust industry insists on holding the exclusive franchise on 20th century genocide in order to push its fundraising and propaganda efforts. An even more important contemporary reason for Israeli and US Zionist Armenian holocaust denial is the close military collaboration between Israel and Turkey, and more recently the heavy presence of Israeli military advisers and secret police (Mossad) operations in Kurdish-controlled Northern Iraq, dubbed Kurdistan.

The entire ZPC was on maximum alert to block or defeat the Armenian resolution in the US Congress in order to show Turkish Prime Minister Erdogan that Israel is using its power over the US Congress on Turkey's behalf. Even on an issue as palpable as genocide, the ZPC had no fear or shame in opposing a symbolic resolution recognizing a world-historic crime. Following the Israeli lead, prominent Zionist Democrats played a major role in undermining a Congressional resolution condemning as genocide the Turkish murder of 1.5 million Armenians.

What is particularly pointed for Americans in this brief episode is the fact that the Israeli fifth column in the US Congress has extended the scope of its control beyond narrow focus on the contemporary Middle East and Israel's quest for regional dominance to encompass historical issues involving non-Arab, non-Muslim peoples who indirectly affect Israeli strategic interests.

The fact that many Congress-members, including the majority of Democrats, were initially convinced of the justice of passing the resolution, and later under the pressure of the Zionist Congressional leadership withdrew their support, is indicative of just how far Congress has degenerated into a Zionist-colonized institution.

Anti-Iraq War Democratic Candidates Pro-War on Iran

The centerpiece of activity for all the major national, state and local pro-Israeli Jewish organizations is to isolate and destroy Iran, by economic sanctions and a massive military attack by the US. There is absolutely no consideration of the millions of Iranians who would be killed, injured or made homeless by a US or Israeli effort to 'wipe Iran off the map.'

The major recipient of 'New York (and Los Angeles, Miami and Chicago) Jewish money' is Hillary Clinton, the most hawkish Democratic warmonger in the 2008 president race—in fact the most hawkish Democratic candidate since the Vietnam era. Clinton, in a recent article in *Foreign Affairs*, has all but written the date and weapons with which the US will strike Iran. She argues that 'Iran poses a long-term strategic challenge to America and its allies and that it must not be permitted to build or acquire nuclear weapons…" If Iran does not comply, all options must remain on the table.[26]

Israel keeps a box-score on how servile US presidential candidates are to Israeli state interests and how obedient to the dictates of the Israel lobby. Clinton started out as the Zionist choice, by far, among Democratic presidential candi-dates, though the realities of American politics have since demanded (and received) a redefining of position by Barrack Obama as well— to the extent of his wearing an Israeli flag next to the US flag on his lapel, as all three candidates vied in loyalty to Israel at the 2008 annual AIPAC meeting. The ZPC has forgiven Clinton for kissing Suha Arafat over a decade ago, because she has kissed both cheeks of each and all male and female Zionist lobbyists and Israeli officials in Washington, and applauded the repression of Palestinians. Clinton aroused the passion and pleasure of the pro-Israel Conference of Presidents of Major American Jewish Organization by being the only Democratic presidential candidate to support the Senate resolution calling on the US government to declare the Iranian government's Revolutionary Guards, an elite division of Teheran's military, to be a 'terrorist entity', thus providing the Bush administration with a justification for financial sanctions and a massive pre-emptive military attack against Iran and its infrastructure.

Both in terms of financing war resolutions and sanctions campaigns against Iran, in terms of lobby-authored legislation and Congressional speeches, of hours campaigning for an attack on Iran, of op-ed columns published and media pundits comments, the Zionist Power Configuration exceeds by a multiple of ten any other group in pushing for a war with Iran.

Not only do the Zionists monopolize the 'attack Iran' propaganda, but they are leading all other authoritarian groups in silencing US critics of this aggressive military option.

Let us be perfectly clear that the ZPC, the Conference of Presidents of Major American Jewish Organizations, the Rahm Emanuels (Israeli-Americans) controlling the Democratic Caucus agenda...do not always and everywhere speak for the majority of American Jews, especially on the denial of the Turkish genocide of the Armenians. Pugnacious ADL President Abraham Foxman found out in Watham, Massachusetts, that both the local Armenian-American community and their Jewish-American compatriots and neighbors do not tolerate the denial of genocide—even by the ADL. Substantial sectors of American Jews object to Clinton's warmongering and find her servile truckling to Israeli officials offensive, even obscene. Zionist polls reveal the majority of educated young American Jews are less and less interested in Israel and its local Fifth Column—much to the chagrin of the self-styled 'leaders' of the community. Saying that a Jewish minority only speaks in the name of, but does not actually represent the views of, an unwilling Jewish majority, however, does not lessen its power and stranglehold over US political institutions and public opinion with regard to policy or appropriations touching on the Middle East or Israeli-defined interests. Jewish power in the United States—all the talk of the "Jewish vote" notwithstanding—has never been based on their numbers, which by now are tied with the numbers of Muslim Americans, but rather on the power of the ZPC elite.

'Jew-haters' became the agitation slogan animating the Zion-Con purge of public forums and a call for mass direct action by hundreds of local Jewish notables and 'community' councils. Even Presbyterian elders were browbeaten by Jewish Zionists because of their mild stand on divesting from US companies involved in oppressing Palestinians.

There is no transcendent event that defines the moment in which Zion-Conservatism became Zion-Fascism. The transition was an evolutionary process, during which racism, militarism and authoritarianism developed a mass community base, took hold over time, and became the definitive modus operandi of the ZPC.

Like earlier fascist movements, Zion-fascism subscribes to racialist doctrines of knowledge. According to Zionist epistemology only Jews can (if they dare) criticize Jews as knowledge of Jewry is monopolized by a closed communally defined people. This Zion-fascist theory of knowledge is buttressed by the frequent utterances of progressive or leftist Zionists who frequently dismiss or warn non-Jewish writers that they enter the 'Jewish' debate at their peril.

Zion-fascism is not merely an ideological expression of a marginal group of unbalanced extremists—its ideology and practice, in full or part, has been taken over by mainstream Jewish organizations.

The Impact of Zionist Authoritarianism on American Democracy

Grassroots Zionist-led authoritarianism, practicing coercion, repression and financial blackmail in defense of Israel and the ZPC, is occurring in every region of the country, in every sphere of social, cultural and academic life at an accelerating pace. Below we cite a small sample of cases which have gotten national and even international attention, which illustrate a far more extensive pattern. We lack a comprehensive data bank to cover the hundreds of incidents of Zionist intimidation and thought control which occur on a weekly basis and go unreported by their victims for fear of retaliation or because they would not receive sympathetic public attention due to media bias, or because they did not want to be viewed as either anti-Semites or Nazis. Most people are sufficiently aware of the negativities of stereotypes to be reluctant to engage in what might be regarded as such—particularly as it relates to Jews, though not as strongly as it relates to many other of the world's peoples.

The theoretical and practical point is that *the ZPC includes hundreds of local organizations and tens of thousands of individuals* who take local initiatives in defending Israeli policy, its image and interests by trampling on the Constitutional and academic freedom of other Americans.

For every play that is banned, producer chastised and theater put in the red, *thousands of other cultural workers and institutions are intimidated*. They *internalize* the repressive codes imposed by the Zionists, and self-censor. They submit to ZPC dictates of what can and cannot be performed, what is or is not offensive to 'Jewish sensibilities', that exquisitely stated euphemism for Zionist power.

Manifestations of Zionist cultural authoritarianism are found at the local level and linked with national campaigns to monopolize the entire discussion of US Middle East policy, and in particular, to exclude any criticism of Israel and the powerful role of the Zionist Lobby. That monopoly is most evident in any systematic study of the op-ed pages of the big circulation print media and the panels of 'experts' included in the major broadcast media. The role of the pro-Israel repressive cultural-ideological hydra especially finds expression among the great majority of 'progressive' critics: 'Marxist' ideologues and 'peace' advocates who deliberately and totally ignore the ZPC's influence in Congress, the Executive and in cultural life. Instead they repeatedly criticize Bush, Cheney, the Republicans and Democrats without mentioning their prime movers among the hundreds of thousands of Zionist zealots and thousands of prime political donors.

It is no wonder that the Zionist power configuration has greater power than any other lobby in Washington—they are the only power group which has no opposition, no organized group willing to *name* them, let alone challenge and fight their stranglehold over Congress. Worse still, some of the most influential critics of the war in Iraq provide ideological cover by *denying* the ZPC's dominant role and deflecting attention to either *non-existent* war-makers (Big Oil) or to the secondary *political actors*, who carry out Lobby initiatives.

The self-styled 'alternative' Jewish lobbies, which claim to speak for liberal Jews critical of Israel, maintain that AIPAC is merely 'one of many factors' influencing US policy, in a 'complex mosaic of changing circumstances'. Using the argument of 'complexities' and packaging the ZPC with 'numerous groups', they downplay or eliminate the essential role of the pro-Israel forces and join their mainstream brethren in smearing as 'anti-Semite' those writers who put the ZPC at the center of their analysis of US policy toward Arab and Muslim countries. The liberal Zionists have had a disastrous impact on the peace movement by deflecting its attention away from a prime mover of US military policy and thus giving the ZPC an uncontested and open terrain for continuing its dominance of US Middle East policy. The liberal Jewish lobby willfully ignores *Israeli* geopolitical interests, Israeli reliance on military rather than diplomatic measures, its pursuit of ethnic cleansing and the ZPC influence on US policy, in terms of the *methods* and strategies that Washington should pursue. They deliberately and continuously ignore the opposition of all the major oil companies to US sanctions against Iran.

In informal interviews, writers and journalists have reported to me how they have received 'visits' by local Jewish 'notables' and members of the Jewish Community Councils, as have local newspaper editors to demand the firing of columnists who dared to criticize, for example, Israel's horrific invasion of Lebanon. After one such 'visit' and 'talk', a local columnist never ventured to criticize or even write about the Middle East. This is not a matter confined to the United States. In 2004, after I wrote an article for the Mexico City daily, *La Jornada*, critical of Israel's savage repression of Palestinians in Jena and the US Zionist apology for mass killings, the Israeli Ambassador in Mexico visited the editors to demand they discontinue publishing my articles. The editor refused to accede at that time, but immediately afterwards they published several vicious personal attacks by their regular columnists (one a Troskyist, and the other a Jewish dentist) labeling my critiques as 'Nazi' propaganda in line with the 'Protocols of Zion'. This was in a reputed, independent, progressive daily newspaper.

'Private visits', abusive phone calls by Zionist zealots, including death threats, are not uncommon practices among 'respectable' Zion-fascists. One incident involved a local doctor who received a 'visit' to her office by a fanatical Zionist 'colleague' complaining of her letter to the local newspaper criticizing the role of the Zionists in financing the electoral defeat of Georgia Congresswoman, Cynthia McKinney, because of her criticism of Israeli policy. She was 'warned' that it was anti-Semitic to criticize the activities of organized Jewry in destroying politicians, especially black politicians, for their support of Palestinian civil rights. African Americans, she was told, were increasingly ungrateful to American Jews, who had led and financed the civil rights struggle, and therefore had to be taught a history lesson. (The colleague did not, of course, mention the Jewish community's role in opposing and rolling back affirmative action, a policy of central concern to African Americans.) A local 'group' of notables had chosen her Harvard-educated Zionist colleague to deliver this message. When he declared himself 'a Jew and a Zionist', she countered that she was 'an anti-fascist and an anti-Zionist' and pointed to the door but not before asking him how an educated man of high professional standing could stomach such a degrading task as trying to censor a colleague. These types of 'visits' from 'respectable' Zionists intimidate others with less standing and intestinal fortitude.

When presented with the manuscript of my book, *The Power of Israel in the United States*, many of my previous editors informed me that it would make a great book ... but ... they didn't want to face the backlash, threats and vituperation that they expected from the ZPC, Jewish academics, writers on contract and publishers. Even the publisher and editor who finally agreed to publish my book expressed real recognition of the impact of Zionist hostility—and eventually a dozen or so Jewish academics cancelled book orders for their classes. But more significantly, while the book, published in September 2006, had within a year of its release gone into its fourth printing with translations in Japanese (hardcover), Italian, German, Arabic, Indonesian and Spanish, it was (and continues to be) largely ignored by independent bookstores. More interestingly, given the volume of sales, the book was only offered for sale through three out of four Ingram (the major wholesaler in the US) regional outlets; for over a year, not a single copy was ordered for Ingram's office in the North-Eastern sector. Despite the numerous requests for review copies (including from the American Jewish Committee and *Commentary*), the only print medium to review the book was the Canadian publication, *Canadian Dimension*. One online journal of high repute not only refrained from reviewing the book but also, while continuing to publish my articles on other topics, omitted any reference to the book in my bio, instead continuing to cite my earlier publications: such are the fears or passions awakened by the subject, that they refused to even mention the book, let alone review it.

A sample of the most publicized cases of Zionist efforts to silence and purge American society of critics of Israel and the Zionist Power Configuration includes the case of over one thousand Zionist alumni of Barnard College campaigning to deny tenure to Professor Nadia Abu el-Haj for publishing *Facts on the Ground*, her ground-breaking critique of Israeli archeologists' efforts to erase centuries of continued Palestinian presence in the Holy Lands.[27]

More recently there was the public campaign to rescind Columbia University's invitation to Iranian Prime Minister Mahmoud Ahmadinejad which culminated in an unprecedented insulting introduction of its invitee by the university's president. Is it too much to surmise that when Columbia University President Lee Bollinger originally invited Iranian President Ahmadinejad to speak at his university, he had not intended to do so in order to deliver a withering stream of invective against him before a distinguished gathering, but rather had later felt compelled to do so in the interests of protecting both his university and his personal career?

The successful British play, 'My Name is Rachel Corrie' based on the writings of the American activist murdered in Gaza by Israeli Defense Forces as she sought to prevent a Palestinian home from destruction, was banned from scheduled performances in New York, Miami and Toronto, causing consternation among theater-goers and actors on both sides of the Atlantic. The cancellation by Toronto-based CanStage, one of Canada's leading theatres, was reported by the CBC as a decision based on the play's merits, rather than the political controversy that dogs it, CanStage artistic producer Martin Bragg said in an interview with CBC.ca. "It was an artistic decision," said Bragg, who saw the play [when ultimately performed] in New York. "It just didn't work on stage."[28]

The *Toronto Star* revealed the true reason for the cancellation—fear of the response of influential supports in Toronto's Jewish community:

> The alternate version being told among CanStage insiders: Members of Bragg's board were alarmed by negative response from influential supporters of the theatre, especially in Toronto's Jewish community, who were canvassed for their opinion. Many were dismayed and openly critical when confronted with the prospect of the city's flagship not-for-profit theatre producing a play that could be construed as anti-Semitic propaganda, especially during a frightening period when Israel's existence is threatened by Iran, Hezbollah and Hamas.[29]

However, it did so in a manner which sought to defend the cancellation rather than freedom of expression, reiterating the "existential threat" canard to nuclear Israel, which has done all in its power to sink any peace options which might have resolved any purported threat to its existence put forward over the past several decades. The Israeli soldier who murdered the young woman was exonerated in Israel while Rachel's words were banned from the cultural capital of her own country.

Even more recently, the Chicago Council of Global Affairs bowed to pressure from the Zionist lobby and cancelled a lecture by the respected professors of political science, John Mearsheimer and Stephan Walt because of their critical study *The Israel Lobby*.

The list goes on to include the cancellation of a concert by Marcel Khalife in San Diego, California and the cancellation of an invitation to Nobel Peace Prize winner, South African Bishop Desmond Tutu because of his criticism of Israeli apartheid policies in the occupied territories.

Then there was a successful campaign to prevent author Susan Abulhawa from presenting her gripping novel, *The Scar of David*, at a Barnes and Noble Bookstore in Bayside, New York. This was followed by a cyberspace attack on the author to undermine a scheduled speaking tour. This pro-Israel attack was led by 14 rabbis and the President of the Queens Jewish Community Council.

In the fall of 2007, the distribution of Pluto Press by the University of Michigan Press became the subject of a controversy when a pro-Israel advocacy organization, StandWithUs, criticized the University of Michigan Press for distributing "anti-Semitic" books issued by Pluto Press, including those by Israel Shahak and *Overcoming Zionism*, by professor of social studies at Bard College, Joel Kovel. When the University of Michigan caved to organized Zionist pressure, it required extensive protest by social forces defending the right of academic freedom to push University of Michigan to resume distribution of Pluto titles.[30]

The recent Congressional Hearings of a blue ribbon committee, which finally got around to investigating the Israeli military attack on the *USS Liberty* (after 40 years of successfully preventing an official investigation through the pressure of the Israel lobby) found Israel guilty of the deliberate killing and maiming of over 100 US service personnel. Its explosive findings, published in the Congressional Record, never appeared in the print and broadcast media.

But then, the media has done little over the years to make plain to Americans the extent of public treasure which is regularly doled out in aid to Israel. Even as they were in violation of United Nations resolutions, Israel's military aggressions against Lebanon, Syria and Palestine, were rewarded by the US Congress with an additional $30 billion dollars in military aid over the next 10 years, making the US annual 'tribute to Israel' in excess of $6 billion dollars a year.[31] At a time of record US deficits and cuts in domestic health programs for poor children and educational services, the vote to give Israel an additional $30 billion dollars passed with virtually no opposition or even discussion. While it might be argued that the US also dispenses an extraordinary (though lesser) sum in aid to Egypt, this aid in turn is in actuality aid to Israel, since its intent is to protect the Egyptian government from the outrage of its own people occasioned by its cooperation with and assistance to Israel despite its treatment of Palestinians in the occupied territories.

Australian journalist and documentary maker, John Pilger produced a searing critique of Israel entitled "Palestine is Still the Issue" which has been viewed all over the world. Its scheduled showing on the public educational channel in San Francisco was blocked by a campaign led by the Jewish Community Relations Council.

The bilingual Arabic-English public middle school in New York City named after the Lebanese Christian poet, Kahil Gibran, was attacked by the ZPC leading to the firing of its Arab American principal.[32] Her 'crime' was accurately translating the Arabic word 'intifada' into 'shaking off' instead of ranting against the Palestinian rights movement in the Occupied Territories. The Zionist-controlled United Federation of Teachers actively backed the blatant purge of one of its own members for her thought crimes.

The world-renowned Palestinian American scholar and literary theorist, Edward Said, was persecuted and slandered up to his recent death by the attack hounds of the Lobby.

At San Francisco State College there was a campaign led by the executive director of the Jewish Community Relations Council of San Francisco to ban a mural depicting a famous Palestinian cartoon character, a little boy defiant before Israeli occupiers. The subject in question was a child holding a key in his hand, which, according to the local Jewish leadership represented a 'veiled reference to Palestinian right of return to Israel'.[33]

One of the most bitter and successful Zionist purge campaigns was the denial of tenure to highly respected scholar, Professor Norman Finkelstein, by De Paul University in Chicago. Led by Harvard Law Professor Alan Dershowitz, it was in direct response to Finkelstein's numerous scholarly studies critical of Israel and the exploitation of the Holocaust to further the aims of the Zionist Power Configuration.

Despite the recommendations of three academic committees at Yale University, Zionist millionaire philanthropists were able to block the appointment of renowned Middle East specialist, Professor Juan Cole. The millionaires threatened to withdraw contributions and several Zionist professors prepared a scurrilous attack on Professor Cole (June 1, 2006).

A campaign was mounted to pressure several state pension funds to divest funds from any company doing business with Iran and pushing the funds to invest in Israel bonds. This has so far succeeded in Texas, Florida, New York, and New Jersey. Several state governors were 'persuaded' while on Zionist-paid junkets to Israel.[34] During one of these junkets, the now disgraced New Jersey Governor McGreevy met[35] an Israeli operative with whom he formed a homosexual relation and later installed as 'Homeland Security' Chief for the State of New Jersey, until the FBI intervened. McGreevy resigned from office after denouncing the Israeli, Golan Cipal, for blackmail.

The Anti-Defamation League, a pro-Israel transmission belt, forced the only Muslim Congressman, Keith Ellison, to recant for daring to compare the tactics of the Bush Administration to those of the Nazis.[36] As in the case of Congresswoman McKinney, Zionist 'punishment' against African-American politicians is particularly vehement.

The major Zionist organizations led by the American Jewish Committee successfully mobilized the major US trade union bureaucrats to denounce the United Kingdom's militant trade union's boycotts of Israel.[37] The AFL-CIO unions are under the thumb of the ZPC and have placed over $5 billion dollars of their members' pension funds in Israel bonds which consistently under-perform market indexes, thus costing their 12 million members hundreds of millions of investment returns each year.

The dean of religion Barry Levin, a pro-Israel activist at McGill University, recently fired Professor Norman Cornelt after 15 years of teaching for his support of Palestinian human rights.[36]

Every major newspaper published editorials and scurrilous book reviews attacking former US President Jimmy Carter's critical study, *Palestine: Peace Not Apartheid*. This was part of a high-priority propaganda campaign coordinated by major Zionist organizations and prominently included Professor Alan Dershowitz.[39] Meanwhile, on amazon.com, it took a determined protest and petition from some 13,000 members of the amazon.com book-buying public to roll back amazon.com's prejudicial listing of the book. As the petition stated:

> Under the "Editorial Reviews" heading—a space normally used either for the publisher's own description of a book, or for short, even-handed summaries from listing services such as *Booklist* and *Publishers Weekly*—you insist on running the complete, 20-paragraph, 1,636-word text of a review unabashedly hostile to Carter's viewpoint. You have refused to add information shoppers should have in evaluating this review: the fact that the reviewer, Jeffrey Goldberg, is a citizen of Israel as well as the United States, and that he volunteered to serve in the Israeli Defense Forces, for which he worked as a guard at a prison for Palestinian detainees. And you have refused to balance his negative review by giving comparable space to a favorable assessment of the book, even though positive reviews by qualified experts have appeared in many reputable publications.[40]

The prominent Jewish writer, Professor Tony Judt of New York University was dis-invited from a scheduled talk at the Polish Consulate because of Zionist opposition to his criticism of Israeli policy. The intervention was so egregious that it prompted a letter to the editor published in the *New York Review of Books* regarding the ADL role in the cancellation, supported by over 100 academics, many of them Jewish.[41]

B'nai Brith of Vancouver, Canada attacked a Canadian web site called Peace, Earth and Justice, forcing the removal of 18 articles critical of Israel.[42]

In early 2007 the ZPC intervened in the US Civil Rights Commission and introduced a section equating anti-Zionism with anti-Semitism, and slandered dozens of academic Middle Eastern studies programs as centers of campus 'anti-Semitism'. The Middle East Studies Association of North America (MESA), the major academic group, wrote a reasoned refutation on June 11, 2007. Here are some excerpts from the letter by Zachary Lochman, President of MESA, to the Chair of the US Commission on Civil Rights:[43]

> MESA is concerned that the briefing report and findings issued by the Commission may actually weaken efforts to combat anti-Semitism by expanding its definition to include an indefensibly broad range of legitimate speech and conduct. We are also concerned that false allegations associating Middle East studies programs and faculty with anti-Semitism may contribute to an already troubling environment of harassment, intimidation and censorship of faculty and students on college and university campuses, thereby threatening academic freedom.

> Three issues are of particular concern to MESA. First, we are deeply troubled by the Commission's apparent acceptance of an overly broad and vague definition of anti-Semitism that dangerously blurs the boundaries between actual anti-Semitic speech and conduct, on the one hand, and criticism of Israel, Zionism, or U.S. policy in the Middle East on the other. As a result, the briefing report and the Commission's findings seem to accept or even endorse assertions made by panelists who submitted statements to the Commission that entirely legitimate views and policy positions with which they disagree should be characterized as anti-Semitic. Such assertions are particularly distressing when they involve scholarship and teaching by college and university faculty. Wherever anti-Semitism surfaces, an immediate and vigorous response is necessary. But efforts to demonize academic and other critics of Israel, Zionism, and U.S. policy in the Middle East by tarring them with the brush of anti-Semitism are clearly unacceptable and merit no less urgent and vigorous a response.

Second, we reject as unfounded the allegations and insinuations presented in the briefing report that university departments of Middle East studies promote anti-Semitism. The briefing report presents no evidence whatsoever that would substantiate such scurrilous claims, and none of the instances of anti-Semitism referred to in the report involved a federally-funded Middle East studies center. Unfortunately, the Commission permitted members of the briefing panel to repeat, without challenge, unfounded allegations concerning individual faculty members specializing in the study of the Middle East and/or Islam, all of whom have rejected the charges against them and denied their truthfulness. Several of these faculty members have in fact been subjected to exhaustive investigations by their universities which have not substantiated the allegations repeated in the Commission's briefing.

We also insist that it is inappropriate and inaccurate for the Commission to have included among its findings the assertion that "many university departments of Middle East studies provide one-sided, highly polemical academic presentations and some may repress legitimate debate concerning Israel." This assertion too is completely unsupported by evidence and should be stricken from the Commission's findings.

Third, we are concerned that the procedure by which the briefing report was produced was defective; that much of its tone and contents is highly polemical and fall far short of the standard that Americans have a right to expect the Commission to adhere to; and that it may contribute to an environment on university campuses that undermines academic freedom as well as the kind of first-rate scholarly research and teaching on the Middle East and the Muslim world which our country so desperately needs.

As the briefing report notes, all of the universities invited to take part in the briefing declined to do so. To our knowledge, no representative of university-based Middle East studies programs or of the academic Middle East studies community was invited to participate. The briefing report, and the responses to it by several universities against which allegations were made, make it clear that the panelists presented a very partial, highly ideological, and narrowly partisan understanding of academic Middle East studies in this country and sought to define anti-Semitism extremely broadly and loosely. We fear that their purpose in so doing was to advance their own partisan political agenda, strengthen efforts to impose political litmus tests on college and university faculty, subject federally-funded Middle East studies programs to politically-motivated oversight, undermine academic freedom, and stifle free and open discussion on public issues of critical national importance. We also note that efforts to dilute and expand the definition of anti-Semitism so as to encompass legitimate speech and conduct can have damaging consequences for efforts to address and combat real anti-Semitism. By adopting a vague and politicized definition of this insidious form of hate speech, the Commission increases the risk that attention and resources that are better directed toward combating real anti-Semitism will instead be diverted to politically-motivated efforts to censor unpopular or controversial views expressed by university faculty. We urge the Commission not to pursue or endorse such a course, but rather to focus its efforts on real forms and incidents of discrimination and hate speech, including anti-Semitism.

On the basis of secret testimony by Israeli intelligence agents and backed by the ZPC, 'terrorism' charges were made against 16 members of a US Islamic charity. A Texas court convicted them of 'crimes' against Israel, even though many of the accused were US citizens and had no access to challenge their hooded accusers, Israeli secret agents operating in the US. The lead defendant, Dr. Rafil Dhofer received a sentence of 22 years for an 'Israeli' crime—although he was never convicted of any crime committed in the US. The defendants and their attorneys were never allowed to question the secret foreign 'witnesses'.

Plans to construct a mosque for the Muslim community in Roxbury, Massachusetts were attacked in a campaign by the 'David Project', a Zionist front group affiliated with the Jewish Community Council of Greater Boston.[44]

Campus Zion-fascist organizations run by David Horowitz routinely bait blacks, Latinos and Arab Americans by praising the 'benefits' of the African slave trade and defend the use of torture and assassination by Israelis and their US counterparts in Iraq and Guantanamo. In addition, they smear professors not sufficiently favorable to Zionism, spy on instructors, disrupt classes, and bring lawsuits for 'anti-Zionist' bias against teachers, other students and college administrators throughout the US.

Despite the Zionist turn to fascist tactics and embrace of authoritarian-coercive measures, the fact of the matter is they still only have partial control over civil society and political power. Some of the Zion-fascist power plays were, at least temporarily, defeated in specific circumstances. The play, My Name is Rachel Corrie played to packed houses in London, Seattle and other courageous cities even as it was banned in New York, Toronto and Miami. Norman Finkelstein received powerful support throughout the academic world and was able to negotiate monetary compensation for De Paul University's cowardly betrayal of one of its faculty, notably following the intervention of pro-torture Harvard professor, Allen Dershowitz. The distribution of Pluto Books by University of Michigan Press was reinstated.

The lesson is clear: the rise of Judeo-fascism represents a clear and present danger to our democratic freedoms in the United States. They do not come with black shirts and stiff-arm salutes. The public face is a clean-shaven, neck-tied attorney, real estate philanthropist or Ivy League professor. But there is rising anger and hostility in America against the ZPC, against its arrogant authoritarian communal attacks on our democratic values, to say nothing of our national interests. Sooner or later there will be a major backlash—and it will reflect badly on those who, through vocation or conviction, engage in the firings, censoring and intimidation campaigns against the American majority. The American people will not remember their cries of 'anti-Semitism'; they will recall their role in sending thousands of American soldiers to their death in the Middle East in the interests of Israel, and how that war has diminished the United States' image in the world, to say nothing of its economic well-being and democratic freedoms at home.

Let us hope that those who seek justice will not use authoritarian laws such as the Patriot Act, nor the harsh interrogation techniques of degradation (torture) and anti-Arab/Muslim practices promoted by the Zionists in the Pentagon, Congress, Justice Department and Homeland Security. Those who oppose Zionism need to abide solidly by higher moral standards.

ENDNOTES

[1] A September 27, 2006 poll by WorldPublicOpinion.org found that "An overwhelming majority believes that the US military presence in Iraq is provoking more conflict than it is preventing...Majorities believe that the withdrawal of US troops would lead to a reduction in the amount of inter-ethnic violence and improvement in the day-to-day security of Iraqis." See "The Iraqi Public on the US Presence and the Future of Iraq," A Worldpublicopinion.org poll conducted by the Program on International Policy Attitudes, p. 4 <http://www.worldpublicopinion.org/pipa/pdf/sep06/Iraq_Sep06_rpt.pdf> As Mehdi Noorbaksh put it in "Iraq: A Deficit in Foresight", published by Foreign Policy Association on March 20, 2008, "In poll after poll, Iraqis have indicated that the United States presence is the source of instability and insecurity."

[2] See recent statements in September and October and US General John Abazaid (Abizaid: "Of Course It's About Oil, We Can't Really Deny That", *Huffington Post,* October 15, 2007), among others by former Federal Reserve Chairman, Alan Greenspan ("Greenspan claims Iraq war was really for oil," *The Sunday Times,* September 16, 2007)

[3] Colum Lynch "Firm's Iraq Deals Greater Than Cheney Has Said: Affiliates Had $73

Million in Contracts", *Washington Post*, June 23, 2001; Page A01.

4   See Walter Pincus, "Contractors in Iraq Have Become a US Crutch", *Washington Post*, August 20, 2007, A13.

5   See James Petras, *The Power of Israel in the United States*, Clarity Press, Inc., Atlanta, 2006.

6   The paper, "A Clean Break: A New Strategy for Securing the Realm", was written by Richard Perle, Douglas Feith, David and Meyrav Wurmser (a co-founder of the Middle East Media Research Institute). In fact, "September 2002's National Security Strategy (NSS) document simply delighted the members of the PNAC. No wonder: it reproduced almost verbatim a September 2000 report by the PNAC, which in turn was based on the now famous 1992 draft Defense Policy Guidance (DPG), written under the supervision of Wolfowitz for then secretary of defense Cheney." Pepe Escobar, *Asiatimes*, <http://www.atimes.com/atimes/Middle_East/EC20Ak07.html>

7   Glenn Kessler and Robin Wright, "Israel, U.S. Shared Data On Suspected Nuclear Site: Bush Was Told of North Korean Presence in Syria, Sources Say", *Washington Post*, September 21, 2007, p. A01.

8   Demetri Sevastopulo, "U.S. Feared North Korea-Syria Link Before Israeli Strike", *Financial Times*, September 20, 2007, p.4.

9   Ibid.

10   Ibid.

11   David E. Sanger, "U.S. Sees Links to N. Korean Reactor," *The New York Times*, April 24, 2008.

12   A fuller elaboration of this survey is provided below.

13   *Financial Times*, October 18, 2007, p.4.

14   David Barstow, "A Pentagon Campaign: Retired officers have been used to shape terrorism coverage from inside the TV and radio networks," *The New York Times*, April 20, 2008.

15   *Financial Times,* May 10, 2007, p.2.

16   *Financial Times,* Oct. 2, 2007, p.2.

17   See Michael Klare, "Oil, Geopolitics and the Coming War with Iran", which is widely circulated on such leftist sites as CommonDreams.org, MotherJones.com, etc.

18   *Haaretz,* September 21, 2007.

19   *Haaretz,* September 12, 2006.

20   *Haaretz,* October 14, 2007.

21   *Haaretz* October 14, 2007.

22   MSNBC, October 14, 2007.

23   *Guardian*, October 13, 2007.

24   Aljazeera, October 14, 2007.

25   BBC, October 14, 2007.

26   *Guardian*, October 15, 2007.

27   *Chronicle of Higher Education*, August 5, 2007

28   "Toronto theatre won't stage My Name is Rachel Corrie", CBC Arts, December 22, 2006.

29   Martin Knelman, "Theatre scraps play on Mideast 'Martyr', Toronto Star, December 22, 2006.

30   However, the pendulum then swung back again; according to wikipedia, in January of 2008, the University of Michigan Press seemed to be seeking a way to cloak a new refusal to distribute Pluto, by drafting Distribution Guidelines which define its mandate as distributing scholarly works, whereas Pluto Press has "a radical agenda" (as if radical works were ipso facto not scholarly), thereby punishing Pluto while the true reasons for it were disguised. While at this writing, the wikipedia contention is still posted, it has been confirmed that Pluto Press is still being distributed by the University of Michigan Press, as is Joel Kovel. See wikipedia http://en.wikipedia.org/wiki/Pluto_Press#cite_note-0>.

31   *The New York Times*, August 16, 2007.

[32]   Ibid, August 11, 2007.

[33]   *Jewish Forum*, August 10, 2007.

[34]   See *Houston Chronicle*, July 18, 2007.

[35]   It seems fair to question whether such an encounter could indeed be random, or whether it was intentionally set up to implicate, manipulate and control the governor of New Jersey.

[36]   *Jewish Telegraph Agency*, July 20, 2007.

[37]   *Jerusalem Post*, July 22, 2007.

[38]   *Montreal Gazette*, June 2, 2007.

[39]   *Washington Report on Middle East Affairs*, April 2007.

[40]   See <http://www.petitiononline.com/Amazon07>

[41]   See Mark Lilla, Richard Sennett, "The Case of Tony Judt: An Open Letter to the ADL," *New York Review of Books*, Volume 53, Number 18, November 16, 2006.

[42]   See Lila Rajiva, "Loonies Tune Out: B'nai B'rith Shuts Down Peace Activists in Canada," *Dissident Voice,* May 28, 2007.

[43]   See MESA's Webpage, Committee on Academic Freedom,   <http://www.mesa.arizona.edu/about/cafmenaletters.htm#USCCRJune11>

[44]   See Charles Radin, Boston Globe, "Tensions High amid Roxbury Mosque Plan," December 17, 2006.

CHAPTER 2

WAR ON IRAN
THE AMERICAN MILITARY
VERSUS THE ISRAEL FIRSTERS

*"Why must Jewish organizations be and be seen as
the loudest drum-beaters of all?
Why can we not bring ourselves to say that
military intervention is not on the table at all?
Why not stash it under the table, out of sight
and mount instead a diplomatic assault?"*
Leonard Fein
Forward, **November 7, 2007**

Introduction

As the White House and Congress escalate their economic sanctions
and military threats against Iran, some top military commanders (excluding
General Petraeus and his minions) and Pentagon officials have launched a
counter-offensive, opposing a new Middle East War. While some commentators
and journalists privy to this high stakes inter-elite conflict, like Chris Hedges,[1]
attribute this to a White House cabal led by Vice President Cheney,   a more
stringent and accurate assessment puts the Zionist Power Configuration
(ZPC) in the center of the Iran war debate. There is a great deal riding on
this conflict—the future of the American empire as well as the balance of
power in the Middle East. Equally important is the future of the US military
and our already heavily constrained democratic freedoms. The outcome of
the continuous and deepening confrontation between top US military officials
and the Israel Firsters over US foreign policy in the Middle East has raised
fundamental questions over such issues as US self-determination, fifth column
colonization by Israel-First Americans, civilian primacy and military political
intervention, empire or republic. These and related issues are far from being
of academic interest only; they concern the future of America.

Recent History of the Civilian Militarists versus Anti-War Movements

Over the past seven years, the civilian militarists in the executive branch and Congress have resoundingly defeated any and all efforts by Congressional critics and anti-war leaders to end the wars in Iraq and Afghanistan. Since 2003, the peace movement has practically vanished from the streets—in large part a product of its own self-destruction. The great majority of anti-war leaders opted for Democratic Party-electoral politics, a strategy that led to the successful election of a pro-war Democratic majority. The retreat of the anti-war movement turned into a full-scale route when the government moved toward a new war with Iran. Heavily influenced by their loyalty to Israel and its shrill cries of an 'existential' danger from non-existent Iranian nuclear weapons and dependent on 'liberal' Zionist donors, the Zionist-influenced half of the peace movement refused to join forces to oppose the Iran war agenda.

Along with the capitulation of the anti-war leaders and absence of any 'street politics', liberal Democrats, or what passes for them, fell into line with the Israel First Democratic Congress-people pushing for an increasingly bellicose political agenda toward Iran. The White House, especially the Vice President's office, was fully in tune with the Israel Firsters and the ZPC, 'keeping the military option' on the table and priming the US forces in the Gulf for offensive action. Within the military and the intelligence services strong opposition emerged to an attack on Iran.

American Military Fights the ZPC Over Middle East Wars

The battle between the civilian militarists (Zion-Cons) in the Pentagon and the military brass took place, in large part, behind closed doors: From the beginning, the military was severely handicapped insofar as they could not engage in public debate. While the dissident military elite did not possess an army of lobbyists, activist ideologues and the entire mass media apparatus to promote their own point of view, 75 military talking heads were mobilized to promote the White House/Zion-Con bellicose line. The ZPC-Israel Firsters' *Wars-For-Israel* crowd did have all of these 'resources' in abundance, and they used them to the maximum in a spiteful and arrogant fashion, when the occasion arose—such as when military officers testifying before Congress questioned the war-to-be in Iraq. Zion-militarists like Richard Perle, Norman Podhoretz and their influential cohort baited the military for having '*the most advanced arms and refusing to use them*', of being fearful of expending troops to defend US security interests in the Middle East, of being ultra-cautious when audacity and preemptive action was necessary. The Israel-Firsters, who not only never risked a broken fingernail on any battlefield, deprecated the generals to increase their power to order them around through their servile operatives in the Rumsfeld Pentagon, the Vice President's Office and on Bush's National Security Council. The Zion-Cons' armchair military strategists have absolutely no qualms in sending US troops to war in Afghanistan, Iraq and now Iran to enhance Israeli regional power. On the contrary, they ridicule the US military precisely to instigate them to prosecute wars and thereby avoid the loss of Israeli-Jewish lives, resulting from an Israeli attack on Iran to enhance its power in the Middle East.

Israel-Firsters Win Round One

For all of the above-enumerated reasons, the Israel-Firsters overcame the doubts and questions on the war raised by the military in the run-up to and continuation of the Iraq War. The ZPC's success in launching the war over military objections was largely due to their control over US civilian institutions and the primacy of these institutions over any and all military political dissent. However the ZPC was not content with repressing civilian dissent, they aggressively repressed and silenced any opposition from within the military: General Eric Shinseki, Chief of Staff of the Army saw his career destroyed when he questioned US policy on the eve of the Iraq invasion.[2] Two years later, General Peter Pace was denied a second term as chairman of the Joint Chiefs of Staff shortly after he rejected claims by the White House and the ZPC that Iran was supplying weapons to the Iraqi insurgents. Lieutenant General Ricardo Sanchez was retired following his call for the withdrawal of US troops in Iraq, which he later described as *"a nightmare with no end in sight".*[3] General John Abizaid, who "made clear his continued opposition to a major surge of U.S. troops in Iraq beyond the current 140,000"[4] followed, with the *Washington Post* describing him as "outflanked". Captains and colonels in the Pentagon who disagreed with the lies and fabrication of 'intelligence' by the Zion-Cons in the Pentagon leading to the Iraq invasion were marginalized and/or silenced. Zion-Cons in the Pentagon marginalized CIA intelligence reports that didn't fit in with their war propaganda—these studies were written, cut and spliced to serve their ends. The Zion-Cons in the Pentagon established a parallel 'intelligence' office under their exclusive control (the Office of Special Plans) and placed one of their own, Abram Shulsky, in charge.

In the Zion-Con charge to push the US into a new war with Iran, they (along with Vice President Cheney) delayed and forced the rewrite of a collective report by various intelligence agencies, the National Intelligence Estimate (NIE) on Iran, in an effort (albeit ultimately unsuccessful) to make it fit in with their war plans.

The humiliating defeats and gratuitous public insults which the victorious ZPC inflicted on the US military had the effect of raising the backs of senior officers in the run-up to a military attack on Iran. The military went public, fighting back with biting open criticism of the White House and Zion-Con war planners. The underlying deep and widespread hostility of the high-ranking military officials has nothing to do with Zion-Con charges of 'anti-Semitism' and everything to do with the destruction, demoralization and discredit of the US military which has resulted from following Zion-Con war policies in Iraq.

The US armed forces have crumbled and decayed as the Iraq occupation and counterinsurgency progresses into its sixth year. Over half of the officers are refusing to re-enlist, recruiting quotas are not being reached except by drastically lowering standards, and morale of on-duty reservists is at its lowest because of extended tours of duty. Black enlistment has dropped precipitously.[5] Despite the war being portrayed by President Bush and Israeli leaders including Prime Minister Olmert as good for Israel. American Jewish wartime enlistment is at its lowest in almost a century. Public esteem for the military has declined sharply since the war, exacerbated by Zionist (Richard Perle, Frederick Kagan, Kenneth Pollack and Martin Indyk) charges of incompetence against American military occupation forces. The loss of prestige, enlistment and the increasing overstretch of the army, and the abrasive and domineering way in which the Zion-Cons denigrate active US military commanders has raised their ire. At one point in an interview, General Tommy Franks referred to Zion-Con, ex-Under Secretary of Defense, Douglas Feith, as "the fucking stupidest guy on the face of the earth".

Round Two: American Military Resists War on Iran

Recognizing how they were outgunned by the Zion-Con monopoly of public space for political discussion in the run-up to the Iraq invasion, the military went public. Admiral William Fallon, as head of CENTCOM (Central Command) launched a series of interviews designed to counter Zion-Con war propaganda. He formed an anti-War-With-Iran alliance with senior military officers, Secretary of Defense Gates, and sectors of the intelligence services not under Zion-Con influence.[6] However, the Secretary of Defense was not a reliable ally to the officers opposed to an Iran war. When Fallon was forced by the White House and the Zion-Cons to resign, Gates caved in to ZPC pressure and abandoned the admiral.

Every major Israeli public spokesperson has at least raised the issue of a sneak attack ('preventive war' in Zion-speak) on Iran, and many are in favor of an immediate attack. Reliable sources in Israel claim that war preparations are already advanced. Fabricating 'existential threats' to Israeli existence, Israeli Foreign Minister Tzipi Livni has spoken forcefully, even … shrilly, about Iranian President Mahmoud Ahmadinejad's threat to 'wipe Israel off the map'—a much repeated, deliberate mistranslation of the President's reference to Israel (more reliable translations refer to 'the regime currently occupying Jerusalem disappearing into history').

While Israeli officials have placed war with Iran as the second most important priority on their foreign policy agenda, by far their highest priority is convincing and manipulating the US to carry out the war and save Israel the enormous economic cost and loss of Israeli lives—to say nothing of the domestically unsustainable possibility of significant destruction, for the first time, of *Israeli* infrastructure. The Israeli state has made its war policy the central task for their agents and their apparatus in the US. Accordingly, the ZPC has taken up the Israeli line with a vengeance. Several hundred full-time functionaries from all the major Jewish organizations have visited and 'advised' Congress that bellicose support for a war against Iran is the primary way to demonstrate their unconditional defense of Israel's 'survival' and guarantee campaign financing from their wealthy political donor base.

Over the past year, several major daily newspapers and weekly or monthly magazines from *The New York Times* through *Time, Newsweek, The New Yorker*, and the entire yellow press (*New York Post, New York Sun, The Daily News*) have published reams of propaganda articles fabricating an Iranian nuclear threat, demonizing Iran and its leaders and calling for the US to bomb Iran and eliminate Israel's 'existential' (the most nauseating and overused cliché) threat. Several thousand op-ed pieces have been written parroting the Israeli war on Iran line by a small army of Zionist academics and think tank propagandists. Breathless and vitriolic, the Israel Firsters claim that 'time is running out', that Iran's pursuit of diplomacy is a ploy promoting inaction, that Iran's well-documented openness to negotiations is a trick. Venomous attacks are launched against Europeans for not pursuing the military option; Germany is slandered as following in the footsteps of the Nazis because its industries and banks still do business with Iran.

US critics of the ZPC's pursuit of an Iranian war for Israel are accused of being 'soft on terrorism', appeasers, and almost always labeled as overt or covert 'anti-Semites'. The massive, sustained and one-sided dominance by the ZPC of the Iranian war narrative has been successful. US public opinion surveys show over half (52% according to a Zogby Poll)[7] of the US public is in favor of offensive bombing of Iran.

The clearest and most vicious Zion-Con counterattack against the US military's harsh reaction to their leading the United States into the Iraq War came from a predictable ultra-Zionist think-tank, the Foreign Policy Research Center (FPRC) run by Ilan Berman, a close collaborator with the Israeli extremist Likud leader, Netanyahu. Speaking at a meeting co-sponsored by the FPRC and the Reserve Officers Association on October 15, 2007 titled "'Mind the Gap': Post-Iraq Civil-Military Relations in America", senior fellow Frank Hoffman attempted to turn senior military officers' criticism of the disastrous Zion-Con-authored Iraq War into a sinister military plot:

"The nation's leadership, civilian and military, need to come to grips with the emerging 'stab-in-the-back' thesis in the armed services and better define the social compact and code of conduct that governs the overall relationship between the masters of policy and the dedicated servants we [sic] ask to carry it out."[8] Hoffman attempts to deflect military and public anger at the enormous damage in morale, recruitment and lives which the Zion-Con war policies have inflicted on the US Armed Forces by invoking an abstract entity: "Our collective failure [sic] to address the torn fabric and weave a stronger and more enduring relationship will only allow a sore to fester and ultimately undermine the nation's security."[9]

Obfuscating Zionist control over war policy, Hoffman instead refers to *"civilian"* control over the military as being *"constitutionally, structurally and historically well-grounded."* This is nonsense: there is no provision, article or clause in the American Constitution which states that the military should submit to civilian power subordinate to a foreign state...

After a vacuous general discussion of civilian-military relations in the lead-up to the Zion-Con designed Iraq War, Hoffman then tries to paint the military critics of Zion-Con Donald Rumsfeld as attacking an innovative defender of civilian supremacy over the military—even as Rumsfeld embraced torture techniques wholesale and violated every principle of the Geneva Convention of War and US Military Code of Conduct toward prisoners and civilians. Hoffman turns up the Zion-Con venom against military officers who dared to question Rumsfeld's application of Israel's illegal and totalitarian technique of colonial warfare in Iraq. Then, despite having castigated the military for questioning Rumsfeld, he launches a diatribe against the professional competence of senior military advisers, "who failed to provide military counsel because they were intimidated 'yes men' or who failed to recognize the complexity of war".[10] Berman's prodigy, Hoffman, is trying to make a case that the Zion-Con 'masters of Iraq war policy' were not responsible for the disastrous war—It was the military officers "who failed to provide candid advice, who fail in their duty to their immediate superiors and stay in their posts (who) are guilty of dereliction of duty to the President, the Congress and their subordinates."[11] The same Zion-Cons who drove out and forced the resignation of American generals who had dissented with Wolfowitz, Feith, Abrams and Rumsfeld are now judging and condemning these very officers for dereliction of duty.

The Zion-Cons follow the Goebbels principle: 'The Big Lie repeated often enough can convince the stupid masses.'

The Berman-Hoffman FPRC counter-attack against American military officers speaking truth to power is a limp effort to deflect attention from the Zion-Con policymakers' treasonous behavior and their role in degrading the US military. The FPRC document blaming the military and unnamed civilians (exclusively non-Zionist) for the Iraq debacle is one of numerous variants on the same theme by Zionist academic militarists justifying the policy directions advocated by the ZPC under the cloak of promoting and defending civilian supremacy over the military, without spelling out the national loyalties of the 'civilian' masters of career military officers.

According to a detailed report published in the *Financial Times*, the US military did not buy the Zion-Con line: "Admiral William Fallon, head of Central Command which oversees military operations in the Middle East, said that while dealing with Iran was a 'challenge' a military strike was not in the offing." [12] Backed by many active senior officers and numerous retired generals, Fallon dismissed the Zion-Con intellectuals and propagandists as ignorant warmongers. In his own words: "It astounds me that so many pundits and others are spending so much time yakking about this topic [of a military attack on Iran]". [13]

In direct repudiation of the ZPC's frenetic campaigning for economic sanctions leading to a military attack, top US military officials and even Secretary of Defense Gates blocked the military option. Addressing the Zionist strategy of sequential wars against Israel's enemies (Iran, Syria, Lebanon), Fallon stated: "It seems to me that we don't need more problems". His remarks were understood to reflect the views of the majority of senior officers in the Middle East combat zone—but not Bush's politically ambitious General Petraeus, who worked with his Israeli-Mossad partners (in Northern Iraq "Kurdistan") in training and arming the Kurdish militia death squads (Peshmerga).

Retired Generals Anthony Zinni and Joseph Hoar, both former heads of CENTCOM, have pointed their fingers at the menace of the Zion-Cons and Israel-Firsters in the government. According to Gen. Hoar, "There is no doubt that an element in the government wants to strike Iran. But the good news is that the Secretary of Defense and senior military are against it". [14] The forced and voluntary retirement, including the indictment and jailing of some highly placed Zion-Cons in the Pentagon, White House, Treasury and State Departments, has weakened their stranglehold over US policy in the White House. The top Zion-Con policymakers who have left or are in jail include Rumsfeld (Gentile Zionist), Wolfowitz, Feith, Larry Franklin, Shulsky, Perle—in the Pentagon; Irving Libby, Wurmser; plus Ari Fleicher, Frum in the White House and many others too numerous to name.

For a period it seemed that, while the Zion-Cons retained power in the higher circles of government, they would not be able to run roughshod over their military critics and opponents as they did in the run-up to the Iraq war. In part this was because of the horrendous situation resulting from their war on Iraq, which has undermined their credibility and turned the vast majority of the US public against the war. Equally the Zion-Cons' war and the disastrous impact of a prolonged (5 year) urban guerrilla resistance on the US Armed Forces in terms of loss of personnel, morale, junior and senior officers and the over-extension of the US military to the detriment of the defense of the US Empire's interests around the world, has served as a 'wake-up call' for the senior military command.

Drawing on their experience from the invasion of Iraq, few if any accept the Israeli-Zion-Con 'evaluations' of the outcome and response to a military attack on Iran. They remember too well the optimistic propaganda put out by Zionist academic ideologues like Kagan and Cohen that the 'Iraqis will celebrate and welcome American forces into Baghdad as liberators'. And then, there is the fiasco of the Israeli assault on Lebanon, which, together with the quagmire in Iraq, impacts military thinking on the plausibility of successful wars with peoples' armies.

According to a report in the *Financial Times*, retired General Zinni, speaking for the many active senior officers, says 'even a limited American attack could push Teheran to retaliate in a number of ways such as firing missiles at Israel, Saudi oilfields and US bases in Iraq, mining the Straits [sic] of Hormuz and activating sleeper terrorist cells around the world."[15] He concluded by pointing out, "It is not a matter of a one-strike option. It is the classic question of... 'and then what'?". A more circumspect criticism of the Iran war reasoning was voiced by Admiral Mike Muller, who objected to the US-Israeli agents "putting the military option on the table". Admiral Muller added, "We're in a conflict in two countries out there right now. We have to be incredibly thoughtful about the potential of in fact getting into a conflict with a third country in that part of the world."[16]

One of the biggest dangers in forcing the US into a war with Iran is an Israeli sneak air attack, in which it destroys Iranian military installations, causing Iran to retaliate against the US, Israel's ally, main financier and armaments supplier. An Israeli air strike is not the only conceivable war provocation—the Mossad is deeply in involved in training Kurdish commandos to carry out terrorist cross-border attacks from Iraq, killing Iranian civilians and soldiers, bombing military installations and collecting intelligence, hoping to provoke a large-scale Iranian military response against 'Kurdistan'. Iranian retaliation against Mossad-trained Kurdish terrorists could then be twisted by Zion-Con ideologues and their 'political elements in Washington' (to quote Admiral Fallon) into being a major Iranian invasion of Iraq, in the hope of convincing the Bush White House to 'counter-attack in defense of our troops in Iraq'.

The Israeli regime and its Fifth Column in the United States have been pressing for unilateral intervention against Iran, preferably military, ever since 2003. The *Daily Alert*, mouthpiece of the 52 biggest Jewish organizations (Conference of Presidents of Major American Jewish Organizations) has published scores of articles each week, characterizing the Europeans as 'foot draggers', 'weak on Iran', 'playing down' or 'failing' to take serious the 'existential threat to Israel'. The US Zion-Cons have their own 'State

Department' and 'overseas' missions, with their own 'foreign policy-makers and spokespeople'. They meet with European, Asian and Latin American heads of state in the US or during 'visits' overseas, mobilizing, advising, organizing and strengthening Zion-Con outposts throughout Europe and beyond.

The Zionist international reach has succeeded in favorably impacting a number of important decisions and appointments, most notably in Brussels and in Sarkozy's appointment of Zionist fanatic, Bernard Kouchner, as France's Minister of Foreign Relations. In a rather crude and undiplomatic show of Zionist loyalty immediately upon taking office, Kouchner declared France to be in favor of a military option against Iran. While he was later pressured to retract, Sarkozy, himself, is no minor league Israel supporter, and has echoed Kouchner's line. One of Kouchner's first acts was to travel to American-occupied Iraq to express his personal support for the occupation. As a result of Israeli and Zion-Con pressure on the White House, France, Germany and England have all supported the escalation of sanctions against Iran...the same Zionist strategy that was applied to Iraq: 'strangle the economy now and bomb later'.

Making the IAEA Report Safe for American Public Consumption

The Zion-Cons are extremely effective in discrediting any and all impartial international bodies and reports which fail to support the Israeli line that Iran represents an 'existential threat' to its survival (code language for 'challenges or resists Israel's drive to dominate the region'). Predictably taking their cue from the Israeli foreign office's dismissal of the United Nations International Atomic Energy Agency's report[17] which documented that Iran had no nuclear arms program and no capacity to construct a nuclear weapon at least for the next five years, the ZPC unleashed a mass media propaganda campaign attacking the IAEA chairman as a 'pro-Iranian' agent.[18] At the same time the news 'reports' used 'potted quotes' from the Report, mentioning only the IAEA 'reservations' and the 'questions unanswered' and 'issues not addressed', seeking to convey the impression that the IAEA report had been a condemnation of Iran, rather than having numerous positive features.

US Senator from Tel Aviv, Joseph Lieberman, combined both a distorted (or blatantly falsified) version of the IAEA Report and a vicious attack on its Chief, El Baradei, claiming that the Report 'made it clear [sic] that Iran was still hiding [sic] large parts of its nuclear program'.[19] A careful or even casual reading of the IAEA Report shows not a single paragraph, line or word stating that Iran was 'hiding large parts of its nuclear program' as Lieberman accused. In fact, as the BBC reported: "the IAEA also noted the answers Iran had given about the history of its centrifuge programme were consistent with the agency's own findings."[20] Ever mendacious,

Lieberman, who had publicly called for an immediate military attack on 'Iran, Iraq and Syria' just days after the September 11, 2001 terrorist attack, viciously attacked El Baradei for writing in the report that Iran was cooperating, and for not recommending a new round of sanctions. In other words, the Zion-Cons with their mediocre academic mouthpieces can save the UN, the IAEA and El Baradei's time and money in site visits and delicate radiologic and satellite monitoring by simply basing all assessments of Iran's nuclear status on the Israeli Foreign Office's pre-packaged 'press' handouts or 'sexed-up intelligence reports'. The fact that the Report itself was publicly available for anyone who wished to check out what it actually said was no deterrent to broadcasting lies about it, cooking up threats and telling a world eager for peace that Iran is not cooperative and should be heavily sanctioned, starved or bombed into submission. The Zion-Cons follow the guidelines of the Jewish state's agenda, seeking to turn Iran into a Gaza Strip of deprivation and desperation.

The Israeli dismissal of the UN report on Iran, and the Zion-Con falsification of its content and attack on its chief negotiator, El Baradei, was echoed by the White House and the Zion-colonized Congress. With a lack of originality characteristic of US Middle East policymakers, they also cited the potted quotes from the IAEA Report to justify harsher sanctions and a greater degree of confrontation. The purpose is to provoke a breakup of the dialog long established between the IAEA and Iran. The Zion-Con/White House strategy is to implicate the IAEA in their savage attacks on Iran, and via harsher economic sanctions, end Iran's cooperation with the IAEA. Having themselves forced the IAEA out of Iran, they would then accuse Iran of rejecting dialog and cooperation with the United Nations. This contrived scenario (like the earlier phony claims that 'Saddam threw out the weapons inspectors') would set the stage for a US-British-led military attack under the pretext that all diplomatic approaches failed to deter Iran's nuclear program which the IAEA had denied had any military component. It behooves everyone to actually consult the IAEA website and read the reports' favorable account of Iran's willing cooperation in providing site visits, documents and responses in answer to many of the key issues raised by the IAEA, the US and the EU. The report ultimately refutes the major accusations cooked up by the Zion-Cons and their political assets in the White House, State Department and Congress. The most important information contained in the IAEA Report is that its inspectors found no evidence of any Iranian effort to develop nuclear weapons.

Fundamental Issues in Dispute by the US Military and Israel-Firsters

There are at least 5 fundamental issues in dispute between senior American military officials and the ZPC:

1. *The extent of the Iranian threat:* The ZPC argues that Iran represents an immediate deadly threat to the US, Israel, Iraq and the Gulf States. The American officers do not see the Iranians as a threat because they have engaged the Iranians in stopping the flow of arms and fighters to the Iraqi resistance; they recognize Iranian positive diplomatic overtures to all the Gulf States including Saudi Arabia; the US armada in the Persian Gulf is confident they can act as a deterrent to any Iranian attack; and finally, the US Central Command know they are in the Persian Gulf facing Iran because of the White House's provocative offensive strategy— and that Iran has not demonstrated anything but a defensive capability. Senior American officers view favorably Iranian President Mahmoud Ahmadinejad's offer *"to discuss with Arab nations a plan to enrich uranium outside the region in a neutral country such as Switzerland."*[21] Not a single major television or print media in the US ran the Iranian president's offer—as would be predictable in the United States' Zionized media.

2. *Iran's Uranium Enrichment Program:* The Israelis, the only nuclear power in the Middle East, and among the top five nuclear powers, argue that Iran, which does not have a single nuclear weapon or even a weapons program, is an 'existential [sic] threat' to Israel, the Middle East, Europe and the United States. This is one argument that the ZPC has used to convince the Democratic Party majority in Congress, the White House and the pro-Israel wing of the US Peace Movement to escalate economic sanctions and keep the 'military option' on the table.

   The only problem is that most European, Asian, African and Latin American diplomats, experts, the majority of world public opinion, and most senior American officers don't buy Israel's shrill disinformation. All legal experts who have given a perfunctory look at the non-proliferation agreement (NPA) insist that there is absolutely no clause or article prohibiting uranium enrichment. Intelligence experts and US military report that, at the earliest, Iran may have sufficient enriched uranium by 2010 and may be able to produce a low-yield weapon by 2010-2015. The job of the ZPC, pursued at full speed, is to bury the NPA determination of what is in fact internationally legal and legitimate under mountains of fabrications, arguing that enriching uranium itself is a violation of 'international law'. The purpose of this attempt to concoct a full state of belligerency is to escalate US and Israeli attacks on Iran and hasten the timing of a surprise, offensive onslaught. This is exactly the reason why American intelligence briefings and IAEA reports have aroused the fury of Israel and its operatives in the US and their calling for El Baradei's dismissal.

3. *Iranian Arms to Iraq*: The US Military and CENTCOM have repeatedly denied, especially in light of another ZPC onslaught to the contrary, that the Iranian government is supplying arms, especially roadside mines or IEDs to Iraqi 'terrorists' and its allied militia forces. Contrary to the assertion of the leading Israeli spokespeople in the US Senate, the US military categorically denies that the IEDs are made in Iran, having discovered bomb-making factories in Iraq, having conducted interrogations and having actually studied the construction and contents of the IEDs.

Nonetheless, Zionist-colonized Senators led by Hillary Clinton have followed the lead of Israeli Senatorial Spokesman, Joseph Lieberman, rather than consulting with the American military, and are mouthing the rhetoric of Iranian arms killing American soldiers.[22] Following the Lieberman-Israeli-ZPC propaganda blitz, the US Senate voted in favor of the Lieberman-Kyle resolution naming Iran's principle border defense force, the Revolutionary Guard, a 'terrorist organization', moving one step closer to an attack. The hollowness of this resolution is reflected in the fact that not one of the US's servile allies chose to follow its lead in denouncing the Revolutionary Guard. Nothing more clearly demonstrates the Israeli-ZPC colonization of the US Congress than questions of war and peace, when the legislature is more likely to follow the dictates of Israeli propagandists than to consult its own senior military officials.

4. *Consequences of an attack on Iran*: The main concern of the ZPC and its political clients in the White House and Congress is that an attack on Iran will secure the safety of Israel, eliminating a 'mortal enemy', preventing 'another Holocaust' and stopping a 'new Hitler'. In pursuit of this policy, Israel's US agents have repeatedly blocked every open-ended Iranian effort to cooperate with the US against the Taliban, Al Qaeda and other 'terrorists groups' as is profusely documented by two former high-ranking policy experts from the Bush Administration's National Security Council, Hillary Mann and Flynt Leverett.[23] Every Iranian offer of unconditional negotiation and cooperation with the US to fight terrorism, as the US defines it, was rejected by key extremist Zion-Cons in the Pentagon (Feith), the Vice-President's office (Irving Libby), the National Security Council (Elliott Abrams and the President's National Security Adviser, Stephen Hadley, a

zealous Gentile Zion-Con). The Zion-Cons paint a picture of an air attack which would simultaneously blow up all Iranian nuclear research facilities, infrastructure, airfields, military bases and ports... preventing any and all Iranian counter attacks against US strategic interests in the region. They further embellish their apocalyptic vision by arguing that the Islamic republic would then be overthrown by a populace grateful to the Americans for bombing their country, destroying its infrastructure, and killing thousands. The Zion-Cons' infantile delusions (or their political need to serve up a positive line and backup talking points, irrespective of reality) then led them to project the emergence of a pro-Western Iranian secular state favorable to American occupation of the Middle East and, of course, wholeheartedly renouncing any 'existential' threats to the 'survival' of its new ally, Israel.

On the issue of the consequences of an attack on Iran, the US military is totally at odds with the Israeli-ZPC propaganda. Senior military officials estimate, based on real estimates on the ground and from hard data from intelligence experts, that Iran will be in a position to retaliate and cause enormous immediate and long-term damage to strategic US and global interests. CENTCOM estimates that:

- Iran will set off air-to-sea missiles aimed at the US fleet stationed in the Persian Gulf and land-to-land missiles destroying oil production sites in the Gulf States, creating a major world oil shortage, doubling oil prices and provoking a world recession as energy scarcities paralyze production.

- The Iranians will send several tens of thousands of its elite forces across the border into Iraq, joining with its Iraqi Shia allies to overrun US bases and endanger the lives of the 160,000 US troops currently in Iraq. This would undermine the entire Iraq war effort, inflicting a strategic defeat and further undermining US military capacity in the Middle East and elsewhere.

- The Iranians will be able to easily block the Strait of Hormuz so that one third of the Middle East's oil shipments will be paralyzed.

- Military intelligence estimates that Iranian 'sleeper cells' in Asia, Africa, Europe and perhaps in North America will be activated and engage in 'big impact' terrorist missions.

Whatever the likelihood of this scenario, it is clear that the US military anticipates major protests and perhaps even the violent overthrow of its clients in the Middle East, if not elsewhere.

Zion-Cons have neither countered military intelligence estimates with any credible counter-facts, nor even seriously considered the likely disastrous consequences affecting the US, Europe and Asia. They only consider Israel's 'security' and its regional ambitions. They have not thought beyond the initial destruction of Iran, regarding that as signaling Mission Accomplished, irrespective of what might follow. No Zionophile or Zion-Con has considered the enormous costs in terms of US lives and damage to the now fragile US economy and society of a third full scale, prolonged war. In effect, the Zion-cons will kill their own US goose, which has laid golden eggs for Israel for almost 6 decades. It is an example of the Zion-Cons' supreme arrogance and sense of their own power that they feel they can plunge the US into a third Asian war which will devastate the US economy and cause world-wide energy scarcity, and still secure their yearly 'tribute' of $3 billion Dollars foreign aid for Israel as well as guaranteeing oil for Israel by diverting it from the needs of American consumers and industries. It is clear that in doing a cost-benefit analysis on a US attack on Iran, Israeli and ZPC operatives have approvingly figured that the costs are on the US side of the ledger and the benefits are for the Israelis. Were it known, American public opinion might disapprove. Furthermore, it is not the case that Israel would suffer "nothing" beyond the side effects of US devastation of Iran. A million people fled Haifa during the war on Lebanon, and the impact on their "not accustomed to losing" population was huge. In such circumstances, could Israel truly remain out of range?

The main difference is that the US does not have a comparable Washington Power Configuration in Tel Aviv to influence Israeli policy to match the Jewish state's Zionist Power Configuration which shapes and influences US Middle East policy.

Military/Zion-Con: Punch and Counterpunch

By the end of 2007, it was clear that the US military, led by CENTCOM Commander Admiral William Fallon and Secretary of Defense Gates, had successfully, if temporarily, contained the strenuous Israeli-Zion-Con military thrust to war, though Gates backtracked under ZPC pressure and later denied that he had taken the military option 'off the table'. In response, the Zion-Cons launched an around-end tactic by intensifying their efforts to impose a global economic blockade to strangle the Iranian economy. The Zionized White House pressured and secured the support of Gordon Brown of Great Britain, and Sarkozy of France for a set of economic sanctions that has undermined dialog with the IAEA.[24]

This is the strategic goal of the Zion-Cons: no dialog, no diplomacy, and a blockaded, weakened economy, ripe for Anglo-French-American bombing. The Zion-Cons shrewdly avoided a head-on confrontation with Fallon and his allies and eventually succeeded in ousting them. They recognized that a bruising battle would have exposed their Fifth Column credentials. Since the military would be called upon to carry out the military option which it strongly opposes, the Zion-Cons turned to their automatic, rubber-stamp majority in the US Congress and especially their most zealous Zionists in the federal bureaucracy. Treasury Department functionary Stuart Levey has devoted all of his working time browbeating, banning and blacklisting any and all businesses and banks dealing directly or indirectly with Iran or its trading partners.

Both the military/Israel-First confrontation, and Treasury's financial assault on Iran were to intensify, as we will discuss in greater detail, later.

Conclusion

The deepening and all-important conflict between the pro-Israel warmongers and the anti-war American senior officers is reaching a bitter climax. As the US military disintegrates under prolonged colonial warfare, the ZPC intensifies its campaign for a third war for Israel and against Iran, a war which will totally shatter the US military forces.

The fundamental question emerging for most senior officers, in private gatherings and informal discussions, is 'Who commands our Commander in Chief?' The deep animosity of US senior active military officers frequently erupts at the ZPC's careless and callous disregard for American lives. They disdainfully refer to the Zion-Con policymakers as 'arm-chair military strategists' who never fought a war, never shot or been shot. At one level, the senior military officers are appalled by the ignorance of the Zion-Con military 'experts' and policymakers featured by the Zion-Con-controlled mass media. One of the most frequent military criticisms is that the Zion-Con policymakers don't have an 'exit strategy'—attributing it to their lack of knowledge or strategic thinking. In reality, the lack of Zion-Con concern for a realistic exit strategy is because the Zion-Cons are concerned (in light of Israel's priorities) only with an *entry* policy, namely, degrading the invaded countries' military and economic potential. Secondly, the Zion-Cons do not have an exit strategy because they believe the US should stay, colonize, build bases, and engage in a prolonged war for a chimerical total victory, while holding the fort for Israeli commercial expansion.

The question of 'who commands the Commander in Chief' goes to the entire core of our constitutional order, because it raises the deeper question of 'who defines the *national interests*' for which the military are fighting? If, as we have documented, the ZPC has effectively colonized the

White House and Legislative Branches (and the Justice Department and secured the appointment of an ultra-Zionist Attorney General, Michael Mulkasey, and Israel-First Head of Homeland Security, Michael Chertoff), to serve the interests of a foreign power (Israel), in what sense does a colonized political system serve the interests of a democratic public? Does there exist a primary condition that makes it possible to speak of a democracy, namely *national self-determination*, with *de-colonization* necessary for the re-democratization of American political institutions?

So far the only effective resistance to colonization has come from the US military. The military is a *non-democratic*, hierarchical institution but an institution representative of the public's opposition to colonial encroachments.

What would normally be considered the prime movers challenging Zion-Con colonization, namely the President, Congress, the political parties, or even the antiwar movements, have abdicated their responsibilities—they have been, in part or whole, colonized and neutralized.

By default, it fell to senior military commanders who reject being commanded by the ZPC at the service of Israel. Paradoxically, it is the military that has taken over the struggle against an offensive war with Iran where the American peace movement has failed. It is the military, which has challenged the Zion-Con agenda, where the Congress has been corrupted and capitulated for reasons of campaign financing, political blackmail and dual loyalty.

Where does that leave us, as democrats and anti-colonists?

We should be able to have both an independent de-colonized and democratic America, governed by patriotic Americans. But suppose we have to choose between de-colonization led by the military or a corrupt colonized electoral system—what should be done?

The ideal solution would be a revitalized civil society including secularist citizens, Muslims, Christians, and non-Zionist Jews, organized in an anti-war, anti-colonial movement, and political parties allied with patriotic officers to 're-found the republic'. The purpose would be to establish a republic to 'defend the heartland' from fires, floods, economic pillage, terrorists, ecological predators and foreign agents acting on behalf of alien regimes. Can it happen? We shall see. What is becoming clear however is that the anti-colonial imperative is growing stronger by the day. If it doesn't come from below, it may come solely from above, whether we like it or not, and with all the negative ramifications that would accompany it.

ENDNOTES

[1]   Truthdig, November 13, 2007.
[2]   "On August 1, 2003, Donald Rumsfeld replaced General Shinseki as Army Chief of

Staff with General Peter J. Schoomaker after Shineski "questioned the cakewalk scenario, and told Congress (that February) that we would need several hundred thousand soldiers in Iraq to put an end to the violence against our troops and against each other." Cited by SourceWatch, <http://why-war.com/news/2003/09/14/seekingh.html>

3   David S. Cloud, "Former Top General in Iraq Faults Bush Administration", *The New York Times*, October 12, 2007.

4   Anne Scott Tyson and Josh White, "A Soldier's Soldier, Outflanked," *Washington Post*, December 21, 2006.

5   Sarah Abruzzeese, "Iraq War Brings Drop in Black Enlistees," *The New York Times*, August 22, 2007.

6   *Financial Times*, November 12, 2007 p.1.

7   The poll was taken on October 29, 2007. See <http://www.zogby.com/news/ReadNews.dbm?ID=1379>

8   "Dereliction of Duty Redux?" See <http://www.fpri.org/enotes/200711.hoffman.derelictionofdutyredux.html>

9   Ibid.

10   ibid.

11   ibid.

12   *Financial Times*, November 12, 2007, pp. 1 and 9.

13   Ibid.

14   Ibid.

15   Ibid.

16   Ibid.

17   IAEA Report, GOV/2007/58, November 15, 2007. <http://www.iaea.org/Publications/Documents/Board/2007/gov2007-58.pdf>

18   *Jerusalem Post* November 16, 2007.

19   Ibid.

20   "Mixed UN Nuclear Report for Iran," BBC, November 15, 2007.

21   Dow Jones News Service in Saudi Arabia, quoted in "Iran Eyes Nuclear Options Abroad", BBC News November 18, 2007.

22   *Financial Times*, November 12, 2007, p.9.

23   See 'The Secret History of the Impending War with Iran That the White House Doesn't Want You to Know', *Esquire Magazine*, November 2007

24   While initially, Britain said it could act only as part of a general EU decision and, within the EU, countries such as Germany, Austria, Spain and Italy called for a UN decision before they would proceed, it appears that the EU will soon "tighten the screws" on one of Iran's biggest banks. "Bank Melli, Iran's biggest commercial bank, is set to be banned from operating in the European Union under proposals in the final stages of discussion in Brussels. " Daniel Dombey, "EU set to tighten screws on Iranian bank", *Financial Times*, May 15, 2008.

25   For updates on Iraqi deaths, go to <http://www.justforeignpolicy.org/iraq/iraqdeaths.html>

CHAPTER 3

BURYING
THE NATIONAL
INTELLIGENCE
ESTIMATE

"The most important thing [sic] *that should be said about Bush is that had I told him that I was opposed to this move* [the Annapolis meeting], *he wouldn't have embarked on it. I could have blocked the move. Had I been unwilling to co-operate with him, Bush wouldn't have coerced me... I spoke to the President with unparalleled sharpness about these matters* [bombing Iran's nuclear facilities] *and my comments were extremely well received—regarding the freedom* [to bomb Iran] *we are reserving for ourselves and what we will and won't do.*
Israeli Prime Minister Ehud Olmert
Haaretz, November 29, 2007.

Introduction

During and immediately after the Annapolis meetings to discuss peace, Israel abducted the student president of West Bank Bir Zeit University for dissent; launched over 50 attacks on Gaza, killing and wounding over 50 Palestinian civilians, police and militia; set in motion a vast building project of 250 new apartments in Palestinian East Jerusalem; projected permanent Israeli military posts in the West Bank; rejected any time limits or specific goals in their negotiations with the PLO; and launched a virulent dismissal of the major US intelligence report (National Intelligence Estimate) on the non-existence of an Iranian nuclear weapons program.

Israel's presence at Annapolis had absolutely nothing to do with its intent to seek peace or promises to negotiate in good faith. Its purpose was to deflect attention from its meat-grinder-style genocidal policies in Gaza and its relentless drive to savagely dispossess all Palestinians of any territory or semblance of autonomy, literally turning off the lights (energy), gas and water for 1.4 million Palestinians residing in Gaza. Since September 11, 2001 the Israeli state, Zionists inside the US government, and the entire leadership of Conference of Presidents of Major American Jewish Organizations have been entirely devoted to pushing the US into Middle East wars on behalf of Israel.

Israeli and Zion-Con success in destroying Iraq, however, was secured at an enormous cost in US military demoralization that far exceeds the relatively few casualties,[1] and one trillion dollars (and counting) in cost to the US taxpayers. As a result, public opinion dramatically shifted against the war, despite the intervention of the Israeli regime in shaping US public opinion via its army of 'Israel-First' academic and journalistic scribes and propagandists with broad access to the US mass media.

As I pointed out in the previous chapter, the devastating effects that the Israeli-Zion-Con-promoted Iraq War has had on the US military and intelligence agencies led to widespread opposition within the US state to the Israeli-Zionist push for mounting a new war against Iran. This historic struggle over Iran policy split the top echelons of the Washington policymakers. On the one hand, the Israeli Firsters controlled or influenced the White House, the majority of Congress and key Congressional committee chairpersons, the financing of both major political parties, the leading presidential candidates and the bulk of the mass media. The opposition was led by senior active and retired military officers, backed by the great majority of middle level officers and ground troops, especially the reserves. The entire range of top intelligence officials were disgusted by the 'Israel Firsters' in the Pentagon because of their distortion and fabrication of 'intelligence' via newly invented agencies and their reliance on Israeli disinformation over US intelligence.

This monumental struggle within the government was not merely about US military policy toward Iran (which is crucial) but also about who *rules* the US, who commands the US military, and who formulates intelligence reports that inform policy, and most basically: *whose interests are being served*. The military command in the Middle East, led by Admiral William Fallon, came out publicly opposing the Israeli-Fifth Column policy to bomb Iran. The active commanders were meekly backed by the rubber-spined Defense Secretary, Robert Gates, and surreptitiously (at first) by the top intelligence chiefs. The Zion-Cons retaliated by launching the White House and Congress in a crusade to escalate economic sanctions and to 'keep the military option' on the table. Every major Israel-First academic and propaganda think tank followed up the Israeli war planning with a wave of op-ed articles and interviews throughout the mass media about Iran's immediate nuclear threat. The President, who does nothing contrary to Israeli Prime Minister Ehud Olmert (as trumpeted by Olmert himself), pronounced an apocalyptic message to the world in October 2007 (six weeks before the National Intelligence Estimate was finally released) proclaiming the advent of 'World War Three' against Iran's nuclear weapons program and the threat of a nuclear attack (a 'holocaust') by Iran against the people of the US and Israel.

The White House was privy to the findings in the National Intelligence Estimate (NIE) on Iran at least 9 months before they were made public, as witnessed by President Cheney's frequent interventions to alter their content and conclusion, and repeated efforts to postpone their publication because it undermined the basis for their push to attack Iran. The Israeli government and its US Fifth Column, well aware of the forthcoming publication of the findings of sixteen top US intelligence agencies, did everything in their power to precipitate a US war with Iran, from issuing hair-raising tales of the 'existential threats to Israel's survival' to encouraging rousing bellicose speeches by AIPAC, Zionist and Jewish community leaders. Israel bombed Syria which has a mutual security pact with Iran, and escalated Israeli-trained Kurdish terrorist attacks across the Iranian border in order to provoke Iranian retaliation—to no avail. AIPAC and its Congressional allies led by Israeli-US Senator Lieberman pulled out all stops to force a conflict, labeling the national branch of the Iranian military special force, the Revolutionary Guard Corp., as an illegal 'terrorist organization' and thus an automatic target of US military attacks under the doctrine of the 'War against Terror'.[2]

Equally oblivious of the NIE Report almost immediately forthcoming in November 2007—of which he must have been aware—and after UN sanctions against Iran reflected Russian and Chinese skepticism concerning Iran's nuclear threat, US Treasury Secretary Henry M. Paulson moved in to throw the might of the US Treasury behind sanctions on Iran on October 25, 2007:

> The IRGC as a whole—a 125,000-person force—and the Defense Ministry were designated as proliferators of weapons of mass destruction and ballistic missiles. The IRGC's Quds Force was named under a separate executive order as a "specially designated global terrorist" group; beyond Iraq, it is active in supporting groups elsewhere that the United States considers terrorists: Hezbollah in Lebanon as well as Hamas and Palestinian Islamic Jihad in Gaza and the West Bank. In all, more than 20 Iranian entities will be sanctioned, including banks, other firms,

and individuals. The state-owned banks targeted are Bank Melli, Iran's largest; Bank Mellat, which allegedly provides services to Iran's nuclear entities; and Bank Sanderat, which allegedly has been used by the Iranian government to send funds to Hezbollah, Hamas, and Palestinian Islamic Jihad.[3]

Just as sanctions had functioned to weaken Iraq prior to US invasion, the determination to impose same on Iran whether or not this was possible through the UN presaged a similar modus operandi.

Earlier in his tenure, Treasury Secretary Paulson had appeared to be on the opposite side of the ledger[4] to the militarist Zion-Cons, favoring market-over military-driven empire.[5] The innovative leap and ferocity of Paulson's effort to bring the weight of the US Treasury to bear against Iranian state agencies and finance through the global private financial sector, when all other means to further attack the Iranian economy seemed to be failing, seems to give the lie to any notion that Paulson did not belong in the Zion-Con militarists' camp along with Wolfowitz, Feith, Abrams, Schulsky, Scheunemann, Zelikow et al. in the Pentagon and elsewhere. This marks the emergence of yet another powerful figure heading yet another major department in the government of the United States—Treasury—taking unusual measures to wield US power in furtherance of the Israeli line.

The hyperactivity, the vicious military attacks, the strident rhetoric against all critics of the military option, and the urgency with which the Israelis and their US supporters acted, was not due to any imminent Iranian nuclear threat but rather a desperate effort to precipitate the war before the US National Intelligence Estimate became public and undermined their entire war propaganda campaign and military preparations for an attack.

The NIE findings[6] dated November 2007 temporarily closed the book on the White House-Israeli-Zionist Big Lie that Iran was engaged in developing weapons to launch a nuclear war. The NIE report refuted its own previous conclusions of 2005, which were heavily influenced by the White House and its Zionist-Israeli backers. The reversal of conclusions was not based on 'new data' or information techniques, as is claimed. The change resulted from a dramatic shift in the balance of forces within the US government and in particular the strengthening of the US military elite versus the pro-war Zionist Power Configuration, a shift shaped by the enormous and unending American losses in Iraq and Afghanistan.

A key factor in pushing the US intelligence agencies to break with their past subjugation to White House manipulation and Israeli-Zionist fabricated intelligence was the repeated failures and incredible stupidity of the Israeli intelligence agencies—leading to a loss of their credibility. Israeli intelligence had blundered and miscalculated on Hezbollah's strength and organization, which led to a debacle when Israel invaded Lebanon in the summer of 2006. Israeli estimates on Iraqi capacity to resist invasion and foreign occupation (so eagerly accepted and propagated by top Zionist Pentagon officials in the lead up to the invasion) led to a US war of attrition in Iraq with no end in sight—similar to Israel's conflict with the Palestinians. Israel's intelligence totally underestimated Hamas' electoral strength in the run-up to their electoral victory over the PLO. Israeli intelligence overestimated the PLO's military capacity to defeat and destroy Hamas in Gaza. Israel's claim to have detected a nuclear facility in Syria, which it bombed, was an international joke—as it could not have destroyed a (fictional) nuclear facility without producing a speck of radioactive dust! Learning from Israeli intelligence agencies' tendency to feed disinformation to its clients in the US Government in order to further Greater Israel's claims to Mid-East hegemony at the expense of Washington's long term interests, the US national intelligence community asserted its independence and published its report, denying each and every Israeli-Zionist-White House assertion concerning Iran's nuclear weapons program and, in particular, pointing to the end of Iranian research into nuclear weapons as far back as the fall of 2003.

Israel Rejects "the Intelligence Report from the Other Side of the Earth"

While governments, the United Nations and experts around the world recognized the rigorous, systematic, and comprehensive methods used to compile the data leading to the report declaring that Iran was free of nuclear weapons programs, one and only one state objected: the Jewish State of Israel. And in the USA, as the general public breathed a huge sigh of relief, only one nationwide configuration of organizations refused to reconcile itself to the absence of any Iranian military threat to Israel (not to speak of the US, a distant secondary consideration) and that was predictably the Zionist Power Configuration, specifically the Conference of Presidents of Major American Jewish Organizations.

Speaking for the Israeli Government, Defense Minister Ehud Barak dismissed the NIE with the predictable arrogance and contempt that Israeli officials treat any US policy analysis or statement that doesn't pass their editorial approval and toe their line: *'We cannot allow ourselves to rest just because of an intelligence report from the other side of the earth* [sic] *even from our greatest friend'.*[7]

Following Orwellian logic, AIPAC then twisted the NIE report to fit Israel's rejectionist lead (as it never fails to do) by arguing that the NIE report actually bolsters the case for continued confrontation, belligerency and isolation.[8] In fact according to the perverse argument of AIPAC spokesman, Josh Block, the absence of any Iranian nuclear weapons threat should result in greater pressure on Iran! 'All in all, it's [the NIE] a clarion call for *additional and continued* [my emphasis] effort to pressure Iran economically and politically to end its illicit nuclear program.'[9]

Once again the Israel Firsters—embracing all the major Zionist organizations and community councils—defied all logic, and the most comprehensive and in-depth empirical intelligence report to be produced by the US in favor of the propaganda emanating from the failed Israeli intelligence agencies and the Israeli regime. In a continuous barrage of articles and television interviews, the entire Zionist Power Configuration (ZPC) buried the NIE report, refocusing attention on themes like *'Iran's nuclear program still a threat'*.[10] During the entire week (December 3-7, 2007) the Conference of Presidents of Major American Jewish Organizations—covering the entire range of financially powerful Jewish organizations in the USA—published an average of nine articles per day (nearly 50) propagating the Israeli line. The articles disparaged, distorted and dismissed the NIE and continued to push for the 'military option' (euphemism for launching a massive attack on Iran) as well as new economic sanctions to destroy the Iranian economy and the livelihood of its 70 million citizens. The euphoria of anti-war critics who claimed the NIE report laid to rest the threat of a new US war with Iran was premature, as was their notion that the 'Israel Lobby' was dealt a decisive blow. The ZPC never lost a beat: Israel Firster and Zion-Con fanatic, US Treasury Under Secretary responsible for terrorism and financial intelligence, Stuart Levey, succeeded in convincing China to tighten trade credit, making trade more difficult and costly for Iran's private sector.[11]

The "International Community" Climbs on Board

Internationally, the United Kingdom's Foreign Secretary, David Miliband—a long-time supporter of Israel with close family ties to the Zionist state—predictably followed the Bush-Israel-ZPC line in all but dismissing the NIE report and emphasizing the need to *'keep the pressure on Iran'*. Miliband, who on his recent visit to Israel, refused to even pass a glance at Israel's shutdown of electricity and fuel to the 1.4 million Palestinians caged up in Gaza, spent an entire evening exchanging pleasantries with his settler relatives over dinner—in Tel Aviv, not in the West Bank, the *Jewish Chronicle* corrected—as if that venue limited the linkage.[12] He accused the non-nuclear Iran of being a major threat to the international community because it produces what he called *'fissile material'* and *'missiles'*. Every large and medium size country in the world produces enriched uranium and possesses missiles; to impose a sinister construction on Iran's civilian and defense projects is laughable.[13] Miliband dismisses out of hand their civilian application and parrots word for word his Israeli mentors' line about *'hidden programs'* and other such unsubstantiated Zionist propaganda. Recent revelations of large-scale, long-term Zionist financing of the highly indebted Labor Party's electoral campaigns by millionaire moguls and self-proclaimed 'Labor Friends of Israel'[14] suggests that Miliband's rapid rise to head the Foreign Ministry had less to do with his minimal international affairs experience and more to do with the 'special relations' between millionaire Zionist fundraisers and past and present Labor Party leaders, Tony Blair and Gordon Brown.

In France President Sarkozy appointed Zionist zealot Bernard Kouchner (a fervent supporter of humanitarian intervention including the US invasion of Iraq), to head the Foreign Ministry after 'consultations' with leading French Jewish organizations, which had rejected an earlier candidate, deemed not pro-Israel enough. Kouchner and Sarkozy immediately picked up the Israeli line, dismissing the NIE Report and calling for a new UN National Security Council resolution adding greater sanctions against Iran even as the original justification (Iran's so-called nuclear weapons program) was found to be a lie.[15] The Bush-Miliband-Kouchner-Israeli logic parallels Stalinist-Nazi logic—the more the intelligence reports demonstrate the absence of a nuclear weapons program, the greater the nuclear threat; the lesser the present threat, the greater the future threat; the lesser the empirically verifiable threat, the greater the secret threat. The NIE report made liars of the White House and Congressional Democrats and the Presidents of the Major American Jewish Organizations who 'knew' Iran had a nuclear weapons program. Even more revealingly, it demonstrated that for the same warmongers, Iranian nuclear weapons were not the motivating force for their drive to attack Iran. Leaving out the weapons motive, it is abundantly clear that attacking Iran through sanctions and military threats is deeply rooted instead in the Israeli priority of destroying Iran as an adversary to its Middle East power grab and its assault and territorial dispossession of Palestinians.

As a result of the NIE Report, the ZPC, Miliband, Kouchner, Olmert, and the White House efforts to push for a third round of UN sanctions seemed likely to be rejected. On December 4, China's UN Ambassador, Wang Guangya, announced that the NIE report called into question the need for new sanctions, 'I think we all start from the presumption that now things have changed. I think council members will have to consider that'.[16] China, with $17 billion dollars in direct trade with Iran and up to $30 billion via Dubai, and with Iran as a major Middle East oil supplier and with no Zionist lobby to reinforce Israeli diplomatic pressures, could claim to be free to pursue its own national interests. The case could be made that Russia, under President Vladimir Putin, would follow China's lead and object to new sanctions.

Nevertheless, the US Congress, and in particular its influential Committee chairpersons, continued to blindly follow Israeli Prime Minister Ehud Olmert's pronouncement post-NIE: 'It is vital to pursue efforts to prevent Iran from developing a capability like this [sic] in the United States'. Leading Congressional Israeli-American zealot, Thomas Lantos, convoked a congressional hearing on the NIE Report and invited two top ex-government advisers and ultra-Zion zealots, David Wurmser and Martin Indyk, to testify.

Then on March 8, 2008, Security Council Resolution 1803 extended sanctions against Iran for attempting to enrich uranium, as is its right within the NPT, and undeterred by the NIE finding, clung compulsively to the Iranian WMD potential, however distant. As Global Policy Forum website summarized it:

> This Security Council resolution extends sanctions against Iran. It notes that the Iranian government attempts to enrich uranium—potentially a key component in the development of nuclear weapons. The text restricts the import of "dual use" technology used for both peaceful and military purposes, and asks UN member states to inspect cargos suspected of transporting nuclear material to and from Iran. The resolution also adds 13 names to an existing travel ban and asset freeze on companies and individuals thought to be engaged in Iran's nuclear program.[17]

The Drumbeat Goes On

There is no question that the anti-(Iran) war groups in the US military and intelligence agencies struck a serious blow to the ongoing war plans of the White House, Israel and their agents in the ZPC. But it was only a temporary defeat for the ZPC's massive war propaganda and their fabrication of an 'existential threat' to the 'world community' (Israel). The publication of the NIE hit the headlines for only a few days, followed by a barrage of hostile propaganda in all of the US mass media which called into question the peaceful intentions of Iran and even twisted certain probabilistic phrases to contradict the main findings.

From the vantage point of Americans trying to free their government and the American public of Israeli and ZPC tyrannical monopoly of opinion, the NIE Report nevertheless struck a blow against the credibility of the White House and Zionist spokespeople in the Congress, National Security Council, Homeland Security and the Justice and Treasury Departments regarding Iran's so-called nuclear weapons program. But the quickness, depth, and scope of the Israeli response, especially as magnified by its representatives in the US, French and British foreign offices, demonstrates that the pro-war Israel Firsters are still deeply embedded in positions of political power, not just in the US but in Europe, and willing to defy the US intelligence and military establishment. Without shame or substance, with aggressive outbursts and manipulative verbal skills, the ZPC moves forward toward new sanctions, despite the systematic empirical refutation of its principal argument.

Only a blind, irrational, tribal-ethnic loyalty to Israel can account for the ready denial of the NIE report and automatic embrace of Israel's continued fabrications. As in the thirties when overseas Nazi sympathizers defended Hitler's' lies about Communists torching the Reichstag and Communist fellow travelers defended Stalin's purges as exemplary judicial processes, our Zionists continue to deny every systematic empirical report (like the NIE) which contradicts Israel's lies and fabrications about Iran's nuclear weapons programs.

Beyond the important issue of dual loyalties (very much in evidence in the ZPC's response to the NIE report) there is the re-emergence of the question of a US-backed Israeli war with Iran. In fact, a likely pretext was only averted by the timely intervention of Admiral Fallon, then head of CENTCOM:

> In a widely publicized incident last January, Iranian patrol boats approached a U.S. ship in what the Pentagon described as a "taunting" manner. According to Centcom staff officers, the American commander on the spot was about to open fire. At that point, the U.S. was close to war. He desisted only when Fallon personally and explicitly ordered him not to shoot. The White House, according to the staff officers, was "absolutely furious" with Fallon for defusing the incident.[18]

However, if there is an irrevocable will to war, and the gradual buildup of means to accomplish it—from naval movements to covert operations,[19] then despite common sense and the fearsome consequences, perhaps all that awaits is the appropriate pretext (see next chapter) and someone at the helm willing to go along. The military option will be buttressed by Israeli military intelligence propaganda dismissing the NIE. Perhaps it will claim secret Iranian nuclear weapons programs buried somewhere near the center of the earth and therefore undetected by US intelligence informants, satellite photos, UN inspectors, defecting (or kidnapped) Iranian Generals or any other US source. Only Israel's superior intelligence agencies (which failed in Lebanon, Iraq and the Gaza Strip), can be right—even if they have to once again 'cook the data' to make the case to the uninitiated.

The NIE and the US military struck a blow against the planners of World War III. But did it succeed in lifting the US Congress off its collective knees to finally address US interests in the Middle East? Did it re-awaken a currently moribund peace movement, terrified to confront the most virulent organized warmongers? Did it allow Congress and the US public to challenge the ZPC's stranglehold on US Middle East policy?

Did the British public and peace movement dare to challenge a Labor Government and Foreign Office bought and paid for by the 'Labor Friends of Israel'? Did the French public and intellectuals of Paris recover their republican credentials and reject its first and foremost Israel First regime?

It is nothing short of amazing that, despite the scope and stature of the agencies involved in producing it and the collective sigh of relief from the American public at its findings, the National Intelligence Estimate has so quickly passed from public recall, while the drumbeat for war on Iran has not slackened.

As for the Bush effort to address the Palestinian issue, two weeks after the Annapolis Meeting, Israeli Housing Minister Zeev Boim gave US Secretary of State Condeleeza Rice the 'bristly cucumber' (a Mediterranean style 'slap in the face') when she pleaded with the Jewish state to stop building new settlements in Palestinian East Jerusalem because, 'it doesn't help to build confidence'. Boim went on to say, 'Secretary of State Rice should be congratulated for her efforts in re-launching the peace process (sic)...but this cannot be constantly linked to the cessation of construction in Jerusalem...There is thus nothing to prevent construction anywhere else in Israel.'[20]

Ominously, Admiral Fallon, head of US Central Command, and chief of US forces in the region, submitted his resignation on March 12, 2008. While documented earlier as an opponent of war on Iran, Fallon attempted to discredit this notion, even as he asserted that perception of it forced his resignation: "Although I don't believe there have ever been any differences about the objectives of our policy in the Central Command area of responsibility, the simple perception that there is makes it difficult for me to effectively serve America's interests there," Fallon said...[21]

Then on March 20, 2008, a scant 9 days after UNSC1803, and acting through its own agency, FinCEN, the US took the extraordinary step of unilaterally ramping up sanctions on all Iranian banking by threatening banks in the global private financial sector who didn't follow suit. In an article entitled "The US Declaration of War on Iran", John McGlynn writes:

> [W]hen the history of this newly declared war is someday written (assuming the war is allowed to proceed) FinCEN's role will be as important as that played by US Central Command (Centcom) ...
>
> ...As of March 20, however, the US, speaking through FinCEN, is now telling all banks around the world "to take into account the risk arising from the deficiencies in Iran's AML/CFT [anti-money laundering and combating the financing of terrorism] regime, as well as all applicable U.S. and international sanctions programs, with regard to any possible transactions" with—and this is important—not just

the above three banks but every remaining state-owned, private and special government bank in Iran. In other words, FinCEN charges, all of Iran's banks—including the central bank (also on FinCEN's list)—represent a risk to the international financial system, no exceptions.

… What it really means is that the US, again through FinCEN, has declared two acts of war: one against Iran's banks and one against any financial institution anywhere in the world that tries to do business with an Iranian bank.[22]

In support of actions of such drastic scope, the US shamelessly recalled UN Security Council Resolution 1803, whose tenuous language now referred only to the mere "potential" of Iranian development of nuclear weapons—a pallid reminder that the NIE had shot its bolt. And that it wasn't going to make any difference.

Just as Israel has rejected the NIE report on the absence of a nuclear weapons program in Iran and continues to pursue its efforts to create a global climate receptive to war, so too can the Jewish state dismiss its vague promises to the Bush regime on the so-called 'peace process' in short order. By the time of Bush's May 2008 visit to Israel, his Annapolis project, too, was distant history, as the focus returned relentlessly to Iran:

> The United States and Israel agree on the need for "tangible action" to prevent Iran from developing nuclear weapons, Israeli Prime Minister Ehud Olmert's spokesman said after a visit by U.S. President George W. Bush.
>
> "We are on the same page. We both see the threat … And we both understand that tangible action is required to prevent the Iranians from moving forward on a nuclear weapon," Olmert spokesman Mark Regev said on Friday.[23]

And at this point in time, with General Petraeus now at the helm, it seems there are now military leaders in place who are willing to go along. Accordingly:

> A US House of Representatives Resolution effectively requiring a naval blockade on Iran seems fast tracked for passage, gaining co-sponsors at a remarkable speed, but experts say the measures called for in the resolutions amount to an act of war. H.CON.RES 362 calls on the president to stop all shipments of refined petroleum products from reaching Iran. It also "demands" that the President impose "stringent inspection requirements on all persons, vehicles, ships, planes, trains and cargo entering or departing Iran…

Congressional insiders credit America's powerful pro-Israel lobby for the rapid endorsement of the bills....The Resolutions put forward in the House and the Senate bear a resounding similarity to AIPAC analysis and Issue Memos in both its analysis and proposals even down to its individual components."[24]

The military struck back, with the Chief of the Joint Chiefs of Staff, Admiral Mike Mullen, issuing a public warning that a strike on Iran's nuclear facilities would be "extremely stressful".

But has it taken the possibility off the table?

ENDNOTES

[1]   Compared, as it often has been, to other wars, or indeed, to the estimated casualties of Iraqis.
[2]   "The designation of the Revolutionary Guard will be made under Executive Order 13224, which President Bush signed two weeks after the Sept. 11, 2001, attacks to obstruct terrorist funding. It authorizes the United States to identify individuals, businesses, charities and extremist groups engaged in terrorist activities. The Revolutionary Guard would be the first national military branch included on the list, U.S. officials said—a highly unusual move because it is part of a government, rather than a typical non-state terrorist organization." Robin Wright, "Iranian Unit to be Labeled ' Terrorist'", *Washington Post*, August 15, 2007.
[3]   Thomas Omestad, "Hitting Iran Where It Hurts: *US News & World Report*, October 25, 2007.
[4]   See James Petras, *Rulers and Ruled in the US Empire*, Clarity Press, Atlanta, 2007.
[5]   See Chapter 7.
[6]   See <http://www.dni.gov/press_releases/20071203_release.pdf>
[7]   *Guardian*, December 4, 2007.
[8]   *Jewish Telegraph Agency*, December 4, 2007.
[9]   Ibid.
[10] *Daily Alert*, December 7, 2007.
[11] *Financial Times*, December 6, 2007, p. 1.
[12] "David Miliband denies visiting family in West Bank settlement", *The Jewish Chronicle*, November 23, 2007.
[13] *Financial Times*, December 6, 2007.
[14] *Independent*, December 6 2007.
[15] AFP, December 7, 2007.
[16] *Al Jazeera*, December 5, 2007.
[17] See <http://www.globalpolicy.org/security/sanction/indxiran.htm>
[18] Andrew Cockburn, "Democrats OK Funds for Covert Ops: Secret Bush 'Finding' for War on Iran", Counterpunch.org, May 2, 2008. <http://www.counterpunch.org/andrew05022008.html>
[19] Ibid.
[20] *Al Jazeera*, December 8, 2007.
[21] "Fallon Resigns as Chief of US Forces in Middle East," CNN.com, March 12, 2008. <http://edition.cnn.com/2008/WORLD/meast/03/11/fallon.resigns/index.html> A clearly different perspective was provided by the *London Times*, as indicated in the title of its notice: "Admiral William Fallon Quits Over Iran Policy," *The Times*, March 12, 2008.
[22] John McGlynn, "The U.S. Declaration of War on Iran," JapanFocus, < http://japanfocus.org/products/details/2707> As of this writing, Barclays Bank in the UK has been the first to cave.
[23] "Israel: US Sees Need for 'Tangible Action' on Iran," Reuters, May 16, 2008.
[24] Andrew W. Cheetham, "House Resolution Calls for Naval Blockade Against Iran", Global Research.ca, June 18, 2008.

CHAPTER 4

PROVOCATIONS AS PRETEXTS FOR IMPERIAL WARS

FROM PEARL HARBOR TO 9/11

'Behind every imperial war there is a Great Lie'

Wars in an imperialist democracy cannot simply be dictated by executive fiat; they require the consent of highly motivated masses who will make the human and material sacrifices. Imperialist leaders have to create a visible and highly emotionally charged sense of injustice and righteousness to secure national cohesion and overcome the natural opposition to early death, destruction and disruption of civilian life, and to the brutal regimentation that goes with submission to absolutist rule by the military.

The need to invent a cause is especially pressing for imperialist countries because their national territory is not under threat. There is no visible occupation army oppressing the mass of the people in their everyday life. The 'enemy' does not disrupt normal life—while forced conscription would and does. Under normal peaceful times, who would be willing to sacrifice their constitutional rights and their participation in civil society to subject themselves to martial rule that precludes the exercise of all their civil freedoms?

The task of imperial rulers is to fabricate a world in which the enemy to be attacked is portrayed as an 'invader' (an emerging imperial power like Japan) or an 'aggressor' in the case of revolutionary movements (Korean and Indo-Chinese communists) engaged in a civil war against an imperial client ruler, or a 'terrorist conspiracy' linked to anti-imperialist, anti-colonial Islamic movements and secular states. Imperialist-democracies in the past did not need to consult or secure mass support for their expansionist wars; they relied on volunteer armies, mercenaries and colonial subjects led and directed by colonial officers. Only with the confluence of imperialism, electoral politics and total war did the need arise to secure not only consent, but also enthusiasm, to facilitate mass recruitment and obligatory conscription.

Since all US imperial wars are fought 'overseas'—far from any immediate threats, attacks or invasions—US imperial rulers have the onerous task of making the *casus bellicus* immediate, dramatic, and self-righteously defensive. To this end US presidents have routinely created circumstances, fabricated incidents and acted in complicity with their enemies to incite the bellicose temperament of the masses in favor of war.

The pretext for wars are acts of provocation which set in motion a series of counter-moves by the enemy, which are then used to justify an imperial mass military mobilization leading to and legitimizing war.

State provocations require uniform mass media complicity in the lead-up to open warfare: namely the portrayal of the imperial country as a victim of its own over-trusting innocence and good intentions. All four major US imperial wars over the past seven decades resorted to a provocation, a pretext, and systematic, high-intensity mass media propaganda to mobilize the masses for war. An army of academics, journalists, mass media pundits and experts 'soften up' the public in preparation for war through demonological writing and commentary: each and every aspect of the forthcoming military target is described as totally evil—hence 'totalitarian'. Even its most benign policy is linked to the surreptitious demonic ends of the regime.

Since the 'enemy to be' lacks any saving graces and worst, since the so-called totalitarian state controls everything and everybody, no process of internal reform or change is possible. Hence the defeat of 'total evil' can only take place through 'total war'. The targeted state and people must be destroyed in order to be redeemed. In a word, the imperial democracy must regiment and convert itself into a military juggernaut based on mass complicity with imperial war crimes. The war against 'totalitarianism' becomes the vehicle for total state control for an imperial war.

In the case of the US-Japanese war, the US-Korean war, the US-Indochinese war and the post-September 11 war against an independent secular nationalist regime (Iraq) and the Islamic Afghan republic, the Executive branch (with the uniform support of the mass media and Congress) provoked a hostile response from its target and fabricated a pretext as a basis for mass mobilization for prolonged and bloody wars.

Provocation as Pretext for the US War Against Japan

President Franklin Delano Roosevelt set high standards for provoking and creating a pretext for undermining majoritarian anti-war sentiment, unifying and mobilizing the country for war. Robert Stinnett, in his brilliantly documented study, *Day of Deceit: The Truth About FDR and Pearl Harbor*, demonstrates that Roosevelt provoked the war with Japan by deliberately following an eight-step program of harassment and embargo against Japan developed by Lt. Commander Arthur H. McCollum, head of the Far East desk of the Office of Naval Intelligence. He provides systematic documentation of US cables tracking the Japanese fleet to Pearl Harbor, clearly demonstrating that *FDR knew in advance* of the Japanese attack on Pearl Harbor, following the Japanese fleet virtually every step of the way. Even more damaging, Stinnett reveals that Admiral H.E. Kimmel, in charge of the defense of Pearl Harbor, was systematically excluded from receiving critical intelligence reports on the approaching movements of the Japanese fleet, thus preventing the defense of the US base. The 'sneak' attack by the Japanese, which caused the death of over three thousand American service men and the destruction of scores of ships and planes, successfully 'provoked' the war FDR had wanted. In the run-up to the Japanese attack, President Roosevelt had ordered the implementation of Naval Intelligence's October 1940 memorandum, authored by McCollum, for eight specific measures, which amounted to acts of war, including an economic embargo of Japan, the shipment of arms to Japan's adversaries, the prevention of Tokyo securing strategic raw materials essential for its economy and the denial of port access, thus provoking a military confrontation.

To overcome massive US opposition to war, Roosevelt needed a dramatic, destructive immoral act committed by Japan against a clearly 'defensive' US base to turn the pacifist US public into a cohesive, outraged, righteous war machine. Hence the Presidential decision to undermine the defense of Pearl Harbor by denying the Navy Commander in charge of its defense, Admiral Kimmel, essential intelligence about the anticipated December 7, 1941 attack. The United States 'paid the price' with 2,923 Americans killed and 879 wounded, Admiral Kimmel was blamed and stood trial for dereliction of duty, while FDR got his war. The successful outcome of FDR's strategy led to a half-century of US imperial supremacy in the Asia-Pacific region. An unanticipated outcome, however, was the US and Japanese imperial defeats on the Chinese mainland and in North Korea by the victorious communist armies of national liberation.

Provocation and Pretext for the US War Against Korea

The incomplete conquest of Asia following the US defeat of Japanese imperialism, particularly the revolutionary upheavals in China, Korea and Indochina, posed a strategic challenge to US empire builders. Their massive financial and military aid to their Chinese clients failed to stem the victory of the anti-imperialist Red Armies. President Truman faced a profound dilemma—how to consolidate US imperial supremacy in the Pacific at a time of growing nationalist and communist upheavals when the vast majority of the war-wearied soldiers and civilians were demanding demobilization and a return to a civilian life and economy. Like Roosevelt in 1941, Truman needed to provoke a confrontation, one that could be dramatized as an offensive attack on the US (and its 'allies') and could serve as a pretext to overcome widespread opposition to another imperial war.

Truman and the Pacific military command led by General Douglas MacArthur chose the Korean peninsula as the site for detonating the war. Throughout the Japanese-Korean war, the Red guerrilla forces led the national liberation struggle against the Japanese Army and its Korean collaborators. Subsequent to the defeat of Japan, the national revolt developed into a social revolutionary struggle against Korean elite collaborators with the Japanese occupiers. As Bruce Cumings documents in his classic study, *The Origins of the Korean War*, the internal civil war preceded and defined the conflict prior to and after the US occupation and division of Korea into a 'North' and 'South'. The political advance of the mass national movement led by the anti-imperialist communists and the discredit of the US-backed Korean collaborators undermined Truman's efforts to arbitrarily divide the country 'geographically'. In the midst of this class-based civil war, Truman and MacArthur created a provocation: they intervened, establishing a US occupation army and military bases, and arming the counter-revolutionary former Japanese collaborators. The US hostile presence in a 'sea' of anti-imperialist armies and civilian social movements inevitably led to the escalation of social conflict, in which the US-backed Korean clients were losing. As the Red Armies rapidly advanced from their strongholds in the North and joined with the mass revolutionary social movements in the South, they encountered fierce repression and massacres of anti-imperialist civilians, workers and peasants by the US armed collaborators. Facing defeat, Truman declared that the civil war was really an 'invasion' by (north) Koreans against (south) Korea. Truman, like Roosevelt, was willing to sacrifice US troops by putting them in the direct fire of the revolutionary armies in order to militarize and mobilize the US public in defense of imperial outposts in the southern Korean peninsula.

In the run-up to the US invasion of Korea, Truman, the US Congress and the mass media engaged in a massive propaganda campaign and purge of peace and anti-militarist organizations throughout US civil society. Tens of thousands of individuals lost their jobs, hundreds were jailed, and hundreds of thousands were blacklisted. Trade unions and civic organizations were taken over by pro-war, pro-empire collaborators. Propaganda and purges facilitated the propagation of the danger of a new world war, in which democracy was threatened by expanding Communist totalitarianism. In reality, democracy was being eroded to prepare for an imperial war to prop up a client regime and secure a military beachhead on the Asian continent.

The US invasion of Korea to prop up its tyrannical client was presented as a response to 'North' Korea invading 'South' Korea and threatening 'our' soldiers, who were defending democracy. The heavy losses incurred by retreating US troops belied the claim of President Truman that the imperial war was merely a police action. By the end of the first year of the imperial war, public opinion turned against the war. Truman was seen as a deceptive warmonger. In 1952, the electorate elected Dwight Eisenhower on his promise to end the war. An armistice was agreed to in 1953. Truman's use of military provocation to detonate a conflict with the advancing Korean revolutionary armies and then using the pretext of 'US forces in danger' to launch a war did not succeed in securing a complete victory. The war ended in a divided Korean nation. Truman left office disgraced and derided, and the US public turned anti-war for another decade.

The US Indochinese War: Johnson's Tonkin Pretext

The US invasion and war against Vietnam was a prolonged process, beginning in 1954 and continuing to the final US defeat in 1975. From 1954 to 1960, the US sent military combat advisers to train the army of the corrupt, unpopular and failed collaborator regime of President Ngo Dinh Diem. With the election of President Kennedy, Washington escalated the number of military advisers, commandos (the so-called 'Green Berets'), and the use of death squads (Plan Phoenix). Despite the intensification of the US involvement and its extensive role in directing military operations, Washington's surrogate 'South Vietnamese' Army (ARVN) was losing the war to the South Vietnamese National Liberation Army (Viet Cong) and the South Vietnamese National Liberation Front (NLF), which clearly had the support of the overwhelming majority of the Vietnamese people.

Following the assassination of President Kennedy, Lyndon Johnson took over the presidency and faced the imminent collapse of the US puppet regime and the defeat of its surrogate Vietnamese army.

The US had two strategic objectives in launching the Vietnam War: The first involved establishing a ring of client regimes and military bases from Korea, Japan, the Philippines, Taiwan, Indochina, Pakistan, Northern Burma (via the KMT opium lords and Shan secessionists) and Tibet to encircle China, engage in cross border 'commando' attacks by surrogate military forces, and block China's access to its natural markets. The second strategic objective in the US invasion and occupation of Vietnam was part of its general program to destroy powerful national liberation and anti-imperialist movements in Southeast Asia, particularly in Indochina, Indonesia, and the Philippines. The purpose was to consolidate client regimes, which would provide military bases, de-nationalize and privatize their raw materials sectors, and provide political and military support to US empire building. The conquest of Indochina was an essential part of US empire-building in Asia. Washington calculated that by defeating the strongest Southeast Asian anti-imperialist movement and country, neighboring countries (especially Laos and Cambodia) would fall easily.

Washington faced multiple problems. In the first place, given the collapse of the surrogate 'South Vietnam' regime and army, Washington would need to massively escalate its military presence, in effect substituting its ground forces for the failed puppet forces, and extend and intensify its bombing throughout North Vietnam, Cambodia and Laos. In a word, convert a limited covert war into a massive publicly declared war.

The second problem was the reticence of significant sectors of the US public, especially college students facing conscription (and their middle and working class parents), who opposed the war. The scale and scope of military commitment envisioned as necessary to win the imperial war required a pretext, a justification.

The pretext had to be such as to present the US invading armies as *responding to a sneak attack* by an aggressor country (North Vietnam). President Johnson, the Secretary of Defense, the US Naval and Air Force Command, and the National Security Agency, acted in concert. What was referred to as the Gulf of Tonkin Incident involved a fabricated account of a pair of attacks on August 2 and 4, 1964 off the coast of North Vietnam by naval forces of the Democratic Republic of Vietnam against two US destroyers the *USS Maddox* and the *USS Turner Joy*. Using, as a pretext, the fabricated account of the 'attacks', the US Congress almost unanimously passed the Gulf of Tonkin Resolution on August 7, 1964, which granted President Johnson full power to expand the invasion and occupation of Vietnam up to and beyond 500,000 US ground troops by 1966. The Gulf of Tonkin Resolution authorized President Johnson to conduct military operations throughout Southeast Asia without a declaration of war and gave him the freedom 'to take all necessary steps, including the use of armed force to assist any member or protocol state of the Southeast Asia Collective Defense Treaty requesting assistance in defense of freedom.'

On August 5, 1964, Lyndon Johnson went on national television and radio announcing the launching of massive waves of 'retaliatory' bombing of North Vietnamese naval facilities (Operation Pierce Arrow). In 2005, official documents released from the Pentagon, the National Security Agency and other government departments revealed that there was no Vietnamese attack. On the contrary, according to the US Naval Institute, a program of covert CIA attacks against North Vietnam had begun in 1961 and was taken over by the Pentagon in 1964. These maritime attacks on the North Vietnamese coast by ultra-fast Norwegian-made patrol boats (purchased by the US for the South Vietnamese puppet navy and under direct US naval coordination) were an integral part of the operation. Secretary of Defense McNamara admitted to Congress that US ships were involved in attacks on the North Vietnamese coast prior to the so-called Gulf of Tonkin Incident. So much for Johnson's claim of an 'unprovoked attack'. The key lie, however, was the claim that the *USS Maddox* 'retaliated' against an 'attacking' Vietnamese patrol boat. The Vietnamese patrol boats, according to NSA accounts released in 2005, were not even in the vicinity of the Maddox— they were at least 10,000 yards away and three rounds were first fired at them by the Maddox, which then falsely claimed it subsequently suffered some damage from *a single 14.5 mm machine gun bullet* to its hull. The August 4 'Vietnamese attack' never happened. Captain John Herrick of the *Turner Joy* cabled that 'many reported contacts and torpedoes fired appear doubtful...No actual visual sightings (of North Vietnamese naval boats) by *Maddox*".

The consequence of the fabrication of the Tonkin Gulf incident and provocation was an escalation of war that killed 4 million people in Indochina, maimed, displaced and injured millions more, in addition to killing 58,000 US service men and wounding a half-million more in this failed effort at military-driven empire building. Elsewhere in Asia, the US empire builders consolidated their client collaborative rule. In Indonesia, which had one of the largest open Communist party in the world, a CIA-designed military coup, backed by Johnson in 1966 and led by General Suharto, murdered over 500,000 trade unionists, peasants, progressive intellectuals, school teachers and 'communists' (and their family members).[1]

What is striking about the US declaration of war in Vietnam is that the latter did not respond to the US-directed *maritime provocations* that served as a pretext for war. As a result Washington had to *fabricate* a Vietnamese response and then use it as the pretext for war.

The idea of fabricating military threats (the Gulf of Tonkin Incident) and then using them as pretext for the US-Vietnam war was repeated in the case of the US invasions of Iraq and Afghanistan. In fact Bush Administration policymakers, who launched the Afghan and Iraq wars, tried to prevent the publication of a report by the top Navy commander in which he recounted how the NSA distorted the intelligence reports regarding the Tonkin incident to serve the Johnson Administration's ardent desire for a pretext for war.

Provocation as Pretext: 9/11 and the Afghan-Iraq Invasions

In 2001, the vast majority of the US public was concerned with domestic matters—the downturn in the economy, corporate corruption (Enron, World Com etc.), the bursting of the *'dot-com'* bubble, and avoiding any new military confrontation in the Middle East. There was no public sense that the US had any interest in going to war for Israel, nor launching a new war against Iraq, especially an Iraq that had been defeated and humiliated a decade earlier and was subject to ongoing brutal economic sanctions. The US oil companies were negotiating new agreements with the Gulf States and looked forward, with some hope, to a stable, peaceful Middle East, albeit marred by Israel's savaging the Palestinians and threatening its adversaries. In the Presidential election of 2000, George W. Bush was elected despite losing the popular vote—in large part because of electoral chicanery (with the complicity of the Supreme Court) denying the vote to blacks in Florida.

Bush's bellicose rhetoric and emphasis on 'national security' resonated mainly with his Zionist advisers and the pro-Israeli lobby—otherwise, for the majority of Americans, it fell on deaf ears. The gap between the Middle East war plans of his principal Zionist appointees in the Pentagon, the Vice President's office and the National Security Council and the general US public's concern with domestic issues was striking. No amount of Zionist-authored position papers or anti-Arab, anti-Muslim rhetoric and theatrics emanating from Israel and its US-based spokespeople, was making any significant impact on the US public. There was widespread disbelief that there was an imminent threat to US security through a *catastrophic terrorist attack*—which is defined as an *attack using chemical, biological or nuclear weapons of mass destruction*. The US public believed that Israel's Middle East wars and their US lobbyists' unconditional promotion of direct US involvement were not part of their lives nor in the country's interest.

The key challenge for the militarists in the Bush Administration was how to bring the US public around to support the new Middle East war agenda, *in the absence of any visible, credible and immediate threat from any sovereign Middle Eastern country.*

The Zionists were well placed in all the key government positions to launch a worldwide offensive war. They had clear ideas of the countries to target (Middle East adversaries of Israel). They had defined the ideology ("the war on terror", "preventive defense"). They projected a sequence of wars. They linked their Middle East war strategy to a global military offensive against all governments, movements and leaders who opposed US military-driven empire building. What they needed was to coordinate the elite into actually facilitating a 'catastrophic terrorist incident' that could trigger the implementation of their publicly stated and defended new world war.

The key to the success of the operation was to encourage terrorists and *to facilitate calculated and systematic 'neglect'*—to deliberately *marginalize* intelligence agents and agency reports that identified the terrorists, their plans and methods. In the subsequent investigatory hearings, it was necessary to foster the image of 'neglect', bureaucratic ineptness and security failures in order to cover up Administration complicity in the terrorists' success. An absolutely essential element in mobilizing massive and unquestioning support for the launching of a world war of conquest and destruction centered in Muslim and Arab countries and peoples was a 'catastrophic event' that could be linked to the latter.

After the initial shock of 9/11 and the mass media propaganda blitz saturating every household, questions began to be raised by critics about the run-up to the event, especially when reports began to circulate from domestic and overseas intelligence agencies that US policymakers had been clearly informed of preparations for a terrorist attack. After many months of sustained public pressure, President Bush finally named an investigatory commission on 9/11, headed by former politicians and government officials. Philip Zelikow, an academic, former government official and prominent advocate of 'preventative defense' (the offensive war policies promoted by the Zionist militants in the government) was named executive director to conduct and write the official '9-11 Commission Report'. Zelikow was privy to the need for a pretext like 9/11 for launching the permanent global warfare, which he had advocated. With a prescience which could only come from an insider to the fabrication leading to war, he had written in 1998: *"Like Pearl Harbor, this event would divide our past and future into a before and after. The United States [sic] might respond with draconian measures, scaling back civil liberties, allowing wider surveillance of citizens, detention of suspects and use of deadly force (torture)"*.[2] Speculation on the Pearl Harbor pretext became common among the neo-con think-tanks; one year before 9/11, the Project for a New American Century, (co-founded by William Kristol and Robert Kagan) also cited "some catastrophic and catalyzing event, like a new Pearl Harbor," which would serve to galvanize US public opinion in support of a war agenda, in their 2000 report, *Rebuilding America's Defenses*.

Zelikow directed the Commission report, which exonerated the administration of any knowledge and complicity in 9/11, but convinced few Americans outside of the mass media and Congress. Polls conducted in the summer of 2003 on the findings of the Commission proceedings and its conclusions found that a majority of the American public expressed a high level of distrust and rejection—especially New Yorkers. The general public suspected government complicity, especially when it was revealed that Zelikow conferred with key figures under investigation, Vice President Cheney and Presidential 'Guru,' Karl Rove. In response to skeptical citizens, Zelikow referred to criticisms of the Commission cover up as a *'bacteria (that) can sicken the larger body (of public opinion)'*.[3]

Throughout the 1990s the US and Israeli military-driven empire building took on an added virulence as Israel continued to dispossess Palestinians and further extend its colonial settlements. Bush Senior invaded Iraq and systematically destroyed Iraqis' military and civil economic infrastructure and fomented an ethnically cleansed Kurdish client state in the north. Like his predecessor, Ronald Reagan, President George H.W. Bush backed anti-communist Islamic irregulars against the leftist secular nationalist regime in Afghanistan. At the same time, Bush Senior attempted to 'balance' military empire building with expanding the US economic empire by not occupying Iraq and unsuccessfully trying to restrain Israeli colonial settlements in the West Bank.

With the advent of Clinton, all restraints on military-driven empire building were thrown over. Clinton provoked a major Balkan war, viciously bombing and dismembering Yugoslavia, periodically bombing Iraq, and extending and expanding US military bases in the Gulf States. He bombed the largest pharmaceutical factory in Sudan, invaded Somalia, and intensified a criminal economic boycott of Iraq leading to the death of an estimated 500,000 children. Within the Clinton regime, several liberal pro-Israel Zionists joined the military-driven empire builders in the key policymaking positions, inter alia, Madeleine Albright, Secretary of State (with deputy/undersecretaries Peter Tarnoff, James P. Rubin, Stuart Eizenstat); Robert Rubin, Secretary of the Treasury, William Cohen, Secretary of Defense; George Tenet, Director of the CIA; Allen Greenspan, Chair of the Federal Reserve, and Sandy Berger, Head of the National Security Council. Israeli military expansion and repression reached new heights as US-financed colonial Jewish settlers and heavily armed Israeli military forces slaughtered unarmed Palestinian teenagers protesting the Israeli presence in the Occupied Territories during the First Intifada. In other words, Washington extended its military penetration and occupation deeper into Arab countries and societies, discrediting and weakening the hold of its Arab client regimes over their people.

Military-driven empire building against existing nation-states was not an easy sell to the US public or to the market-driven empire builders of Western Europe and Japan and the newly emerging market-driven empire builders of China and Russia. Washington needed to create conditions for a major provocation, which would overcome or weaken the resistance and opposition of rival economic empire builders. More particularly, Washington needed a 'catastrophic event' to 'turn around' domestic public opinion, which had opposed the first Gulf War and subsequently supported the rapid withdrawal of US troops from Iraq in 1990.

The events that took place on September 11, 2001 served the purpose of American and Israeli military-driven empire builders. The destruction of the World Trade Center buildings and the deaths of nearly 3,000 civilians served as a pretext for a series of colonial wars, colonial occupations, and global state terrorist activities, secured the unanimous support of the US Congress, and triggered an intense global mass media propaganda campaign for war.

The Politics of Military Provocations

Ten years of starving 23 million Iraqis under the Clinton regime's economic boycott, interspersed with intense bombing within and beyond the US/UK self-declared "no fly" zones, was a major provocation to Arab communities and citizens around the world. Support for Israel's systematic dispossession of Palestinians from their lands, interspersed with encroachment on the Islamic holy sites in Jerusalem, was a major provocation, which detonated scores of suicide bomb attacks in retaliation. The construction and operation of US military bases in Saudi Arabia, home of the Islamic holy city of Mecca, was a provocation to millions of believers and practicing Muslims. The US and Israeli attack and occupation of southern Lebanon and the killing of 17,000 Lebanese and Palestinians were a provocation to Arabs and to Muslims worldwide.

Ruled by pusillanimous Arab regimes, which were servile to US interests, and impotent to respond to Israeli brutality against Palestinians, Arabs and devout Muslim citizens were constantly pushed by the Bush Senior and especially the Clinton regime to respond to their continued provocations without the assistance of their respective states. Against the vast disproportion in firepower between the advanced weaponry of the US and Israeli occupation forces (the Apache helicopter gunships, the 5,000 pound bombs, the killer drones, the armored carriers, the cluster bombs, napalm and missiles) the secular Arab and Islamic resistance had only light weaponry consisting of automatic rifles, rocket-propelled grenades, short-range and inaccurate Katyusha missiles, and machine guns. The only weapons they possessed in abundance to retaliate were the suicidal 'human bombs'.

Up to 9/11, US imperial wars against Arab and Islamic populations were carried out in the targeted and occupied lands where the great mass of Arab people lived, worked and enjoyed shared lives. In other words, all (and for Israel most) of the destructive effects of their wars (the killings, home and neighborhood destruction and kinship losses) were products of US and Israeli *offensive wars*, perpetrated by states that were seemingly immune to retaliatory action on their own territory.

September 11, 2001 was the first successful large-scale Arab-Islamic offensive attack on US territory in this prolonged, one-sided war. The precise timing of 9/11 coincided with the highly visible takeover of US Middle East war policy by extremist Zionists who inhabited the top positions of the Pentagon, the White House and National Security Council and exercised dominance over Congressional Middle East policies. Arab and Islamic anti-imperialists were convinced that military-driven empire builders were readying for a frontal assault on all the remaining centers of opposition to Zionism in the Middle East, i.e. Iraq, Iran, Syria, Southern Lebanon, the West Bank, Gaza, as well as Afghanistan in South Asia, and Sudan and Somalia in North-East Africa.

This offensive war scenario had already been spelled out by the American Zionist policy elite headed by Richard Perle for the Israeli Institute for Advanced Strategic and Political Studies in a policy document, entitled

"A Clean Break: A New Strategy for Securing the Realm". This was prepared in 1996 for far-right Israeli Prime Minister Bibi Netanyahu prior to his taking office.

On September 28, 2000, despite the warnings of many observers, the infamous author of the massacre of Palestinian refugees in Lebanon, General Ariel Sharon, profaned the Al Aqsa Mosque with his huge military entourage—a deliberate religious provocation that guaranteed Sharon's election as Prime Minister from the far right Likud Party. This sparked the Second Intifada and the savage response of the Israelis. Washington's total support of Sharon merely reinforced the worldwide belief among Arabs and Muslims that the 'Zionist Solution' of massive ethnic purges was on Washington's agenda.

The pivotal group linking US military-driven empire builders with their counterparts in Israel was the major influential Zionist public policy group, PNAC, promoting what they dubbed the 'Project for a New American Century". In 1998 they set out a detailed military-driven road map for US world domination (that *was* the so-called project for a New American Century'), which just happened to focus on the Middle East and just happened to coincide exactly with Tel Aviv's vision of a US-Israel-dominated Middle East. In 2000 the PNAC Zionist ideologues published a strategy paper, 'Rebuilding America's Defenses', which laid down the exact guidelines which incoming Zionist policymakers in the top spheres of the Pentagon and White House would follow. PNAC directives included establishing forward military bases in the Middle East, increasing military spending from 3% to 4% of GNP, a military attack to overthrow Saddam Hussein in Iraq, and military confrontation with Iran using the pretext of the threat of 'weapons of mass destruction'.

The PNAC agenda could not advance without a catastrophic 'Pearl Harbor' type of event, as US military-driven empire builders, Israelis and US Zionist policymakers recognized early on. The deliberate refusal by the White House and its subordinate 16 intelligence agencies and the Justice Department to follow up precise reports of terrorist entry, training, financing and action plans was a case of deliberate 'negligence'. The purpose was to allow the attack to take place and then to immediately launch the biggest wave of military invasions and state terrorist activities since the end of the Indochina War.

Israel, which had identified and kept close surveillance over the terrorists, insured that the action would proceed without any interruption. During the 9/11 attacks, its agents even had the presumption to video and photograph the exploding towers, while dancing in wild celebration, anticipating Washington's move toward Israel's militarist Middle East strategy.

Military-Driven Empire Building: The Zionist Connection

US militaristic empire building (see Chapter 7) preceded the rise to power of the Zionist Power Configuration (ZPC) in the George W. Bush

Administration. The pursuit of it after 9/11 was a joint effort between the ZPC and longstanding US militarists like Rumsfeld and Cheney. The provocations against Arabs and Muslims leading up to the attacks were induced by both the US and Israel. The current implementation of the militarist strategy toward Iran is another joint effort of Zionist and US militarists.

What the Zionists did provide, which the US militarists lacked, was an organized mass-based lobby with financing, propagandists and political backing for the war. The principle government ideologues, media 'experts', spokespeople, academics, speechwriters and advisers for the war were largely drawn from the ranks of US Zionism. The most prejudicial aspect of the Zionist role was in the implementation of war policy, namely the systematic destruction and dismantling of the Iraqi state. Zionist policymakers promoted the US military occupation and supported a massive US military build-up in the region for sequential wars against Iran, Syria and other adversaries of Israeli expansion.

In pursuit of military-driven empire building in accord with Israel's own version, the Zionist militarists in the US government exceeded their pre-9/11 expectations, raising military spending from 3% of GNP in 2000 to 6% in 2008, growing at a rate of 13% per year during their ascendancy from 2001-2008. As a result they raised the US budget deficit to over $10 trillion dollars by 2010, double the 1997 deficit, driving the US economy and its economic empire toward bankruptcy.

The Zionist American policymakers were blind to the dire economic consequences for US overseas economic interests because their main strategic consideration was whether US policy enhanced Israel's military dominance in the Middle East. The cost (in blood and treasure) of using the US to militarily destroy Israel's adversaries was of no concern.

To pursue the Zionist-US military-driven imperial project of a *New Order in the Middle East*, Washington needed to mobilize the entire population for a series of sequential wars against the anti-imperialist, anti-Israeli countries of the Middle East and beyond. To target the multitude of Israeli adversaries, American Zionists invented the notion of a 'Global War on Terrorism'. The existing climate of national and international opinion was decidedly hostile to the idea of fighting sequential wars, let alone blindly following zealous Zionist extremists. Sacrificing American lives for Israeli power and the Zionist fantasy of a US-Israeli 'Co-Prosperity Sphere' dominating the Middle East could not win public backing in the US, let alone in the rest of the world.

Top policymakers, especially the Zionist elite, nurtured the notion of a fabricated pretext—an event which would shock the US public and Congress into a fearful, irrational and bellicose mood, willing to sacrifice lives and democratic freedoms. To rally the US public behind a military-driven imperial project of invasion and occupation in the Middle East required 'another Pearl Harbor'.

The Terror Bombing: White House and Zionist Complicity

Every level of the US government was aware that Arab extremists were planning a spectacular armed attack in the United States. The FBI and the CIA had their names and addresses; the President's National Security Adviser, Condoleezza Rice, publicly admitted that the Executive branch knew that a terrorist hijacking would occur... only they had expected, she claimed, a 'traditional hijacking' and not the use of 'airliners as missiles'. Attorney- General John Ashcroft was acutely aware of the possibility and refused to fly on commercial airliners. Scores of Israeli spies were living blocks away from some of the hijackers in Florida, informing headquarters on their movements. Overseas intelligence agencies, notably in Germany, Russia, Israel and Egypt claimed to have provided information to their US counterparts on the 'terrorist plot'. The President's office, the CIA, the Defense Intelligence Agency and the FBI allowed the attackers to prepare their plans, secure funding, proceed to the airports, board the planes and carry out their attacks... all carrying US visas (mostly issued in Jeddah, Saudi Arabia—once a prominent site for processing Arabs to fight in Afghanistan) and with 'pilots' who were US-trained. As soon as the terrorists took control of the flights, the Air Force was notified of the hijacking but top leaders 'inexplicably' delayed moves to intercept the planes, allowing the attackers to reach their objectives ... the World Trade Center and the Pentagon.

The military-driven empire builders and their Zionist allies immediately seized the pretext of a single military retaliatory attack by non-state terrorists to launch a worldwide military offensive against a laundry list of sovereign nations. Within 24 hours, ultra-Zionist Senator Joseph Lieberman, in a prepared speech, called for the US to attack 'Iran, Iraq and Syria' without any proof that any of these nations—all full members of the United Nations— were behind the hijackings. President Bush declared a 'Global War on Terror' (GWOT), launched the invasion of Afghanistan, and approved a program of extraterritorial, extra-judicial assassinations, kidnappings and torture throughout the world. Clearly the Administration put into operation a war strategy that had been publicly advocated and prepared by Zionist ideologues long before 9/11. The President secured nearly unanimous support from Congress for the first Patriot Act, suspending fundamental democratic freedoms at home. He demanded that US client-states and allies implement their own versions of authoritarian anti-terrorist laws to persecute, prosecute and jail any and all opponents of US and Israeli empire building in the Middle East and elsewhere.

In other words, September 11, 2001 became the pretext for a virulent and sustained effort to create a new world order centered on a US military-driven empire and a Middle East built around Israeli supremacy.

Provocations and Pretexts: the Israeli/US War Against Iran

The long, unending, costly and losing wars in Iraq and Afghanistan undermined international and national support for the Zionist-promoted New American Century project. US militarists and their advisers and ideologues needed to create a new pretext for the US plans to subdue the Middle East and especially to attack Iran. They turned their propaganda campaign to Iran's legal non-military nuclear energy program and fabricated evidence of Iran's direct military involvement in supporting the Iraqi resistance to US occupation. Without proof, they claimed Iran had supplied the weapons, which bombed the American 'Green Zone' in Baghdad. The Israeli lobby argued that Iranian training and weapons had been instrumental in defeating the American-backed Iraqi mercenaries in the major southern city of Basra. Top Zionists in the Treasury Department organized a worldwide economic boycott against Iran. Israel secured the support of top Democrat and Republican Congressional leaders for a military attack on Iran. But is Iran's *existence* a sufficient pretext for an attack on Iran, or will a *'catastrophic'* incident be necessary?

One of the most important political implications of our discussion of the US government's resort to provocations and deception to launch imperial wars is that the vast majority of the American people are opposed to overseas wars. Government lies at the service of military interventions are necessary to undermine the American public's preference for a foreign policy based on respect for the self-determination of nations. The second implication, however, is that the peaceful sentiments of the majority can be quickly overturned by the political elite through deception and provocations, if amplified and dramatized through their constant repetition through the unified voice of the mass media. In other words, peaceful American citizens can be transformed into irrational, chauvinist militarists through the 'propaganda of the deed' where executive authority disguises its own imperial attacks as 'defensive' and its opponent's retaliation as unprovoked aggression against a 'peace loving' United States.

All of the executive provocations and deceptions are formulated by a Presidential elite but willingly executed by a chain of command involving anywhere from dozens to hundreds of operatives, most of whom knowingly participate in deceiving the public, but rarely ever unmask the illegal project either out of shared intent, fear, loyalty or blind obedience.

The notion, put forward by upholders of the 'integrity' of the war policy, that given such a large number of participants, 'someone' would have 'leaked' the deception, the systematic provocations, and the manipulation of the public, has been demonstrated to be false. At the time of the 'provocation' and the declaration of 'war', when Congress unanimously approved 'Presidential Authority' to use force, few if any writers or journalists raised serious questions: executives operating under the mantle of 'defending a peaceful country' from 'unprovoked treacherous enemies' have always secured the complicity or silence of peacetime critics who choose to bury their reservations and investigations in a time of 'threats to national security.' Few academics, writers or journalists are willing to risk their professional standing when all the mass media editors and owners, political leaders and their own professional cohorts froth over 'standing united with our President in times of unparalleled mortal threat to the nation'—as happened in 1941, 1950, 1964 and 2001.

With the exception of World War Two, each of the subsequent wars led to profound civilian political disillusion and even rejection of the fabrications that initially justified the war. Popular disenchantment with war led to a temporary rejection of militarism… until the next 'unprovoked' attack and call to arms. Even in the case of the Second World War there was massive civilian outrage against a large standing army and even large-scale military demonstrations at the end of the war, demanding the GIs' return to civilian life. The demobilization occurred despite government efforts to consolidate a new empire based on occupation of countries in Europe and Asia in the wake of Germany and Japan's defeat.

The underlying structural reality, which has driven American presidents to fabricate pretexts for wars, is informed by a military-driven conception of empire. Why did Roosevelt not answer the Japanese imperial economic challenge by increasing the US economic capacity to compete and produce more efficiently instead of supporting a provocative boycott called by the decaying European colonial powers in Asia? Was it the case that, under capitalism, a depression-ridden, stagnant economy and idle work force could only be mobilized by the state for a military confrontation?

In the case of the US-Korean War, could not the most powerful post-World War US economy look toward exercising influence via investments with a poor, semi-agrarian, devastated but unified Korea, as it was able to do in Germany, Japan and elsewhere after the war?

Twenty years after spending hundreds of billions of dollars and suffering 500,000 dead and wounded to conquer Indochina, European, Asian and US capital entered Vietnam peacefully at the invitation of its government, hastening its integration into the world capitalist market via investments and trade.

It is clear that Plato's not-so 'noble lie', as practiced by America's Imperial Presidents to deceive their citizens for 'higher purposes', has instead led to the use of bloody and cruel means to achieve grotesque and ignoble ends.

The repetition of fabricated pretexts to engage in imperial wars is embedded in the dual structure of the US political system, a military-driven empire and a broad-based electorate. To pursue the former it is essential to deceive the latter. Deception is facilitated by the control of the mass media whose war propaganda enters every home, office and classroom with the same centrally-determined message. The mass media undermine what remains of alternative information flowing from primary and secondary opinion leaders in the communities and erode personal values and ethics. While military-driven empire building has resulted in the killing of millions and the displacement of tens of millions, market-driven empire building imposes its own levy in terms of massive exploitation of labor, land and livelihoods.

As has been the case in the past, when the lies of empire wear thin, public disenchantment sets in, and the repeated cries of 'new threats' fail to mobilize opinion. As the continued loss of life and the socio-economic costs erode the conditions of everyday life, mass media propaganda loses its effectiveness and political opportunities for positive change appear. As after WWII, Korea, Indochina and today with Iraq and Afghanistan, a window of political opportunity opens. Mass majorities demand changes in policy, perhaps in structures, and certainly an end to the war. Possibilities open for public debate over the imperial system, which constantly reverts to wars and lies and provocations that justify them.

Our telegraphic survey of imperial policymaking refutes the conventional and commonplace notion that the decision making process leading up to war is open, public and carried out in accordance with the constitutional rules of a democracy. On the contrary, as is commonplace in many spheres of political, economic, social and cultural life, but especially in questions of war and peace, the key decisions are taken by a small Presidential elite behind closed doors, out of sight and without consultation, and in violation of constitutional provisions. The process of provoking conflict in pursuit of military goals is never raised before the electorate. There are never investigations by independent investigatory committees.

The closed nature of the decision making process does not detract from the fact that these decisions were 'public' in that they were taken by elected and non-elected public officials in public institutions, and directly affected the public. The problem is that the public was kept in the dark about the larger imperial interests that were at stake and the deception that would induce them to blindly submit to the decisions for war.

Defenders of the political system are unwilling to confront the authoritarian procedures, the elite fabrications and the unstated imperial goals. Apologists of the military-driven empire builders resort to irrational and pejorative labeling of the critics and skeptics as 'conspiracy theorists'. For the most part, prestigious universities and academics conform closely to the rhetoric and fabricated claims of the executors of imperial policy.

Everywhere and at all times, groups, organizations and leaders meet in closed meetings before going 'public'. A minority of policymakers or advocates meet, debate and outline procedures and devise tactics to secure decisions at the 'official' meeting. This common practice takes place when any vital decisions are to be taken whether it is at local school boards or in White House meetings. To label any taking account or observation of the fact of small groups of public officials meeting and taking vital decisions in 'closed' public meetings (where agendas, procedures and decisions are made prior to formal 'open' public meetings) as 'conspiracy theorizing' is to deny the normal way in which politics operate. In a word, the 'conspiracy' labelers are either ignorant of the most elementary procedures of politics or they are conscious of their role in deflecting criticism of the abuses of power of today's state terror merchants.

Zion-Con Zelikow, the 2002 National Security Strategy, and 9/11

The key figure in and around the Bush Administration who actively promoted a 'new Pearl Harbor' and was at least in part responsible for the policy of complicity with the 9/11 terrorists, was Philip Zelikow. Zelikow, a prominent Israel-Firster, is a government academic, whose expertise was in the nebulous area of *'catastrophic terrorism'*—events which enabled US political leaders to concentrate executive powers and violate constitutional freedoms in pursuit of offensive imperial wars and developing the *'public myth'*. Philip Shenon's book, *The Commission: The Uncensored History of the 9/11 Investigation* pinpoints Zelikow's strategic role in the Bush Administration in the lead up to 9/11, in the period of 'complicit neglect' in its aftermath, in the offensive global war period, and in the government's cover-up of its complicity in the terror attack.

Prior to 9/11 Zelikow provided a 'blueprint' for the process of an executive seizing extreme power for global warfare. He outlined a sequence in which a 'catastrophic terrorist event' could facilitate the absolute concentration of power, followed by the launching of offensive wars for Israel (as he publicly admitted they were). In the run-up to 9/11 and the multiple wars, he served as a member of National Security Adviser Condoleezza Rice's National Security Council transition team (2000-2001), which had intimate knowledge of terrorist plans to seize US commercial flights, as Rice herself publicly admitted ('conventional hijackings' was her term). Zelikow was instrumental in demoting and disabling the counter-terrorism expert, Richard Clark, from the National Security Council, the one agency tracking the terrorist operation. Between 2001-2003, Zelikow was a member of the President's Foreign Intelligence Advisory Board. This was the agency that had failed to follow up and pursue the key intelligence reports identifying the terrorist plans. After having played a major role in undermining intelligence efforts to prevent the terrorist attack, Zelikow then became the principal author of the 2002 National Security Strategy of the United States, which prescribed Bush's policy of military invasion of Iraq and targeted Syria, Iran,

Hezbollah, Hamas and other independent Arab and Muslim countries and political entities. Zelikow's 'National Security Strategy' paper was the most influential directive shaping the global state terrorist policies of the Bush regime. It also brought US war policies into the closest alignment with the regional military aspirations of the Israeli state since the founding of Israel. Indeed, this was why former Israeli Prime Minister Netanyahu stated at Bar Ilan University that the 9/11 attack and the US invasion of Iraq were 'good for Israel'.[4]

Finally Zelikow, as Bush's personal appointee as the Executive Director of the 9/11 Commission, coordinated the cover-up of the Administration policy of complicity in 9/11 with the Vice President's office. While Zelikow is not considered an academic heavyweight, his ubiquitous role in the design, execution and cover-up of the world-shattering events surrounding 9/11 and its aftermath mark him as one of the most dangerous and destructive political 'influentials' in the shaping and launching of Washington's past, present and future catastrophic wars.

ENDNOTES

[1]   Robert Cribb, "Genocide in Indonesia, 1965-1966," *Journal of Genocide Research* 3 no. 2 (June 2001), pp. 219-239. According to Cribb, most scholars cite 500,000; in my view it was closer to one million.

[2]   See "Catastrophic Terrorism—Tackling the New Dangers", by Ashton Carter, John Deutch and Philip Zelikow, *Foreign Affairs*, Vol. 77, No. 6, 1998.

[3]   Carol Morello, "Conspiracy Theories Flourish on the Internet," *Washington Post*, October 7, 2004.

[4]   See *Haaretz*, April 16, 2008.

Part II

EMBRACING
THE ISRAELI
MODUS OPERANDI
OF ENDLESS WAR

CHAPTER 5

THE PALESTINEAN SEWAGE DISASTER

THE POLITICAL ECOLOGY OF US/ISRAELI RESPONSIBILITY IN MICROCOSM

On Monday, March 26, 2007 in Northern Gaza, a river of raw sewage and debris overflowed from a collapsed earth embankment into a refugee camp, driving 3,000 Palestinians from their homes. Five residents drowned, 25 were injured, and scores of houses were destroyed.

The New York Times, *Washington Post* and the television media blamed shoddy infrastructure. The *Daily Alert* (the house organ of the Conference of Presidents of Major American Jewish Organizations) blamed the Palestinians who, they claimed, were removing sand to sell to construction contractors, thus undermining the earth embankment. The disaster at Umm Naser, the village in question, is emblematic of everything that is wrong with US-Israeli politics in the Middle East. The disaster in this isolated village has its roots first and foremost in Washington, where AIPAC and its political allies have successfully secured US backing for Israel's financial and economic boycott of the Palestinian government subsequent to the democratic electoral victory of Hamas. AIPAC's victory in Washington reverberated throughout Europe and beyond—as the European Union also applied sanctions, shutting off financing of all new infrastructure projects and the maintenance of existing facilities. At the AIPAC conventions of 2005 through 2007, the leaders of both major American parties, congressional leaders and the White House pledged to re-enforce AIPAC's boycott and sanctions strategy. AIPAC celebrated its victory for Israeli policy and claimed authorship of the legislation. In addition to promoting Palestinian malnutrition, the policy undermined all public maintenance projects, including the maintenance of sewage treatment plants and cesspools.

Equally central to the sewage disaster, Israel's massive sustained bombing attack on Gaza in the summer of 2006 demolished roads, bridges, sewage treatment facilities, water purification and electrical power plants. Northern Gaza was one of its many targets, putting severe strain on already precarious infrastructure and government budgets—again including the maintenance of sewage treatment plants and cesspools.

The Israeli economic blockade of Gaza increased unemployment, poverty and hunger to unprecedented levels. Over 60% of the Gaza population was now unemployed—large families with young children were reduced to one meal a day. Family heads desperately looked for any way to earn funds to buy a pound of chickpeas, oil, rice and flour for bread.

It is possible that, forced by the AIPAC-induced US-EU boycott and Israeli bombing and blockade, some desperate workers removed some sand around the cesspool. This in turn served as the pretext cited by the Conference of Presidents of Major American Jewish Organizations (PMAJO) to blame the Palestinian victims for their own suffering, and exonerate the Israelis, AIPAC and their congressional clients.

The PMAJO is in actuality seeking to justify nearly four decades of Israeli occupation and criminal neglect of Gaza's basic sewage treatment facilities. Israel spends less than 2% on a per capita basis for basic services in the Occupied Territories—services that it is obligated under international law to provide responsibly—of what it spends in Israel. The United Nations and Israeli human rights groups have documented Israel's callous "irresponsibility" toward the Palestinian civilians under its brutal occupation—as if this policy were due to inattention, rather than yet another calculated assault upon the living conditions of the Palestinian population at large, aimed at driving them from their homelands. It is not surprising that the Conference of Presidents of Major American Jewish Organizations should choose to blame the destitute Palestinians for the collapse of a primitive earth embankment and the horrific deaths, rather than address events within their politico-economic context.

To the extent that any Palestinian leader can be held responsible, the finger points to the US- and Israeli-backed PLO and its titular head, Mahmoud Abbas, who receives whatever 'humanitarian' aid flows into Palestine, and now lives in the West Bank. The tens of millions of dollars of Palestinian import taxes withheld by Israeli banks were handed over to Mahmoud Abbas and his CIA-Mossad liaison, Mohammed Dahlen, to arm their anti-Hamas vigilantes, rather than address basic Palestinian socio-economic and infrastructure needs. Over the past two decades, the US-backed 'moderate' PLO leaders and crony 'capitalists' have diverted tens of millions of dollars and euros to their private overseas bank accounts, with the acquiescence of their European, US and Israeli patrons. What is a bit of Palestinian corruption if it means propping up an incompetent group of pliant 'leaders' in total disregard of the Palestinian democratic elections?

The plight of the Umm Naser villagers deluged by their own sewage was neither an act of fate nor a result of local negligence or theft: it was a direct consequence of all that is wrong in US-Middle East politics, the taking sides with a brutal colonial power and its powerful voices and supporting organizations in Washington. Umm Naser is written large throughout Palestine, Iraq and Lebanon: Millions of Arab villagers suffer the consequences of pre-emptive wars to secure Greater Israel, as both President Bush and Vice President have publicly stated in justifying their aggression. Their commitments follow the Lobby's script, which 'coincidentally' is exactly whatever pleases the Israeli Foreign Office.

CHAPTER 6

GENERAL PETRAEUS
FROM SURGE TO PURGE
TO DIRGE

> *General Petraeus:* "President Ahmadinejad and other
> Iranian leaders promised to end their support for the special
> groups but the nefarious activities of the Quds Force have
> continued."
> *Senator Joseph Lieberman:* "Is it fair to say that the
> Iranian-backed special groups are responsible for the
> murder of hundreds of American soldiers and thousands of
> Iraqi soldiers and civilians?"
> *General Petraeus:* "It certainly is…That is correct."
>
> **General Petraeus testimony**
> **to the US Senate, April 8-9, 2008**

Introduction

When President Bush appointed General David Petraeus Commander
(head) of the Multinational Forces in Iraq, his appointment was hailed by *The
New York Times*, the *Wall Street Journal* and the *Washington Post* as a
brilliant decision: a general of impeccable academic and battlefield credentials,
a warrior and counterinsurgency (counter-terrorist) intellectual. The media
and the President, the Republicans and Democrats in the Senate and Congress,
all described his appointment as 'America's last best hope for salvation in
Iraq'. Senator Hillary Clinton joined the chorus of pro-war politicians in praise
and support of Petraeus' 'professionalism and war record' in Northern Iraq. In
contrast, Admiral William Fallon, his predecessor and former commander,
had called Petraeus' briefings 'a piece of brown-nosing chicken shit'.

In both his theory and strategy in pursuit of defeating the Iraqi
resistance, General Petraeus was a disastrous failure, an outcome

predictable from the very nature of his appointment and his flawed wartime reputation.

In the first instance, Petraeus was a political appointment. He was one of the few high military officials who shared the Bush and Zion-Con assessment that the 'war could be won'. Petraeus argued that his experience in Northern Iraq was replicable throughout the rest of the country. Moreover Petraeus, unlike most military analysts, was willing to ignore the heavy costs of multiple prolonged tours of duty on US troops. Petraeus' willingness to ignore the larger costs of prolonged military engagement in Iraq has weakened the capacity of the US to sustain its worldwide imperial interests. For Petraeus, sacrificing the overall cohesion and structure of the US military in Iraq, the global interests of the empire and the US domestic budget were worth securing Bush's appointment as 'Commander of the Forces in Iraq'. Shortly after taking office and in the face of massive domestic, international and Iraqi demands for the withdrawal of US troops, Petraeus took the path dictated by the pro-Israeli US militarists in the Bush Administration and their powerful 'Lobby'. He escalated the war by calling up more troops, which he euphemistically referred to as 'the surge'—a massive call-up of 30,000 more mission-weary infantry and marines.

An analysis and critique of the failure of military-driven imperialism and its militarily dangerous consequences requires an objective critical analysis of Petraeus' media-inflated military record prior to taking command. Equally important, Petraeus' close ideological and political linkages with Israel's militarist approach toward Iran (and the rest of the Middle East countries opposing it) dates back to his close collaboration with Israel's (unofficial) military advisers and intelligence operatives in Kurdish Northern Iraq.

Petraeus' Phony Success in Northern Iraq

Petraeus' vaunted military successes in Northern Iraq—especially in Nineveh province—were based on the fact that it is dominated by Kurdish warlord tribal leaders and party bosses eager to carve an independent country. The relative stability of the region has little or nothing to do with Petraeus' counterinsurgency theories or policies and more to do with the high degree of Kurdish 'independence' or 'separatism' in the region. Put bluntly, the US and Israeli military and financial backing of Kurdish separatism has created a *de facto* independent Kurdish state, one based on the brutal ethnic purging of large concentrations of Turkmen and Arab citizens. By giving license to Kurdish irredentist aspirations for an ethnically purified 'Greater Kurdistan' encroaching on Turkey, Iran and Syria, General Petraeus secured the loyalty of the Kurdish militias, and especially the deadly Peshmerga 'special forces', in eliminating resistance to the US occupation in Nineveh. Moreover, the Peshmerga has provided the US with special units to infiltrate the Iraqi resistance groups, and to provoke intra-communal strife through incidents of terrorism against the civilian population. In other words, General Petreaus' 'success' in Northern Iraq is *not replicable* in the rest of Iraq. In fact, his very success in carving off Kurd-dominated Iraq has heightened hostilities in the rest of the country and provoked Turkish attacks in the region.

An Armchair Strategist

His theory of 'securing and holding' territory presumes a highly motivated and reliable military force capable of withstanding hostility from at least eighty percent of the colonized population. Petraeus, like Bush and the Zionist militarists, ignores the fact that the morale of US soldiers in Iraq and those scheduled to be sent to Iraq is very low. The ranks of those who are seeking a quick exit from military service now include career soldiers and non-commissioned officers—the backbone of the military.[1] The soldiers being recruited include convicted felons, mentally unstable young men, uneducated and impoverished immigrants and professional mercenaries. Unauthorized absences (AWOLs) have shot up—14,000 between 2000-2005.[2] In March 2007, over one thousand active-duty and reserve soldiers and marines petitioned Congress for a US withdrawal from Iraq. By April 2008, a record 69% opposed Bush's war strategy and economic policy.[3] The opposition of retired and active generals to Bush's escalation of troops percolates down the ranks to the 'grunts' on the ground, especially among reservists on active duty whose tours of duty in Iraq have been repeatedly extended (the 'backdoor draft'). Demoralizing prolonged stays or rapid rotation undermines any effort of 'consolidating ties' between US and Iraqi officers, and certainly undermines most efforts to win the confidence of the local population.

If the US troops are deeply troubled by the war in Iraq and increasingly subject to desertion and demoralization, how less reliable is the Iraqi mercenary army? Iraqis recruited on the basis of hunger and unemployment (caused by the US war), with kinship, ethnic and national ties to a free and independent Iraq, do not make reliable soldiers. Every serious expert has concluded that the divisions in Iraqi society are reflected in the loyalties of the soldiers. The attempt by Petraeus and US puppet Prime Minister Maliki to invade Basra in Southern Iraq turned into a military fiasco as thousands of Iraqi soldiers joined the insurgents.

General Petraeus could not count on his Iraqi troops, because scores were defecting and perhaps thousands will in the future. An empty drill field, or worse, a widespread barracks revolt, is a credible scenario. The continued high casualty rates among US soldiers and Iraqi civilians during his 18 months as Commander suggests that Petraeus' plan of 'holding and securing' Baghdad failed to alter the overall situation.

While the addition of 30,000 US troops saturating Baghdad initially reduced civilian and military casualties there, fighting intensified in other regions and cities. More important, the decline of violence had less to do with Petraeus' 'surge' and had more to do with the temporary political ceasefire reached with the anti-occupation forces of Muqtada al Sadr. This was clear when the US and its client prime minister, Nouri al-Maliki, launched an offensive against Sadr's forces in March-April, 2008—casualties shot up, and even the US Green Zone bunker came under daily rocket attacks. After 18 months under Commander Petraeus, the Iraqi troops showed little willingness to fight their own compatriots engaged in resistance. Thousands turned their arms over to the anti-colonial popular militias and several hundreds joined them.

Madness in His Method: The Petraeus *Manual*[A]

Petraeus' 'rule book' prioritizes "security and task sharing as a means of empowering civilians and prompting national reconciliation." 'Security' is elusive because what the US Commander considers 'security' is the free movement of US troops and collaborators based on the *insecurity* of the colonized Iraqi majority. They continue to subject the civilian Iraqis to arbitrary house-to-house searches, break-ins and humiliating searches and arrests.

While the death toll of civilians declined from 'hundreds a day' to 'hundreds a week', it nonetheless demonstrated Petraeus' failure to achieve his most elementary goal. 'Task Sharing' as defined by Petraeus and his officers is a euphemism for Iraqi collaboration in 'administrating' his orders. 'Sharing' involves a highly asymmetrical relation of power: the US orders, and the Iraqis comply. Petraeus defines the 'task' as informing on insurgents. The Iraqi population is supposed to provide 'information' on their families, friends and compatriots—in other words, betray their own people. The concept sounded more feasible in his manual than in practice. US troops still are ambushed on a daily basis and insurgents, operating among the population, bomb their armored carriers.

'Empowering civilians', another prominent concept in Petraeus' manual, assumed that those who 'empower' give up power to the 'others': in other words, that the US military cedes territory, security, financial resource management and allocation to a colonized people or to the local armed forces. During his 18 months in command, the 'empowered' people have instead protected and supported insurgents, and oppose the US occupation and its puppet regime. But then, what Commander Petraeus really meant was 'empowering' a small minority of civilians who would be willing collaborators of an occupying army. Instead, they were frequently the target of the insurgents. The civilian minority to be 'empowered' by the Petraeus version of the empowerment formula would require heavy US military protection to withstand retaliation. In practice no neighborhood civilian collaborators have been delegated *real* power, and those who were delegated authority are dead, hiding or secretly allied with the resistance.

Petraeus' goal of 'national reconciliation' has been a total failure. The Iraqi regime is paralyzed into squabbling sects and warlords. Reconciliation between warring parties is not on the horizon. What Petraeus fails to recognize, but even his puppet allies publicly state, is that US colonization of Iraq is a blatant denial of the conditions necessary for reconciliation. Commander Petraeus and his army and the dictates of the Zionist White House play off the warring parties, wilfully undermining any negotiations toward 'conciliation'. Like all preceding colonial commanders, Petraeus fails to recognize that Iraqi popular sovereignty is the essential precondition for national reconciliation and stability—or more likely, he simply regards popular sovereignty as among the obstacles that have to be surmounted—presuming national reconciliation and stability were indeed the intended aim of the game... Military-imposed 'reconciliation' among warring collaborator groups with no legitimacy among the Iraqi electorate has been a disaster.

Former Clintonite, Sarah Sewall (ex-Deputy Assistant Secretary of Defense and Harvard-based 'foreign affairs expert') was ecstatic over Petraeus' appointment. Yet she claimed the 'inadequate troop to task ratio' would undermine his strategy.[5] The 'troop to task ratio' forms the entire basis of the critique of Bush's Iraq policy by Israel and the Zion-Con Democratic Senators, Hillary Clinton and Charles Schumer. The assault on Iraq was neither illegal, nor morally wrong, nor even counterproductive to US interests: simply, it was poorly implemented. Their solution is 'send more troops'. While Petraeus did increase the troops with the surge, the US is militarily and politically unable to mobilize 500,000 more to meet Sewall's 'troop to task ratio'. This argument begs the question: inadequate numbers of troops reflects the massiveness of popular opposition to the US occupation. The need to improve the 'ratio' (i.e. increase the number of troops) is due to the level of mass Iraqi opposition and is directly related to increasing neighborhood support for the Iraqi resistance. If the majority of the population and the resistance did not oppose the imperial armies, then *any ratio would be adequate*—down to a few hundred soldiers hanging out in the Green Zone, the US Embassy or some local brothels.

Historical evidence seems to suggest that the converse is also true.

Petraeus' prescriptions borrowed heavily from the Vietnam War era, especially General Creighton Abrams' 'Clear and Hold' counterinsurgency doctrine. Abrams ordered a vast campaign of chemical warfare spraying of thousands of hectares with the deadly 'Agent Orange' to 'clear' contested terrain. He approved of the Phoenix Plan—the systematic assassination of 25,000 village leaders[6] to 'clear' out local insurgents. Abrams implemented the program of 'strategic hamlets', the forced re-location of millions of Vietnamese peasants into concentration camps. In the end Abram's plans to 'clear and hold' failed because each measure extended and deepened popular hostility and increased the number of recruits to the Vietnamese national liberation army. Israel's brutal occupation policies in the West Bank have followed the same strategy with equally disastrous results, which doesn't prevent its advisers from selling it to the US military.

Petraeus is following the Abrams-Israeli doctrine with the same disastrous civilian casualties. Large-scale bombing of densely populated Shia and Sunni neighborhoods has taken place since he took command. Mass arrests of suspected local leaders have been accompanied by the tight military encirclement of entire neighborhoods. Arbitrary, abusive house-to-house searches have turned the poor sectors of Baghdad into one big shooting gallery and concentration camp. Paraphrasing his predecessor, General Creighton Abrams, Petraeus wants to 'destroy Iraq in order to save it'. But maybe the Zionists/Petraeus want just that? As it stands, his policy is merely punishing the civilians and deepening the hostility of the population. In contrast, the insurgents blend into the huge slum neighborhood of Sadr City or into the surrounding provinces of Al-Anbar, Diyala, and Salah ad Din. Petraeus was able to 'hold' a people hostage with armored vehicles but he has not been able to rule with guns. The failure of General Creighton Abrams was not due to the lack of 'political will' in the US, as he complained, but was due to the fact that 'clearing' a region of insurgents is temporary, because the insurgency is founded on its capacity to blend in with the people and then re-emerge to fight the occupation army.

Petraeus' fundamental (and false) assumptions are based on the notion that the 'people' and the 'insurgents' are two distinct and opposing—or at least potentially opposing—groups (which can happen, depending on the success/effectiveness/depth of the insurgency and extent of grievance). He assumed that his ground forces and Iraqi mercenaries could distinguish between them and exploit this divergence—'clear out' the insurgents and 'hold' the people. The history of the 2003 US invasion, occupation and imperial war, including his 18 months in command, provides ample evidence to the contrary. With upward of 159,000 US troops in Iraq at the peak of the "surge"[7] and close to 200,000 Iraqi and over 50,000 foreign mercenaries, Petraeus has failed to defeat the insurgency. The evidence points to very strong, extensive and sustained civilian support for the insurgency. The high ratio of civilian to insurgent killings by the combined US-mercenary armies suggests that US troops have not been able to distinguish (nor are they interested in the difference) between civilians and insurgents. Even the puppet government complains of civilian killings and widespread destruction of popular neighborhoods by US aerial bombing. The insurgency draws strong support from extended kin ties, neighborhood friends and neighbors, religious leaders, nationalists and patriots: these primary, secondary and tertiary ties bind the insurgency to the population in a way which cannot be replicated by the US military or its puppet politicians.

Early on, General Petraeus' plan to 'protect and secure the civilian population' was a failure. He flooded the streets of Baghdad with armored vehicles but was quickly forced to acknowledge that the 'anti-government... forces were regrouping north of the capital'. Petraeus was condemned to play what Lt. General Robert Gaid un-poetically called 'whack-a-mole: Insurgents will be suppressed in one area only to re-emerge somewhere else'.

General Petraeus made the presumptuous assertion that the Iraqi civilian population did not know that the 'special operations' forces of the Occupation, which he directed, is responsible for fomenting much of the ethno-religious conflict. Investigative reporter Max Fuller, in his detailed examination of documents, stressed that the vast majority of atrocities... attributed to 'rogue' Shiite or Sunni militias "were in fact the work of government-controlled commandos of 'special forces', trained by the Americans, 'advised' by Americans and run largely by former CIA agents".[8] Petraeus' attempt to play 'Good Cop/Bad Cop' in order to 'divide and rule' has been unable to weaken the opposition and has instead destabilized and fragmented the Maliki regime. While Petraeus was able to temporarily buy the loyalty of some Northern Sunni tribal leaders, their dubious loyalties depend on multi-million dollar weekly payoffs.

In theory, Petraeus recognized the broader *political* context of the war: "There is no military solution to a problem like that in Iraq, to the insurgency... In Iraq, military action is necessary to help improve security... but it is insufficient. There needs to be a political aspect".[9] Yet the key 'political aspect' as he put it, is the *reduction*, not escalation, of US troops, the *ending* of the endless assaults on civilian neighborhoods, the *termination* of the special operations and assassinations designed to foment ethnic-religious conflict, and above all, a timetable to withdraw US troops and dismantle the chain of US military bases. During his 18-month tenure, Petraeus increased the number of troops, increased the bombing of the very people he was supposed to win over, and fortified the 102 acres of US bases. General Petraeus was neither willing nor in a position to implement or design the appropriate political context for ending the conflict because of his dogged implementation of the Bush-Zionist 'war to victory' policy.

The gap between Petraeus' 'theoretical' discourse on the centrality of politics and his practice of prioritizing military victory can only be explained by his desire to please the Bush-Zion-Cons in Washington in order to advance his own military career (and future political ambitions). The result was an exceptionally mediocre military performance, underwritten by dismal political failures *and the achievement of his personal ambitions.*

In April 2008, the Bush Administration named Petraeus as head of the US Central Command, overseeing the wars in Iraq, Afghanistan, Somalia and the rest of the Horn of Africa. Petraeus replaced Navy Admiral William Fallon who was forced to resign his command by the White House and the Zion-Cons over his opposition to their war plans against Iran. Even prior to his retirement Fallon had expressed his contempt for Petraeus' shameful truckling to the Zionists in Northern Iraq and the Bush ' Know Nothings' in charge of Iraq and Iran policy planning. It is clear that Petraeus ensured his promotion on April 16, 2008 through his Senate testimony one week earlier (April 8-9, 2008), where he delivered a bellicose speech implicating Iran in the fighting deaths of US troops in Iraq. With the purge and intimidation of military officials not willing to act as White House/Zionist poodles, Petraeus had few competitors. His promotion to the top military post, just days after his Senate testimony pointing to war with Iran, could not be attributed to his (failed) military performance, but rather to his slavish adherence to Bush's and Israel's push for heightened confrontation with Iran. Blaming Iran for his failed military policies served a double purpose—it covered up his incompetence and it secured the support of leading Zionist senators like Joseph Lieberman.

Petraeus' reference to the "need to engage in talks with some groups of insurgents" fell on deaf ears. His proposal was seen by the insurgents as a continuation of the divide and conquer (or 'salami') tactics. The only 'talks' Petraeus secured were with tribal leaders who demanded millions of dollars up front. Otherwise he failed to attract any sector of the insurgency. Petraeus proved to be an armchair tactician, wise on public relations techniques, but constrained from coming to grips with the decolonization political framework in which such tactics might work.

Petraeus' Double Discourse

Commander Petraeus was quick to grasp the difficulty of his colonial mission. Just a month after taking command, he engaged in the same sophistry and double discourse of any colonial general confronted with an unwinnable war. To keep the flow of funds and troops coming from Washington, he talked of the "reduction of killings and discontent in Baghdad", cleverly omitting the increase of civilian and US deaths *elsewhere.* He mentioned 'a few encouraging signs' but also admitted that it is 'too early to discern significant trends'.[10] In other words, the 'encouraging signs' he expressed to the White House were of no military importance!

From the beginning Petraeus gave himself an *open-ended mission* by extending the time frame to secure Baghdad. He shifted the goal posts from days and weeks to 'months' and years. Playing with indefinite time frames in which to evaluate his performance was a coy way to prepare the US public for prolonged warfare—with few positive results. There is nothing like a failed general acting as a political panderer covering his ass in anticipation of military defeat.

As a military intellectual, Petraeus surely has read George Orwell's *1984* because he was so fluent in double-speak. In one breath he spoke of "no immediate need to request more US troops to be sent to Iraq'; on the other he called for 30,000 additional troops as part of what he called 'the surge'. In March 2008, he spoke of big advances in security and one month later he demanded a 'pause' because the puppet regime and army were not capable of defending themselves without US backing.

Petraeus' political manipulation of troop numbers and his blatant lies about the security situation in Iraq prepared the ground for a greater military escalation in the region. "Right now we do not see other requests (for troops) looming out there. That's not to say that some *emerging mission* or *emerging task* will not require that, and if it does then we will ask for that [my emphasis]".[11] First there's a 'surge', then there is an 'emerging mission', and suddenly there are another fifty thousand troops on the ground in the meatgrinder that is Iraq, along with seven battleship and aircraft carriers off the Persian and Lebanese coasts, thousands more troops in Afghanistan and nearly $170 billion dollars in military spending scheduled to be added to the 2008 federal budget.

Petraeus' Political Ambitions

The General is a fine master of 'double speak'. Yet despite superb media performances before his colleagues in the White House and Congress, Petraeus' military strategy is doomed to go down the same road of political-military defeat as his predecessors in Indo-China. His military police have jailed tens of thousands of civilians and killed and injured many more. They were interrogated, tortured, and perhaps some were 'broken'. But many more took their place, turning the Green Zone into a war zone under siege. Petraeus' real security policy through intimidation 'held' only as long as the armored cars patrolled each neighborhood, pointing their cannons at every building. That proved to be a temporary solution. As soon as the troops moved on, the insurgents returned. The insurgents re-emerge after a week because they live and work there, whereas the Marines do not and neither do the Iraqi collaborators dare. Petraeus was running a costly colonial army, which suffers endless casualties and, which is not politically sustainable. Petraeus knew that, so he chose a political route upward and out of immediate command in Iraq, shifting the burden for failure to his replacement, Lieutenant General Ray Odierno.

General Petraeus' long-term political ambitions exceeded his military abilities. He realized that military success is a stepping-stone to a higher post in Washington. So Petraeus, like McCain, must present failure as success.

In his Senate testimony of April 8-9, 2008, Petraeus lied to Congress and the American people about the US military failures, fabricating accounts of progress in order to bolster the sagging fortunes of his political patron, President Bush. His Senate testimony and press conferences were designed to bolster Bush's total loss of credibility: he claimed that the war was being won, Iraq was stabilized, security and peace were 'around the corner', and that we should go to war with Iran.

If the media uncritically swallowed Petraeus testimony, the public didn't and a host of former generals and admirals were chagrined, embarrassed and outraged that he was advancing his career by sucking up to President Bush and Israel at the expense of the troops serving under him.

Petraeus Panders to Israel's Fifth Column: "The Iran Threat"

By the spring of 2008, as the war turned from bad to worse, as the insurgency grew in power and his leadership and strategy was transparently a sham, Petraeus played his last formidable political card. To sustain his position and cover up his defeats in Basra, and his inability to lower US casualties or even defend the Green Zone, he blamed Iran. Petraeus was the first general to charge Iranian weapons were blowing up US armored carriers; Iranian agents were training the Iraqi resistance and defeating his army of 200,000 Iraqi collaborators. Petraeus could not face the fact that he was losing Iraq. He deflected attention from the failure of his entire military-political strategy in Iraq by dragging in Iran as a key military player.

That Petraeus would make such an inflammatory *public* statement against Iran—given all its implications and possible politico-military use as a *casus belli* for future US action against Iran—without having it "vetted" beforehand by his "civilian overseers" is highly unlikely. Given his awareness of the agenda and power of the Zion-Cons in the administration, it is conceivable that, as a politically alert and ambitious general, he was indeed the originator of the "blame-Iran-for-Iraq" pretext (subsequently strongly discredited by the Iraqi government), to please and facilitate the neo-con forces driving for war. Or he was simply saying what they told him to say, parroting a Zion-Con-developed Pretext Two for war on Iran to counter the NIE destruction of Pretext One. (Indeed, who else could better put forward Pretext Two?) Either way, in Petraeus, the neo-cons finally found their stooge general who would do whatever necessary to stay in the game.

In pointing to Iran, Petraeus played the dangerous game of echoing the Israeli line and providing support for a military attack on Iran promoted by the leadership of the Major American Jewish Organizations.

Even as Petraeus was covering up his failure by blaming Iran and launching Pretext Two, the Iraqi puppet government was praising the Iranian government for helping to stabilize the country, using its influence on the Shia militias to hold their fire. Puppet Prime Minister Maliki invited the Iranian President to Baghdad, signed trade agreements, and praised their co-operation and efforts to stabilize the country.

The only organized group that took up Petraeus' campaign to blame Iran for the US defeats was the Zionist Power Configuration in the US. In the Congress, media and public forums, Zionists amplified and backed Petraeus. They see him as a critical ally in countering the National Intelligence Estimate absolving Iran of having a program to develop nuclear weapons. No other high military commander, in Europe or the US, took up Petraeus' call to arms against Iran... except the Israeli military command. It is a sad commentary on the state of the US military when generals advance to the highest posts by flattering and propagandizing for the most discredited American president in memory while advancing the agenda of power brokers for a foreign government.

General Petraeus, in his advance from Commander of US and 'allied' forces in Iraq to head of the US Central Command overseeing current US wars in Iraq, Afghanistan, Somalia and future wars with Iran, Lebanon and Syria, has left behind a bitter legacy of hundreds of thousands of Iraqi civilian deaths, an unreliable Iraqi 'quisling' army, a failed client regime, and a vast US bunker under constant attack. Every military official and most experts know that he was 'Bush's man' and his advances were very much a product of the White House and its pro-Israel backers in the Congress.

The opposition to Petraeus cropping up among leading Zio-Democrats was purely for domestic political purposes; as Rahm Emanuel put it to the *Washington Post*, "We needed to stay away from General Petraeus and focus on making this Bush's war". Obligingly, the *Post* writers titled their article, "Petraeus Returns to War That Is Now His Own."[12]

Conclusion

The advance of Petraeus has been a victory of the Zionist Power Configuration in its quest for American military leaders willing to pursue Israel's agenda of sanctions and war against Iran. That is why the ZPC was a factor in the ousting of Admiral William Fallon, and why the main propaganda bulletin (the *Daily Alert*) of the Conference of Presidents of Major American Jewish Organizations worked for and hailed his promotion to military overseer of the Middle East wars. AIPAC and their bought and bonded Senators ensured Petraeus an easy time during his confirmation hearing and his unanimous endorsement. His appointment marks the first time that the Zionist Power Configuration has trumped the views and opinions of the majority of active and retired American military officers. How far Petraeus will go in 'paying back' his debt to his long-term Zionist backers for his meteoric rise remains to be seen. What is certain is that they will demand that he line up with the State of Israel in pushing forth toward a war with Iran.

It is neither military honor, nor patriotism, which will restrain Petraeus from pursuing the Zionist War for Israel agenda—but his future presidential ambitions. He will have to calculate whether a second Middle East war, which will please Israel and billionaire American (?) Zionist political fundraisers, can offset voter discontent resulting from a war in which the price of oil will rise to $300 dollars a barrel and cost several tens of thousands of American casualties, and further his political ambitions.

The US has degenerated into a sorry state of affairs when its future course depends on the political calculations of a feckless general/failed counterinsurgency 'expert'/ambitious politician pandering to billionaire political contributors working for a foreign colonial power.

ENDNOTES

[1]   *Financial Times*, March 3-4, 2007 p.2.
[2]   Ibid.
[3]   *USA Today*, April 22, 2008.
[4]   *Counterinsurgency Field Manual* (No. 3-24). hastily published in December, 2006 by the US Army and Marine Corps, republished in July 2007 by the University of Chicago Press. For a review of the extent of "unacknowledged borrowing" from other sources in the manual, see "Pilfered Scholarship Devastates General Petraeus' *Counterinsurgency Manual*", David Price, Counterpunch.org, October 30, 2007, <http://www.counterpunch.org/price10302007.html>
[5]   As at May 12, 2008, according to *US News & World Report*.
[6]   *Guardian*, March 6, 2007.
[7]   "According to official South Vietnamese statistics, Phoenix claimed nearly forty-one thousand victims between 1968 and 1972; the U.S. counted more than twenty thousand in the same time span." Seymour M. Hirsch, "Moving Targets", *The New Yorker*, December 13, 2003.
[8]   Chris Floyd, 'Ulster on the Euphrates: The Anglo-American Dirty War', www.truthout.org/docs. 2006/021307J.sthml
[9]   BBC, March 8, 2007.
[10] *Aljazeera*, March 8, 2007.
[11] Ibid.
[12] Peter Baker and Thomas E. Ricks, "Petraeus Returns to War That Is Now His Own," *Washington Post*, September 13, 2007.

Part III

MILITARISM AND THE DECLINE OF US POWER

CHAPTER 7

MILITARY-DRIVEN OVER MARKET-DRIVEN EMPIRE BUILDING

1950-2008

Introduction

From the middle of the 19th century but especially after the Second World War, two models of empire building competed on a world scale: one predominantly based on military conquests, involving direct invasions, proxy invading armies and subsidized separatist military forces; and the other predominantly based on large-scale, long-term economic penetration via a combination of investments, loans, credits and trade, in which 'market' power and superiority (greater productivity) in the means of production led to the construction of a virtual empire.

Throughout the 19th to the middle of the 20th centuries, European and US empire building resorted to the military route, especially in Asia, Africa, Central America, North America and the Caribbean. The British and US primarily colonized the territories through military force, which was followed by the introduction of state-directed mercantile systems—the Monroe Doctrine for the US and imperial preference for the British. Following independence, South America became the site of the growth of market-powered empire building. British and later US capital successfully captured the commanding heights of these economies, especially the agro-mining and petroleum export sectors, trade, and finance; in some cases they attached customs and treasury to cover debt collection.

As late developing capitalist countries and emerging imperial powers (EIP), the US, Germany and Japan faced the hostility of the established European empires and limited access to strategic markets and raw materials. The EIP adopted several strategies in challenging the existing empires.

These included demands for free trade with their colonies and for the end of imperial (colonial) privilege/preference. The EIP established parallel colonial settlements and concessions bordering the old empires. They fomented and financed 'anti-colonial' revolts to replace existing colonial collaborators, and pursued economic penetration via superior production. They disseminated political propaganda promoting 'democratic' values within a market-driven empire. World War Two marked the decline of the European military-based colonial empire and the US transition from a *predominantly* market-based to a military-based empire. This 'transition' was facilitated by earlier military occupations in the Philippines and the Caribbean, and a multitude of invasions in Central America.

Nationalist liberation movements, based on liberal, nationalist and socialist leaders and programs, drawing on returning soldiers, weakened colonial control and post-war European anti-fascist and anti-war sentiments, led to the dismantling of European military-based empires. Internal reconstruction and domestic working class radicalism influenced the agenda for most European colonial powers. The attempts by the European powers to re-impose their colonial empires failed despite bloody wars in Indo-China, Kenya, Algeria, Malaya and elsewhere. The French, English and Israeli invasion and occupation of the Egyptian Suez (1956) marked the last major European attempt at military-driven imperialism.

The US opposition to this effort at European re-colonization marked the supremacy of US-centered empire building and, paradoxically, the beginning of US military-driven empire building. The European powers, especially Great Britain, engineered a strategic shift from colonial-military empires toward market-driven empires based on supporting pro-capitalist nationalists against socialist revolutionaries (India, Malaysia, Singapore, etc.). While Europe transited to the market-driven empire building model based first and foremost on the reconstruction of their war-torn domestic capitalist economy, the US quickly moved toward a military-based empire building approach. The US established military bases throughout Europe, militarily intervened in Greece, elaborated a complex and comprehensive military buildup to challenge Soviet spheres of influence in Eastern Europe, and intervened in the Chinese, and especially the Korean and Vietnamese, civil wars.

Immediate Post-World War II:
The Combination of Market and Military Roads to Empire

Because the US economy and military came out of the victory following WWII with enormous resources far surpassing any other country or group of countries, the US was able to pursue a dual approach to empire building, engaging in both military and economic expansion. The US dominated over 50% of world trade and had the greatest surplus public and private capital available to invest overseas. The US possessed technological and productivity advantages enabling it to gain most from the promotion of 'free trade' among its would-be competitors, and to increase its domestic living standards.

These advantageous circumstances, directly related and limited to the first decade of the post-WWII period, became embedded in the strategic thinking and resultant practice of US policymakers, Congress, the Executive branch and both major parties. The conjunctural 'world superiority' generated a plethora of elite ideologies and a mass mindset in which the US was seen to be—'by nature', by 'divine will', by 'history/destiny', and its 'values', by its 'superior education, technology and productivity'—to rule over the world. The specific economic and political conditions of the 'decade (1945-1955) were frozen into an unquestioned dogma, which denied the dynamics of changing market, productive and political relations that gradually eroded the original bases of the ideology.

Divergence in the World Economy: US-Europe-Japan

Beginning with the massive military buildup during the Cold War and the subsequent hot war in Korea, the US allocated a far greater percentage of its budget and GNP to war and military empire building than Western Europe or Japan.

By the mid-1950s, while the US vastly expanded its state military apparatus (armed forces, intelligence agencies and clandestine armies), Western Europe and Japan expanded and built up their state economic agencies, public enterprises, and investment and loan programs for the private sector. Even more significantly, US military spending and purchases stimulated Japanese and European industries. Equally important state-private procurement policies subsidized US industrial inefficiency via cost overruns, non-competitive bidding and military-industrial monopolies.

US empire building via projections of military power absorbed hundreds of billions of dollars in government expenditures in countries with low economic payoffs in the Caribbean, Central American, Asia and Africa.

While military-driven empire building did increase short term domestic growth and led to rising income, some important civilian spin-offs, and technological breakthroughs that entered the civilian economy, European and Japanese market-based empire building moved with greater dynamism from domestic to export-led growth and began to challenge US predominance in a multiplicity of productive sectors.

The prolonged and costly war by the US against Indo-China (roughly 1954-74) epitomized the replacement of European colonial-military empire building by the US version. The hundreds of billions of dollars in US government war spending spilled over into Japanese and South Korean high-growth manufacturing industries. Western European manufacturing achieved productivity gains and export markets in former African and Asian colonial nations, while the US Empire's murderous wars in South East Asia discredited it and its products throughout the world. Domestic unrest, widespread civilian protests, and military demoralization further weakened the US capacity to pursue its imperial agenda and defend strategic collaborating regimes in key regions.

The relative decline of US manufacturing exports was accompanied by the massive growth of US public debt, which in turn stimulated the vast expansion of the financial sector which then shaped regional and national policy toward de-industrializing central US cities and converting them into finance/real estate and insurance monocultures.

The contrasting and divergent roads to empire building between the US on the one hand and Europe and Japan on the other, deepened with the advent of the 'Second Cold War' during the Carter-Reagan years. While the US spent billions in proxy wars in Southern Africa (Angola and Mozambique), Latin America (Nicaragua, Chile, El Salvador and Guatemala) and Asia (Afghanistan), the Europeans were expanding economically into Eastern Europe, China, Latin America and the Middle East. Even at the moment of greatest imperial success, the overthrow of Communism in the USSR and East Europe and China's transition to capitalism, the US militarily-driven empire failed to reap the benefits. Under Clinton, the US promoted the raw pillage of the Russian economy and destruction of the state (civilian and military), market, and scientific base rather than stabilizing and jointly exploiting its existing markets and human and material resources. The US spent billions undermining Communism, but the Europeans, primarily Germany, and to a much lesser degree France, England and Japan, were the prime beneficiaries in terms of securing the most productive industries and employing the better part of the skilled labor and engineers in the former Soviet bloc. By the end of the Clinton era and with the bursting of the information technology speculative bubble, the European Union had eclipsed the US in GNP, and outperformed the US in accumulating trade surpluses and foreign debt management.

Market Versus Military Empire Building in the 1990s

During the Bush-Clinton years, US military-driven empire building vastly expanded its commitments in financing and providing troops for the Balkan and Iraq wars, military entry into Somalia, the bombing of the Sudan, the increased subsidy of Israel's colonial wars, the Afghan wars, Colombia's counterinsurgency and to a lesser extent, the Philippines' counterinsurgency and counter-separatist wars. While the US spent billions to prop up a gangster-ridden and corrupt KLA regime in order to spend billions more in building a huge military base in Kosova, Germany was reaping the economic benefits of its economic hegemony in the relatively prosperous regimes of Croatia, Slovenia and the Czech Republic. While the US spent hundreds of billions in the First and Second Gulf Wars, China, the new emerging market-driven empire builder, was looking to sign lucrative oil and gas contracts in the Middle East, especially with Iran. While the US was backing an unpopular minority regime through applying the military force of its Ethiopian client in Somalia, China was signing major oil contracts in Sudan, Angola and Nigeria, and even in Northern Somalia (Puntland). While the US military-centered empire-building state was giving away over $3 billion in military aid per year (plus transferring its most up-to-date military technology to competitor firms) to Israel, European, Asian and Latin American private and public enterprises were signing long-term lucrative contracts with the Gulf oil states as well as with Iran.

A clear sign of the long-term economic decay of the US global competitive position between 2002-2008 is evidenced by the fact that a 40% depreciation of the dollar since 2002[1] has failed to substantially improve the US balance of payments, let alone produce a trade surplus. Despite the handicap of appreciating currencies, China, Germany and Japan continued to accumulate trade surpluses, especially with the US. While the US spent hundreds of billions in Asian wars, CIA propaganda and subversive operations in the former USSR, Eastern Europe, the Baltic States, the Caribbean (Cuba/Venezuela) and the Caucuses, the principle beneficiaries were the revitalized European market-driven empire builders and the newly emerging market-driven empire builders.

While the US spends enormous sums in building new military bases surrounding Russia, including new offensive operations in Kosova, Poland and the Czech Republic, with new preparations for NATO bases in Georgia and the Ukraine, Russian, Chinese and European capital expands, buying out or investing in privatized and public-private strategic mining, petrol and manufacturing enterprises in Africa, Latin America, Australia and the Gulf.

While China harnesses foreign capital, including major US MNCs, to make itself the 'manufacturing workshop of the world', Germany with its high precision heavy manufacturers is prospering by constructing the workshops for the Chinese. US manufacturers and productive capital flee to state-subsidized (via tax reductions and low interest rates) financial, real estate and speculative sectors, and go overseas to avoid high rent and fringe payments to US labor. The resulting decline of the domestic market and the shrinking base of industrially trained labor reinforce the overseas and speculative movements of US capital. These *capitalist structural changes undermined the economic fundamentals underlying* the financial sector.

The deterioration of the US economy became apparent as the speculative paper pyramid (sub-prime and credit crises) collapsed during the 2007-08 recession. The recycling of multiple layers of 'exotic' financial 'instruments', each more precarious than the last, each more divorced from any tangible productive unit in the real economy, characterized this period. Their predictable collapse dragged the US into recession. Even among the big banks and financial houses, there is no knowledge of the real value of the paper being traded or of the 'material collateral' (housing and commercial property being held). The fictitious economy revolves around unloading the devalued paper to cover costs and lessen losses... and letting the next holder of the paper face the risks and uncertainties. As a result there is a total lack of confidence in the market because the 'objects' up for sale have become so lacking in value, i.e. so intangible and unrelated to the real economy.

The decline of the real producer basis of goods and social services and the predominance of the paper economy accentuated the divergence between military-directed empire building and the global economic interests of the US. The paper economy is not directly influenced by imperialist militarism, as is the case with US MNCs which face the possibilities of their physical assets being put at risk by imperial wars, armed resistance, the disruption of trade routes, the destruction of overseas markets, and the disarticulation of access to minerals and energy sources.

The ascendancy of speculative finance capital coincides with the greater autonomy of the militarist empire builders over and against the residual influence of American manufacturing and commercial interests supporting market imperialism. The extraordinary role that the pro-Israel power bloc plays in shaping a bellicose US Middle East foreign policy over and above what US oil companies looking to sign contracts with Arab countries exercised, can only be understood within the large upsurge of 'militarist-driven imperial policy'.

Washington's unconditional support of Israel's militarist colonial regime reflects two important structural changes in US empire building. One is the extraordinary organization and influence of the principle pro-Israel Jewish organizations over local, regional, and national legislative and executive bodies, and in the mass media and financial institutions. The second change is the rise of a political class of executive and legislative militarist policy-makers, which has an affinity with Israeli colonialism and its offensive military strategy. Israel is one of the few—if not the only—military-driven 'emerging imperial powers' and that is part of the reason for the 'resonance' between Jewish leaders in Israel and Washington policymakers. This is the real basis of the often stated and affirmed 'common interests and values' between the two countries. Military-driven imperial powers, like the US and Israel, do not share 'democratic values'—as even the most superficial observer of their savage repression of their conquered peoples and nations (Iraq and Palestine) can attest—what they really share is the military route to empire building.

Historic Comparison of Market- and Military-Driven Imperialism

A rational cost efficient evaluation of the US major and minor military invasions demonstrates their high economic cost and low economic benefits to both the capitalist system as a whole and even to many key economic enterprises.

The US blockade of and subsequent war with Japan ultimately unleashed the Asian national liberation movements, which undercut European and US colonial-style military imperialism. The Korean War ignited the massive re-industrialization of Japan and created optimal conditions for Korea's model of protectionism at home and free trade with the US (so-called Asian state-led export model). The result was the creation of two major manufacturing rivals to US economic expansion in Asia, in North America, and later in the rest of the world.

The US invasion, colonial occupation and imperial war in Indochina and its subsequent defeat severely weakened the military capacity to subsequently defend global imperial interests and client states in Southern Africa, Iran and Nicaragua. More to the point, by concentrating resources on war making, the US lost markets to the emerging market empire builders and diverted capital from increasing the productivity and productive forces which create market dominance.

In the broader picture, military- and market-driven imperialism, which coexisted and seemed to complement each other, diverged in the period between 1963-1973, with the militarist faction gaining supremacy in directing US empire building. The divergence was papered over by several instances of complementary activity such as the overthrow of President Allende in Chile on behalf of US MNCs and similar earlier instances in Guatemala (1954), Iran (1953), and in other countries where quick imperial victories over smaller countries did not seem to carry any significant economic or political costs.

The ascendancy of Reagan and the negative long-term economic impact of the new arms buildup were obscured by the breakup of the communist system and the Chinese and Vietnamese transitions to capitalism. The windfall gains to US economic interests in the former European communist countries, especially Russia, were largely based on pillaging existing resources in alliance with gangster-capitalists. Long-term, large-scale benefits were not due to US capitalists taking over and developing the forces of production and developing the internal markets of the ex-communist countries. The political and military gains that accrued to US military empire building obscured its continued loss of economic power in the world marketplace to the market-driven imperial powers. Moreover, China unleashed a large-scale, long-term process of dynamic capital accumulation, which in less than two decades displaced the US from manufacturing markets and challenged its access to energy markets.

In other words, favorable resolution of the US-Soviet conflict led to their mutual economic decline. What is worse from a practical historical perspective, the military-driven empire builders saw their 'victory' over communism as a vindication and license to escalate their militarist approach to empire building. According to this line of argument, the Soviets fell because of military pressure backed by ideological warfare. Moreover in the absence of a countervailing military pole, the Bush-Clinton-Bush presidencies saw an open field for pursuing the military road to empire building.

From the Gulf, to the Gulf and Back to the Gulf: 1990-2008 (and beyond)

The first Bush presidency assumed the military road to empire building but tried to avoid the high costs of occupation and colonization. The Israeli colonial model had to await the Zionist occupation of policymaking positions in later US administrations. The first Iraq War was intended to project US imperial military power, secure US economic interests among the Gulf oil states (Kuwait and Saudi Arabia) as well as expand Israeli influence in the Middle East. Most of all, it was seen as the launching of a 'New World Order' centered in US world supremacy, supported by docile allies, and financed by rich Arab oil states.

Shortly after the Gulf War, the triple alliance, which emerged during the war, collapsed as Europe pursued its own market-driven empire in competition with the US, Saudi Arabia paid some of the US military expenditures and then abruptly ended its funding, and domestic opposition grew as the electorate demanded less imperial expenditure and the rebuilding of the domestic economy.

Military-Driven Empire Building and Zionism

The Zionist Power Configuration in the United States successfully secured from the White House and Congress massive and sustained multi-billion dollar military and economic grant and aid packages for Israel throughout the 1980s, ensuring Israel's military superiority in the Middle East. Yet both Presidents Reagan and Bush (Senior) tried to maintain a balance between the interests of major US oil multinationals working with Arab regimes on the one hand, and Israeli and Washington's military-driven empire building (MDE), on the other.

Bush Senior's attack on Iraq in the First Gulf War greatly reduced Baghdad's military capability but he refrained from destroying its armed forces or overthrowing Saddam Hussein, as Israel and the ZPC were demanding at the time. Above all Bush did not want to destabilize the region for US oil deals in the Gulf, even as he imposed a US military presence to ensure dominance.

With the election of Clinton and the Democratic-controlled Congress, the MDE and the ZPC gained strategic positions in the elaboration and implementation of foreign policy. Madeleine Albright (Secretary of State), 'Sandy' Berger (National Security Adviser), Dennis Ross (Director of Policy Planning, State Department), William Cohen (Secretary of Defense), and Martin Indyk (US Ambassador to Israel), and an army of lesser known functionaries, militarists and Zionists launched a series of wars, military attacks and severe sanctions against Yugoslavia, Somalia, Sudan and Iraq. They devastated their populations (over 500,000 children died in Iraq as a direct result of US starvation sanctions), destroyed their national productive facilities and, intentionally disarticulated and fragmented their nations into violent ethno-tribal and religious mini-states. While Clinton embraced the military road to empire building, he was also totally committed to the financial sector of the US economy (in particular, the most speculative activities) by de-regulating all controls, oversight and constraints on 'hedge funds', investment banks and equity houses. Under the tutelage of the Chairman of the Federal Reserve Bank, the pro-Israel Alan Greenspan, the Clinton regime became the launching pad for the full conversion of the US into a speculation-driven economy, culminating in the dot-com bubble which burst in 2000-2001, and the massive Enron and World Com swindles leading up to the current financial meltdown of 2006-2008.

While the MDE gained a dominant role under Clinton, the ascendance of speculative capital marginalized and eroded the political influence and economic weight of productive capital, forcing it overseas and/or to transfer funds into the financial-speculative sector. The socio-economic basis of market-driven empire building was weakened relative to the militarists and the ZPC in setting the US foreign policy agenda. This new power configuration opened the door for the total takeover by these same forces during the eight years of the Bush (Junior) presidency. The latter quickly eliminated any residual influence of the market-driven imperialists, forcing the resignation of his first Treasury Secretary, Paul O'Neal, and others. Even hybrid market-militarists like Colin Powell who went along with the global war strategy but raised tactical questions, were subsequently forced into retirement.

MDE were in total control of the government in all spheres, from the elaboration of war propaganda, the build-up of a global network of terror and assassination teams, to colonial wars and the systematic use of torture abroad, to the savaging of elementary freedoms at home. Within the MDE, the ZPC gained dominance, especially in the formulation and the implementation of total war strategies in Iraq and the unconditional backing of Israel's genocidal politics in Gaza and the West Bank. Every sector of the government was geared to war, bellicose action, and especially to subordinating economic policies to military practices informed by the military-driven Israeli colonization.

The convergence of policy and practice between the MDE and the ZPC within the highest levels of government and their mutual reinforcement, gave US foreign policy its extremist military character. Zionist cultural and media power provided an army of academic and journalistic ideologues and mass media platforms which the MDE previously lacked—and amplified their message. As *The New York Times* revealed,[2] the Pentagon prepped 75 retired officers to serve as military analysts and flood the media with views supportive of its policy—but without certainty of access to the ZPC-dominated media, such a program would have been futile. Don Meyer (former assistant to Victoria Clarke, Assistant Secretary of Defense, Public Affairs) said "a strategic decision was made in 2002 [*sic*] to make the analysts the main focus of the public relations push to construct a case for war.". Was it truly plausible that the media had been duped into thinking that in engaging retired military officers, they were hiring independent commentators rather than supporters of DoD policy? The military analysts knocked, but it was the media that opened the door.

The linking of traditional US MDE and the emerging power of the Israeli-ZPC buttressed the spread of authoritarian controls and harsh and widespread censorship over any politician, intellectual or media critic of Israel and its unconditional supporters in the ZPC.

The joint forces of the MDE and ZPC have reshaped the US military command to serve their plans for new major wars—against Iran—and the prolongation and extension of wars against Iraq, Afghanistan, Somalia, Lebanon and elsewhere. The MDE have failed to pursue the free trade openings in Latin America, Asia and the Middle East—leaving the field wide open for entirely new trading and investment networks involving China, Europe, Japan, India, Russia and the Middle Eastern sovereign funds. Even with the onset of the recession in the US and the meltdown of the financial markets, the militarists have refused to change or alter their stranglehold on the budget and foreign policy, causing the government to resort to printing currency to finance the bailout of speculators and their investment banks.

Imperial Wars, Social Revolutions and Capitalist Restorations

The historical record demonstrates that imperial wars destroy the productive forces and social networks of targeted countries. In contrast, market-driven economic empire building gains hegemony via collaboration with local political and economic elites, taking control of strategic industries, minerals and energy via direct investments and loans, privatizations and denationalization, and favorable trade and monetary agreements. Market-driven empire building takes over; it does not destroy the productive forces, it does not demolish the social fabric, it reconstructs or 'adjusts' it to accommodate its accumulation needs.

Was Socialism a Detour to Capitalism?

The evolution of social revolutionary regimes in a post liberation period shows a common pattern reflecting the political-economic external constraints imposed by military imperialism. The revolutionary regimes expropriate and nationalize the major means of production, control foreign trade and organize the planning of the economy. They eliminate foreign control over strategic economic sectors, centralize political and economic control as well as redistribute land and income. In many cases these radical measures were imposed upon the revolutionary governments by imperial economic boycotts, the flight of capitalists and landlords, the non-cooperation of managers and technicians and by the necessity of reconstruction in the face of large-scale destruction. The US embargo and similar constraints on external financial aid have forced revolutionary governments to rely on the rationing of scarce resources for priority public projects, limiting their capacity to increase individual consumption.

As a result, the post-revolutionary regimes were forced to deal with market-driven empire builders. They contracted large-scale short-term and long-term trade agreements and joint investment ventures through equitable profit sharing agreements and a broad range of technological contracts involving royalty payments. In other words, given the unfavorable position of the revolutionary economy in the world market and the low level of development of the forces of production, the market-driven empire-building countries were in a position to secure lucrative economic opportunities. In contrast, the military-driven empires attempted to inflict maximum economic damage to compensate for their military defeat.

The revolutionary regimes under Communist leadership featured characteristics which foreshadowed positive future relations with market-driven imperial countries. Their vertical leadership and concentrated political power facilitated quick and relatively easy changes from collectivist to neo-liberal policies, while hindering the development of democratic mechanisms, which might have corrected erroneous and harmful economic decisions. Secondly, unchecked power at the top in a time of scarcity led to the conversion of power into privilege, corruption and social inequalities. These developments created a wealthy nepotistic elite with an interest in deepening ties with their capitalist counterparts from the imperial states. These internal changes coincided with the interests of market-driven capitalists willing to establish lucrative 'beachheads' and relations with elite groups in the post-revolutionary society and state. Market-driven empire builders were attracted by the tight controls exercised over labor and the lack of competition from military-driven imperial states.

Post-revolutionary economies continued to be embedded in the world capitalist marketplace and subject to its competitive demands. In the best of circumstances, even with a democratic and socially egalitarian leadership and relatively favorable world commodity prices, the revolutionary regime would need to balance the social demands of a socialist domestic economy (with its demands for increases in income, social services, workplace improvement and consumer goods) with the world market demands for greater efficiency, increased capital investments, rising productivity and labor discipline. Given the built-in biases toward political and military security embedded in the bureaucratic centralist structures, it was not surprising that production would stagnate. The constraints and the centralized elites' inability to micro-manage the economy beyond the period of reconstruction was one reason for stagnation. The other was that the regime would prefer a hierarchical organized capitalist structure (over any democratic changes from below), which would not challenge, but rather strengthen, the communist elite's position in a 'new' eclectic system.

In other words, a dual transition from imperial-dominated extractive capitalism to centralized socialism would be sought, which would entail a period of reconstruction and national unification with an organized and disciplined labor force. This would be followed by a transition to a centralized mixed state capitalist economy, increasingly penetrated by market-driven imperial capital.

Were Imperial Wars Necessary for Capitalist Expansion?

The historical record documents the continued growth and expansion of market-driven empire building throughout the post World War II period, *without* wars, significant military intervention, boycotts, embargos or other offensive belligerent actions. The expansion took place in the context of non-revolutionary, revolutionary and post-revolutionary regimes. Germany's market-driven empire builders traded with the Communist East, China and Russia before, during and after the fall of Communism, accumulating huge trade and productive advantages over the US. The same occurred with Japan with regard to China and other Asian communist countries.

The market imperialists did not depend, as some apologists for military imperialists argue, on 'the protective umbrella' of US militarism, but on their superior position in the world market and the greater development of the forces of production, which allowed them to enter and secure favorable and lucrative economic positions.

In contrast, the US empire builders, who started the post-war 1945-50 period in a uniquely favorable position in the world market, wasted their massive economic resources in funding wars against successful revolutions—in China, Korea, Indochina, Cuba, and now in prolonged colonial wars in Iraq and Afghanistan. Billions more have been spent in numerous surrogate wars in Angola, Nicaragua, Guatemala and Chile with no economic payoffs for US MNCs over and against its European and Asian competition. The US imperial wars failed to enhance its economic empire. US empire builders shifted massive resources away from producing goods for the international market and upgrading their industrial productivity in order to retain world and domestic market shares to its monstrous and wasteful military budgets. The result has been a steady decline of the US economic empire relative to its competitor market-driven empires. Ironically, when the centralized collectivist regimes eventually made the transition toward capitalism, it was *because of their inner social and economic contradictions* and not because of US military policies. The restoration of capitalism had little to do with the hundreds of billions of dollars in US military spending.

In contrast, the market-driven empires from the end of the 1940s benefited from US imperial wars by securing lucrative US military contracts, and were able to concentrate their state expenditures and investment policies on securing overseas markets. They were in an ideal position to reap the benefits resulting from the socialist regimes' transition to capitalism.

Given the emergence of post-Communist political and social ruling elites who blindly adhered to free market dogma with their corrupt, authoritarian and privileged political practices, in retrospect 'socialism' *did* appear as a 'detour' to capitalist restoration. However the structural changes implemented by some communist political elites, especially in China and Vietnam, created the essential foundations for a capitalist take-off. They unified the country, educated and trained a healthy, disciplined workforce, launched basic industries, and eliminated warlords and local ethnic fiefdoms. Subsequently Communist-led liberalization opened the door to the peaceful economic invasion of market-driven imperialism, safeguarded by a strong centralized state limiting any working class or nationalist opposition or protest. The Communist elites established a framework ideal for subsequent imperialist reentry and expansion.

The historical record makes it clear that imperial wars were not necessary for economic expansion. Empire-driven militarism thoroughly undermined the US long-term competitive position. If the driving impetus for empire building is economic conquest, then market-driven empires are far superior to military-driven empires. The goal of 'colonial political dominance', pursued by military-driven imperialists, is in the modern period, a chimera, as demonstrated by a history of political defeats in Asia, Africa, Latin America and now in Iraq and Afghanistan.

Military-Driven Imperialism Today
and the Newly Emerging Imperial Powers

One might conclude that the US imperial leadership would have 'learned the lessons' of failed military-driven empire building from their experience over the past 50 years. But as we pointed out earlier, the internal structural dynamics of the US economy and the reconfiguration of the political elite directing the political system have led in the opposite direction. The 21st century has witnessed the ascendancy within the US of the most zealous exponents of military-driven empire building in the entire post-World War II period—which may be under other influences than simply the impetus to secure economic conquest. An overview of US imperial policy shows the proliferation and intensification of direct wars, surrogate wars, and military confrontations in which the US favors militarist allies over countries with lucrative markets and profitable investment opportunities in natural resources.

Market-Driven Versus Militarist Alliances

The militarist and Zionist takeover of US empire building in the 21st century is manifested in their strategic decisions, alliances and priorities, each and every one of which is diametrically opposed to market-based empire building and ultimately doomed to further erode the position of the US empire.

The newly emerging empire-building states (like China) rely almost exclusively on market-driven strategies designed by political elites linked to industrialists and technocrats. They are quickly dominating manufacturing markets, accessing strategic raw materials, and securing long-term trade agreements at the expense of the increasingly militarist, but internally deteriorating US Empire. Near the end of the first decade of the 21st century, the imperial policies of the US militarists and Zionists have demonstrated their willingness to make deep sacrifices in market growth by choosing to align the US with costly and dubious militarist regimes in all regions of the world, beginning with the US alliance with Israel.

In the Middle East, unlike market-driven empire builders, the US militarists and Zionists have invaded Iraq and Afghanistan, destroying many lucrative oil deals and joint ventures, and leading to quadrupling of the world price of oil. Instead they have invested (and lost) over a trillion dollars in non-productive, non-economic, military activity. Militarist imperialism has weakened the entire economic fabric of the US Empire without any 'compensatory' gains on the military side. The prolonged war in Iraq (6 years and running) has demoralized the US ground troops and weakened US military capability to engage in any 'third front' in which the US has important economic interests. US liberal market-driven imperialists describe this as 'imperial overstretch'. While the US invests in non-productive and unsuccessful military conquests, profoundly indebting the domestic economy, China, India, Korea, Russia, Europe, the Middle East and even Latin America pile up trade surpluses while expanding their economic empires via private and sovereign investments.

Largely because of the political fusion and strategic convergence of interests between militarists and Zionists, the US empire builders choose to sacrifice lucrative ties to the richest markets among the Gulf States in the Middle East and among predominantly Muslim countries in order to favor Israel, a resource-poor militarist-colonial state with a third rate market for goods and investments. US militarists have subjected America's empire building to strategies in the Middle East, which mostly favor Israel's colonial and regional hegemonic drive. This places the US on a direct confrontational path with Lebanon, Syria, Iran, and even the Gulf States, who feel threatened by Israel's constant resort to offensive military power to attack its neighbors. No Arab oil country, no matter how conservative and pro-capitalist, can afford to open its economy to the US, if it believes that Washington will subordinate it to the vision of a militarist Israel/US-dominated sphere of influence. By unconditionally backing Israel's colonial and hegemonic interests, American militarists have gained a strategic domestic political ally (the Zionist Power Configuration) but it has come at an enormous cost to US economic empire building. Moreover the Israeli state has run the biggest and most aggressive espionage operations against the US of any country since the fall of the USSR, thus calling into question its 'security benefits.' The multiplicity of enemies resulting from Israel's racist-colonialist policies ensures that the US will be engaged in decades of war, or as long as the US taxpayers can sustain the demands of the military empire.

Military-driven empire building is manifested not only in the Middle East but throughout the world. In Africa, the US propelled the Ethiopian military regime into supporting its weak and isolated puppet regime in Somalia against an Islamist-secular nationalist coalition representing the majority of Somalis. Washington and Israel finance and arm the Sudanese separatists in Darfur against the oil-rich central Sudanese government. In both Somalia and Sudan, China and other emerging imperial powers have secured access to strategic oil rich sites. While the US spends billions of dollars on endless wars, propaganda campaigns and sanctions, China reaps hundreds of millions in profits. While the US-financed African wars militarize impoverished Ethiopia and destroy the entire fabric of production and society in Somalia, the Chinese build roads and infrastructure to facilitate exports in both the Sudan and Northern Somalia. Pentagon-directed colonial wars in Africa, conducted by surrogates, undermine the political support of economic collaborators while the market-driven empires enhance their ties with local economic elites and political rulers.

In Latin America, the US military imperialists have so far contributed $6 billion dollars in military aid to Colombia's militarist regime during the 21st century, destroying the entire social fabric in the rural areas, while the rest of Latin America expanded their ties with Europe, Asia and the Middle East. Washington has spent hundreds of millions of dollars in failed efforts to destabilize Venezuela's nationalist-democratic Chavez Government. As a result US capitalists have lost out on billions of dollars in investments and trading contracts in Venezuela to China, Russia, Brazil, Argentina and Iran. By making Colombia the centerpiece of their South American policy, US militarist empire builders have lost out on the enormously lucrative economic opportunities accompanying the commodity price boom in Argentina, Brazil, Ecuador and Bolivia.

In Asia, despite the deepening US economic dependence on China to sustain the rapidly depreciating US dollar (China holds $1.5 trillion dollars in foreign reserves which has lost 40% of its value since 2002), the US militarists still engage in sustained anti-Chinese propaganda campaigns and highly provocative incidents. The US-backed violent protests against the Chinese presence in Tibet fomented by the Dalai Lama and CIA-funded exile organizations is only a more recent example. American Zionists have directed a political campaign against the expansion of Chinese investments and contracts (market-driven imperialism) in the Sudan. The Zionist role in the so-called 'Darfur' campaign is based on Sudan's support for the Palestinians and opposition to Israel's genocidal policy in Gaza, and on its Islamic orientation. The same applies to Somalia, where the Ethiopian military was deployed to prevent the Islamic Courts from forming a government. The needs of Israel, whose most steadfast opponents are from the Islamic rather than secular sectors of the Middle East, may have provoked the Bush administration to alienate the entire Muslim world through thinly-disguised attacks on Islam itself through epithets such as "Islamo-fascism".

China has so far generally overlooked US military provocations such as the shooting down of a Chinese fighter plane, spy flights over Chinese offshore territory, the deliberate bombing of its embassy in Belgrade and the sale of advanced missiles to Taiwan. The US financing of the separatist demonstrations among Tibetan exiles is designed to tarnish China's image in the lead up to its hosting the 2008 Summer Olympics. China's market-driven empire builders ignore US military provocations because they have had little effect on Chinese overseas and domestic economic expansion. Nevertheless China has increased spending on modernizing its military defense capabilities. More significantly, as the US economy declines and enters a deep recession in 2008, and as the dollar continues to fall ($1.60 to 1 Euro as of May 2008), China has turned toward the Asian, European, and

Middle Eastern markets. Asian markets now account for 50% of world trade growth as of 2008. In 2007 China increased production and the development of its market to sustain growth rates at least five times higher than the militarist-dominated US Empire. Even more significant, the great majority of Chinese exporters (over 800,000) have shifted payments to Euros, Yen, Pounds Sterling and the Renminbi in their trading with non-US trading partners.

Russia, shaking off the shackles of Clinton-backed pillage during the gangster capitalism of the Yeltsin years in the 1990s, has taken off during the 21st century under the leadership of President Putin. Meanwhile, US military-driven empire builders were able to integrate and subordinate all the former members of the Russia-centered Warsaw Pact into the US-dominated NATO. In the 21st Century, the Russian economy has expanded rapidly between 6% and 8%, established majority control over strategic resources, and sought to lessen its vulnerability to US military encirclement. While Germany, Italy and most of the major Asian trading countries (China, India and Japan) have obtained lucrative trading and investment agreements with Russia, the US militarists have concentrated on military encroachment along Russia's European and Asian borders. The US is pushing to incorporate Ukraine and Georgia into NATO, and preparing to station offensive, so-called 'missile shields' in Poland and the Czech Republic on the absurd pretext that such highly sophisticated installations are intended to *protect* Western Europe from attacks by distant Iran rather than to target Moscow, just 5 minutes away, by missile attack.

Conclusion

US military-driven empire building has made costly military alliances with peripheral countries at a catastrophic economic cost. The persistence of the militarist empire builders has systematically undercut market-driven empire building and has pushed the domestic US economy to near bankruptcy. The twin motors of the contemporary empire and domestic economy—speculative finance and militarism—have driven the US economy backwards at the same time that established and emerging imperial competitors are advancing.

Comparative historical data covering the entire half-century to the present demonstrates that European, Japanese and now Chinese and Indian market-driven expansion have been far more successful in securing market shares, developing the productive forces and accessing strategic raw materials than US military empire building.

Market-driven empire building has both resulted from and created a strong civil society in which socio-economic priorities take precedent in defining domestic and foreign economic policy over military priorities and definitions of international reality. US empire builders, academics and political advisers have interpreted what they call *'the rise of US global power, its victory in the Cold War and the decline of Communism'* as a vindication of military-driven empire building. They have ignored the rise of capitalist competitors and the relative and absolute decline of the US as an economic power. It can be argued that the newly emerging market-driven former Communist countries (like China and Russia) represent a greater global challenge to the US Empire than did the previous stagnant bureaucratic Communist regimes.

Militarism is deeply embedded in the structure, ideology and policies of the entire US governing class, its political parties, the executive and legislative branches, the judiciary and the armed forces. Over the same half-century countervailing *market-driven* empire builders have declined as a defining force in the formulation of foreign policy in the US. The growing encroachment of the militant Zionist Power Configuration within the policy-making directorate has been greatly facilitated by the ascendancy of militarism and the relative decline of economic empire building.

The long period of incremental decline of US economic empire building and the trillions of dollars wasted by military-driven empire building has come to a climax. In the new millennium, with the profound devaluation of the imperial currency (the dollar), huge indebtedness, and loss of markets, Washington is totally dependent on the good will of its commercial partners to keep accepting constantly devalued dollars in exchange for essential commodities.

The immediate outcome is likely to be a major domestic crisis, which could be accompanied by one more desperate and futile military attack on Iran and/or Venezuela or a forced confrontation with China and/or Russia. Desperate acts of declining military empires have historically accelerated the demise of imperial rulers.

Out of the debris of failed empires two possible outcomes could emerge: a new rabidly nationalist authoritarian regime, or the re-birth of a republic based on the reconstruction of a productive economy centered on the domestic market and social priorities, free from foreign entanglements and power configurations whose only purpose is to subordinate the republic to overseas colonial ambitions.

The dismantling of the military-driven empire will not occur 'by choice' but by imposed circumstances, including the incapacity of domestic institutions to continue to finance it. The demise of the militarist governing class will follow the collapse of their domestic economic foundations. The result could be a withered empire, or a democratic republic. When and how a new political leadership will emerge will depend on the nature of the social configurations that undertake the reconstruction of US society.

ENDNOTES

[1]   See Speech, Gov. Frederic S. Mishkin, "Exchange Rate Pass-Through and Monetary Policy," Board of Governors of the Federal Reserve System, March 7, 2008, <http://www.federalreserve.gov/newsevents/speech/mishkin20080307a.htm>

[2]   See David Barstow, "Behind TV Analysts, Pentagon's Hidden Hand," *The New York Times*, April 20, 2008, <http://www.nytimes.com/2008/04/20/washington/20generals.html?_r=1&oref=slogin>

CHAPTER 8

US MILITARISM AND THE EXPANDING ISRAELI AGENDA

Introduction

Never in recent history has US Middle East policy been subject to such a barrage of conflicting pressures from erstwhile allies, clients as well as adversaries. The points of contention involve fundamental issues of war and peace, foremost of which are divergent responses to the Palestinian-Israeli conflict, the US-Iranian confrontation, and the US occupation of Iraq as well as the US-Ethiopian proxy invasion and occupation of Somalia.

The major contenders for influence in the making of US policy in the Middle East include the 'war party' led by the Zionist Power Configuration, its followers in Congress, and its allies among the civilian militarists in the White House led by Vice President Cheney, Secretary of State Rice, and National Security Adviser for Middle East Affairs Elliot Abrams, along with an army of scribes in the major print media. On the other side are a small minority of Congress-people, ex-officials linked to Big Oil, a divided peace movement, the Arab Gulf States, Saudi Arabia, and a number of European countries on specific sets of issues.

To date the Zionist Power Configuration (ZPC) has consistently lined up its Congressional and White House backers and steamrollered domestic opposition in securing unconditional US backing for Israel's position in the Middle East. One of the latest instances illustrating the Zionist Power Configuration's political and media influence is their dismissal of a major document on human and civil rights in Israel issued by the United Nations' Committee on the Elimination of Racial Discrimination (published March 9,

2007). Compiled by two dozen experts, the study offered 19 recommenda-tions for Israel to comply with in 25 areas of racial discrimination against Arab citizens of Israel.[1]   Israel rejected the report, the ZPC automatically followed suit, as did Washington.

Nevertheless there are signs (weak to be sure) that the visible and invisible power of the ZPC is being subjected to critical public scrutiny and even 'put on trial' among US clients. The Council of Gulf Cooperation is made up of conservative, pro-US regimes, housing US military bases, linked to the largest US oil and financial houses. Composed of Kuwait, Qatar, Oman, Saudi Arabia, Bahrein and the United Arab Emirates, the Council members are also the world's biggest oil suppliers (over 40%), and, along with Egypt, among the biggest purchasers of military hardware from the US military-industrial complex. The Council met in late March 2007, and called for the US to engage Iran diplomatically, and not militarily or with economic sanctions. Israel took a diametrically opposing view, pushing for tighter sanctions and a military confrontation. Automatically the ZPC in the United States echoed the Israeli Party line.[2] Congress and Bush ignored Big Oil, the military-industrial complex and its Arab clients, and followed the Zionist line: they escalated sanctions, increased commando operations, added to the warships off the coast of Iran and offered to send fighter-planes into Iran after British sailors, engaged in espionage, were captured (Blair, for once, rejected the war provocation). Once again the ZPC out-muscled Big Oil and the military-industrial complex in dictating US Middle East policy.

Equally important, the US foremost Arab 'allies' in the Middle East have promulgated a series of proposals and policy options, which are directly opposed to the ZPC-Israeli agenda. Saudi Arabia's proposal approved by the Arab League, offering Israel recognition and normal relations in exchange for abiding by UN resolutions and returning territory seized in 1967 is one example. These Arab initiatives have elicited a positive response from many governments in the European Union and Turkey, adding to the forces arraigned against the ZPC/Israeli-promoted direction for US Middle East policy. Defectors from the Israeli lobby's cause have been especially noticeable from among conservatives, including Robert Novak.[3]

New Directions for US Policy: A Moderate Arab Agenda?

The primary preoccupation of the moderate Arab regimes of the Persian Gulf is securing political stability, avoiding disruptive regional and internal conflicts and consolidating a favorable business climate for the dynamic development projects they have undertaken. The US military invasion, occupation and prolonged violent imperial war in Iraq have been a source of instability and internal conflict in the region. Israel's repeated military assaults and violent seizures of Palestinian land, its invasion of

Lebanon and threats against Iran and, most important, its political vehicle—the ZPC's capacity to ensure US backing—have created an environment of permanent 'high tension'. The growing incompatibility between the conservative/business-oriented goals of the moderate Arab states and the 'radical militarist' destabilizing policies of Washington and Tel Aviv has forced a widening breach between the long-time allies and clients. With large trade surpluses and enormous liquidity in dollars and Euros, the Arab East is intent on building economic empires both in the region and throughout the globe. For that they need, above all, a secure 'home base', serving as the headquarters and operating base to sustain the global financial, commercial and real estate networks.

The recent meeting of Arab states in Riyadh, convoked by the Saudis, served as a platform for outlining a program for Middle East stability and the ending of violent destabilizing activities. Both in their formal proposals and informal pronouncements the conservative leaders put forth an agenda to re-direct US Middle East policy away from the ZPC-Israel line of military confrontation and toward diplomatic negotiations, elite reconciliation and the strengthening of regional economic stability. Within this conservative regional frameworks, with the high priority given to economic stability, the 'new facts' on the ground (namely the critical position toward the US and the peace offer to Israel) become key markers in defining Middle East politics.

'New Facts' and the New Middle East Realities

The old clichés lobbed by liberal critics of the Gulf States and Saudi Arabia are highly misleading and fail to capture the new economic and political dynamics of the region. The liberal and Zionist images of reactionary sheiks engaged in conspicuous consumption, luxuriating in their backward and stagnant economies, living exclusively on 'rents' accruing from the gushing oil wells and dependent on US military protection, have largely been superseded. All the Gulf States and Saudi Arabia are heavily engaged in long-term, large-scale economic diversification projects, creating new businesses; financial, commercial and real estate markets based on local capital; and, in some cases, major overseas investment banks. Major joint industrial ventures in energy, refineries, and chemical plants between Saudi Arabia and China and India have been consummated. Multi-billionaire 'princes' are major investors and part owners of global networks of financial enterprises, hotels, ports and other large-scale infrastructure and construction sectors.

Energy wealth from gas and petroleum is the *point of departure* for the new Arab ruling elites, who are reinventing themselves as regional if not global players. While still retaining many of the 'external traditional religious forms' (opposition to usury), vast armies of local financiers have in fact invented financial instruments that pay de facto returns equivalent to interest. Given the growing global and regional economic interests of these conservative elites, they have everything to lose by following US-Israeli destructive-colonial-militarist policies in the region.

Economic diversification and dynamic internal development have created a new bourgeoisie in the Gulf linked to European and Asian capital (state and private), increasingly politically independent from the US and less dependent on 'external' military power. These new economic facts provide clues to the new 'political facts' on the ground, including Saudi Arabia's low key, but forthright, critique of the US occupation of Iraq and demands for troop withdrawal. The Gulf States' backing for the Saudi-initiated "Mecca Agreements" leading to the PLO-Hamas unity government, explicitly went against the White House-Israeli-Zionist policy of isolating Hamas, as did the explicit rejection by Saudi Arabia and the Emirates of US and Israeli war preparations against Iran. They have rejected Washington's and Israeli-Zionist's policy of refusing to meet with Iran by holding separate top level meetings and discussions. The Arab League's offer to Israel—authored and authorized by Saudi Arabia—of peace and recognition of Israel as a state in the region by all Arab states[4] in exchange for Israel's withdrawal from the 1967 regions of occupied Palestine has exposed Israel's pretexts for continued colonization and annexation of Palestinian land and US subordination to the Zionist Power Configuration. This was only the latest in a long succession of opportunities to end the so-called "existential threat" that Israel has snubbed.

The new economic and political facts in the Middle East pit an increasingly *militarized* US foreign policy elite, heavily influenced by the Zionist Power Configuration, against an increasingly *marketized* Arab Gulf elite. Israel's *military industries* (which are central to its economy),[5] the *political* leverage of the settler parties, religious fundamentalists and security apparatus, and the Israeli state's dependence on multi-billion dollar handouts from the US treasury and wealthy Jewish militarist donors, mean that Israel is *structurally incapable* of coming to any peace for land agreement. The re-settlement of a half-million armed fanatical Jewish settlers into pre-1967 Israel, the peaceful re-conversion of Israel's military industries, and the maintenance of support from overseas Zionist plutocrats without the rhetoric of 'existential military threats' are beyond the boundaries of the Israeli political class as it is currently constituted. The deep integration and subordination of the Zionist Power Configuration to the Israeli power structure therefore in actuality results in the demands of Israel's settler-military-industrial complex getting transmitted into the US Congress and Executive, and eventually into US policy.

Insofar as this is the case, the ZPC is responsible for the rigidities of US Middle East policy expressed in its fixation on permanent warfare, and its blindness to the yawning gap between market-driven Arab states and US-Israeli militarism. The ZPC accounts for the unchanging, unconditional support for an anachronistic colonial regime in a time of growing global market relations. The paralysis of US policy is the result of the power of a modern 21st century, extraordinarily wealthy and entrepreneurial lobby[6] acting on behalf of fundamentalist—and mythic[7]—Judaic territorial claims going back to a period almost 2500 years ago. The notion of 'combined and uneven development' certainly applies to Israel's biggest overseas financiers.

The rigid structural parameters of Israeli politics are transmitted via the ZPC into the basic contradictory reality in US-Israeli relations: the rigid structural politics of a tiny 'isolated, militarized, settler-controlled' state blocking economic transactions of a globalized imperial economy by forcing it into disastrous military adventures.

The Iraq War: A Success for Israel

Contrary to many war critics, especially those daring enough to attack the pro-war, neoconservative and Zionist lobby, the US invasion of Iraq has not been a 'disaster', a 'debacle' or a 'defeat'. The corollary of this argument—that the 'Iraq disaster' has led to a 'rout' of the Zion-Cons from the Bush Administration—is also open to question.

The principle goal of the ZPC was the overthrow of Saddam Hussein, the destruction of the Iraqi state (especially its military and intelligence apparatus) and its societal infrastructure in order to permanently eliminate a key backer of the Palestinian resistance to Israeli ethnic cleansing, a staunch focus for secular Arab nationalism in the Middle East and a strong challenger to Israel's attempt to assert hegemony in the region. The Zion-Con-orchestrated war succeeded in each and every one of Israel's strategic objectives. The Palestinian resistance lost a powerful financial and political backer. The Middle East opposition to Israel was reduced largely to clerical Muslim states and movements. The stage was set for a new sequence of wars with Israeli adversaries, including Hezbollah, Hamas, Syria and, most important, Iran.

As a consequence of the US destruction of the Iraqi state, Israel had a free hand in invading and devastating Palestine, especially Gaza, in completing its ghetto wall isolating Palestinian towns and villages from their markets and everyday activities,[8] and in extending its colonial settlements. US Zion-Cons in the Administration were able to scuttle any serious peace negotiations, using their scripted 'war against terror' as a pretext. The departure of *some* of the Zion-Cons from the Administration in the aftermath of the US military occupation of Iraq was due to their having so successfully served Israeli strategic interests through securing a massive commitment of US economic and military resources against Israel's primary enemy. But as the Israel-serving war turned into an unpopular, prolonged and costly war for the United States, public and highly placed critics, investigators and military figures began to point their finger at the key role of the Zionist officials in the Government as the prime movers of the 'disastrous' war, the Zion-Cons 'resigned' from office. This short-circuited any wide-reaching and serious investigation into the inter-face between the US Zion-Con war architects and the Israeli Foreign Office and its military command.

Out of their successful 'war with Iraq' operation, the Zion-Cons suffered a few collateral losses. Paul Wolfowitz, Deputy Secretary of Defense and regarded as the primary architect of the war, swiftly departed for the World Bank, and from there to obscurity. Douglas Feith, Under-Secretary of Defense for Policy joined the faculty of the Edmund A. Walsh School of Foreign Service at Georgetown University. Press Secretary Ari Fleischer quit. Irving 'Scooter' Libby, Chief of Vice President Cheney's military planning office, was convicted on peripheral perjury charges, which did not directly implicate the Zion-Con network's role in the run-up and follow-through on the war. One major and one secondary AIPAC leader were indicted for spying for Israel. The two indicted spies, Steven Rosen and Keith Weiss, did not in any way materially or politically weaken AIPAC's powerful hold over the US Congress or White House. AIPAC continued to receive unconditional support from the US Congressional leaders of both parties, as well as from the Vice President and Secretary of State who gave keynote addresses at the AIPAC's annual conventions in 2006 and 2007, and from the three primary presidential candidates in 2008.

The fact that the ZPC considers the Iraq war a 'done deal' in enhancing Israel's Middle East position and has now moved on to pursuing Israel's next strategic objective, the destruction of Iran, has caused a visible rift with key officials in the White House who are still stuck in a losing war in Iraq.

Vice President Cheney, speaking at the AIPAC annual convention in 2007, directly challenged AIPAC leaders who seemed to be abandoning support for the Administration's Iraq war and pressing for more aggressive economic sanctions and the war option strategy toward Iran. The Zion-Cons seek to maximize support for their new phony 'existential' war against Iran among Jewish liberals who have turned against the Iraq war, thus leaving Cheney and Bush holding the US body bags. At the AIPAC convention, Cheney, no neophyte to backstabbing intrigues, offered to escalate US threats against Iran if the Zionists maintained their support for the Bush-Cheney-Rice war in Iraq. While Israeli Prime Minister Olmert formally reiterated the importance of the US continuing its occupation of Iraq for Israeli 'security', in practice all his ministers attending every major Zionist conference have instead emphasized to their US acolytes the Iranian threat and the need to eliminate the Iranian regime, its nuclear power plants and state structures. Despite the fact that the US is bleeding white from the open wounds of the current war in Iraq, despite the fact that over three quarters of the US population is fed up with US involvement in Middle Eastern wars, this has not prevented or, even more importantly, weakened the ZPC effort to set the US on a course toward new wars with the whole-hearted support of the majoritarian Democratic Party leadership.

With an eye toward campaign financial contributions, every single Democratic and Republican presidential candidate has pledged to unconditionally support Israeli interests, specific pledges to the ZPC-AIPAC included.

Democrats Capitulate to the Pro-Israel Lobby on Bush War Powers

The key factor in the Democrats' withdrawal of constraints governing Bush's management of the occupation of Iraq was the Jewish Lobby. According to the *Associated Press* "Conservative Democrats, as well as lawmakers concerned about the possible impact on Israel, had argued for the change in strategy..."[9] As the *Congressional Quarterly* noted: "Hawkish pro-Israel lawmakers are pushing to strike a provision slated for the war spending bill that would require the President to seek Congressional approval before launching any military force in Iran." On March 8, *CQ Today* added, "The influential American Israel Public Affairs Committee also is working to keep the language out, said an aide to a pro-Israel lawmaker."[10]

The Iran-related proposal stemmed from a desire by some leading Democratic politicians to ensure that Bush did not launch an attack without going to Congress for approval, a measure approved by the vast majority of Democratic rank and file. But during the week of March 5-10, the Zionist elite both in Congress and in the Lobby banged heads in a series of closed door sessions and literally forced the 'leading Democrats' to recant and capitulate. Echoing the Olmert line, one of several Zionist mouthpieces in Congress overtly spoke against constitutional and legislative restraints on President Bush because of its 'effect' on Israel. Representative Shelley Berkley said in an interview, "there is widespread fear in Israel about Iran which...has expressed unremitting hostility about the Jewish State." Democratic Caucus Chairman Rahm Emanuel, who works closely with AIPAC, 'predicted', "It would take away perhaps the most important negotiating tool that the US has when it comes to Iran".[11] He succeeded in excluding the amendment from the Supplemental War Budget Allocation, although it was initially favored by Speaker of the House Nancy Pelosi and Representative John Murtha, Chair of the Defense Appropriations Committee.

A smirking Vice President Cheney pointed out the hypocrisy of the pro-Israel liberal Democratic Congresspeople and liberal Zionists who opposed Bush on Iraq yet were pressing a pro-war policy on Iran. "It is simply not consistent for anyone [including pro-Israel liberals! JP] to demand aggressive action against the menace posed by the Iranian regime while at the same time acquiescing in a retreat from Iraq that would leave our worst enemies dramatically emboldened and Israel's best friend, the United States, dangerously weakened".[12] Once again the interests of Israel took precedence over the voting preferences of the Democratic electorate. Once more, the power of Congressman Rahm Emanuel and his fellow 'conservative' pro-Zionist congressional colleagues overpowered the 'conscience' of other leading Democrats. Once again, AIPAC freed Bush from any Constitutional and Congressional constraints to launch a military attack on Iran. Once again, Israel's bellicose policy dictates were effectively transmitted and implemented in the US Congress. The Democrats abandoned the war authority provision accorded to Congress under the Constitution. Israel once again demonstrated that it is the supreme arbiter of US Middle East war policy through its representatives in the US Congress. *(No wonder Buchanan and others call the Congress 'Israeli-occupied territory').*

Bush got AIPAC backing for his arbitrary war powers; Israel retained a President who is a willing accomplice to its war aims in the Middle East.

Israel-AIPAC-US Middle East Wars

The role of *Israel* in mobilizing the Zionist Lobby in favor of Bush's broad war powers was evident in Israeli Foreign Minister Tzipi Livni's forceful speech to the annual AIPAC conference in Washington in March 2007. According to the Israeli daily, *Haaretz*, Livni "warned the US not to show weakness in Iraq."[13] She went on to emphasize the importance of exercising violence and power… "in a region where impressions are important, countries must be careful not to demonstrate weakness and surrender to extremists." This is another way of stating the familiar Israeli canard that 'Arabs only understand force', a well-worn colonial-racist justification for widespread and continued repression of subjugated Arab people.

Livni instructed the thousands of cheering AIPAC loyalists and hundreds of US Congressional followers at the convention of the Iranian threat and incited them to escalate their attacks on Teheran: "Iran was at the forefront of extremist threats to Israel, the Greater Middle East and the world in general because of its nuclear ambitions. To address extremism is to address Iran, she said, urging tougher UN sanctions over its nuclear program".[14] Livni's closing words touched all the agit-prop code words that fire up the zealotry of the AIPAC leaders, followers and US Congresspeople. Iran, she stated, "is a regime which denies the Holocaust while threatening the world with a new one. To those states who know the threat but still hesitate because of narrow economic and political interests, let me say this: History will remember!"

Livni's speech served several purposes. It laid down the 'line' to pro-Israel loyalists in the US to continue supporting Bush-Cheney's policy on the Iraq war, independently of the sentiments of most American Jewish voters. It strengthened the hand of the Lobby and its US Congressional followers by forcing House liberals—Jews and Gentiles—to retract their American voter-mandated constraints on Bush's war powers. Thirdly it laid out the high priority agenda and campaign for its Zionist followers to pursue with regard to Iran. Finally, it ended any breach between Cheney-Bush and the Lobby over prioritizing a 'new' war against Iran over the 'old' unpopular war in Iraq by tying them together.

The Israeli Foreign Minister's direct intervention in the internal politics of the US, her blatant support for the Bush-Cheney war, and attack on the US public's anti-war sentiments, is reminiscent of the worst diplomatic intrusions by the US in the banana republics of Central America. Not a single Congress member dared to point this out, let alone oppose Israeli interference in US politics for fear of retaliation by the aroused mass of 'Israel Firsters'. Not a single 'leftist' or 'progressive' commentator noted that Livni's attempt to universalize Israel's hostility to Iran was nothing but a demagogic ploy. Extensive opinion surveys in Europe found absolute majorities rating Israel the most threatening and 'negative' country in the world, exceeding Iran, North Korea and Syria.[15] The fact that Iran is a welcome participant in the World Congress of Islamic Countries representing over 500 million people is a slight omission in Livni's rhetorical excesses concerning its threat to "the world". These lapses are no cause for worry in the Israeli Foreign Office, because the propagation of deliberate and verifiable falsehoods is not a problem; the power of lies is a real politik necessity to *arouse to action* its US agents and to discourage any possible US critics. By sounding off on the 'Holocaust' and its corollary, 'History will remember', Israel was guaranteed the blind fanatical adherence of the ZPC to its bellicose war policies and the silence and capitulation of its ineffective Jewish liberal anti-war doubters. The Jewish-based 'AIPAC Alternative', especially the 'Jewish Voice for Peace', spends as much time denying the power of the pro-Israel Lobby as criticizing US policy.[16]

In an ironic and perverse twist of the pro-Israel, anti-war slogan, 'No War for Oil', Livni demanded 'No Peace for Oil'. Livni's warning to those "states who know the threat but still hesitate because of narrow economic or political interests" is a clear reference to the United States. More specifically it is aimed at politicians who might look toward peaceful negotiations with Iran, or accept the Saudi peace plan in order to safeguard US oil interests, rather than sacrificing these interests to serve Israel's political and military supremacy in the Middle East. Livni is clearly directing its 'Israel Firsters' in the US to trump the Oil Appeasers, to browbeat any politicians who raise US market concerns over Israeli and Zionist war demands.

While Livni's perception of the danger to Israel emanates from the peaceful-diplomatic approach of 'narrow [*sic*] economic or political interests' (to the even narrower Israeli concern for land grabs in Palestine and Lebanon), what passes as a US peace movement joins in chorus by blaming the oil industry for US Middle Eastern wars. There is a convenient coincidence of Israeli hawks and US doves in denouncing Big Oil, which is not such a coincidence if we remember that what passes for the US peace movement is inordinately influenced by prominent left Zionists, who combine criticism of 'Bush's war' with exclusion of any mention of Israel or criticism of the war mongering Zionist lobby. Before, during and after the AIPAC conference in Washington several thousand of its zealots blitzed the offices of Congress members and Senators. More than half the Congress members and practically every Senator were browbeaten in over 500 meetings in favor of Israel's war agenda against Iran.

Then, when in late March, 2007, the Arab League led by Saudi Arabia proposed a comprehensive peace plan to end the Israeli-Palestinian conflict, offering Arab recognition, trade and diplomatic relations, an end of the state of belligerency and economic sanctions, in exchange for Israel abiding by United Nations resolutions and withdrawing from all Palestinian lands seized during and after the 1967 war, the Israeli Prime Minister flatly refused to accept the Saudi proposal. It was, he argued, only the 'basis of negotiations'. The ZPC immediately echoed the Israeli party line, calling into question the form and substance of the proposal as well as attacking the Arab regimes. On March 29, 2007 alone, the organ of the Presidents of the Major American Jewish Organizations published four major propaganda pieces attacking the peace proposal and backing Israel's rejection. The Lobby ensured that the US Congress and executive either supported the Israeli position or refused to back the Saudi plan. Once again, AIPAC's 150 full time lobbyists ran circles around pro-Arab US oil multinationals.

Democratic House Majority Leader Serves as Israel's Messenger

Democratic House Majority leader Nance Pelosi's visit to Syria stirred a hostile response from the White House and accolades from liberals and progressives. Bush objected to Pelosi interfering with his foreign policy powers and 'non-negotiation' position *vis à vis* Syria. Liberals hailed Pelosi's visit as opening new vistas for 'diplomacy' rather than saber rattling. Both failed to recognize that Pelosi's main substantive task was to serve as a proxy and messenger for the Israeli state. During her visit to Israel, prior to going to Syria, the Israeli regime instructed Pelosi to pressure Syria to end support for Hamas, Hezbollah and Iran. The Israeli prime minister told his messenger, Pelosi, to relay to the Syrians that breaking ties and isolating itself from its only allies were the conditions for Israel opening negotiations. Up to Pelosi's visit to Syria, AIPAC and the entire Zionist political machine had vilified any Congress member who even mentioned visiting Syria. However when Israel gave the word that Pelosi was running Israeli messages to Syria, the Lobby did not object. The party line from Tel Aviv had shifted and the Israeli Fifth column automatically shifted its line: not one of its 'functionaries' raised a peep. There were far more overseas Communist dissenters when Stalin abruptly changed the party line than there are Zionist defectors under similar circumstances.

The almost comical back flips and ideological contortions which the 'Israel Firsters' engage in to conform to the zigzags of their Israeli handlers is evident in their treatment of the Arab Gulf states. For the longest time the IF did everything possible to discredit them, referring to them as decrepit, absolutist states, and debunking the State Department's characterization of them as 'Arab Moderates'. More recently when Olmert referred to the same states as 'moderate' largely because they engaged in covert trade with Israel through third parties, and criticized Iran, the Lobby then revised its line and spoke favorably of them. Then, when the Saudis brokered the Hamas-PLO unity government, Israel attacked the role of Saudi Arabia as backing the terrorist Hamas and the Zionist propaganda machine followed suit, labeling the Saudis as financiers of Hamas terrorism. The blind servility of the Israel Lobby to a 'foreign power' would simply be a matter for the Justice Department if it didn't have such a profound impact on US Middle East policy, where every Israeli change in policy is automatically reflected in US policy.

Buying Israeli Permission for Arms Sales to Saudi Arabia

With the US trade deficit exceeding $500 billion dollars, one of its few competitive export sectors is its arms industry, which is number one in world arms sales, followed by Israel in fourth place as of 2007, ahead of Great Britain. The Bush Administration's planned arms sale to Saudi Arabia and other Persian Gulf allies has been blocked by Israeli action through its Zionist Lobby.[17] The Administration officials twice scheduled and canceled briefings for members of the Senate Foreign Relations Committee because of AIPAC's influence over the Committee and the likelihood that the arms deal would be rejected. As a result the Administration accepted that Israel would call off its Lobby attack dogs in exchange for a 20% increase in US military aid and grants to Israel—upping the total of military aid from $2.4 billion dollars to $3 billion annually—only $1 billion less than total Israeli arms exports for 2007.[18] Secretary of Defense Gates, who was unable to shake the Lobby's influence over Congress, had to fly to Israel to plead with Israel to allow the sales to go through—in exchange for receiving more advanced US military technology.[19]

US grants to Israel of advanced military research, design and technology has increased Israel's competitive position in the world's military high-tech market, increasing its share at the expense of the US, as seen in Israel's recent $1.5 billion dollar military sales to India. In brief, the Israel Lobby runs circles around the US military-industrial complex in terms of influencing the US Congress, blocking lucrative deals and advancing Israel's sales in the world market.

Democratic Party Presidential Candidates Truckle to the Lobby

All major Democratic Party Presidential hopefuls have made an extraordinary effort to secure the Lobby's approval: all back Bush's 'military option' toward Iran; all support the annual $2.4 billion dollar foreign aid package to Israel, despite Israel's $30,000 per capita income and booming high tech industry.[20] Speaking before the National Jewish Democratic Council, New York Senator Hillary Clinton called on the US to confront Iran militarily.[21] Taking advantage of the fawning behavior of all the candidates, the Israeli newspaper, *Haaretz*, promoted a panel of Israeli 'experts' to evaluate US Presidential candidates on the basis of their servility to Israeli interests. This, in turn, led Senator Obama to send his latest, most crass and bellicose pronouncements regarding Iran to the Israeli panel.[22]

Nonetheless, it is Hillary Clinton who leads the pack in securing Jewish campaign financing. The Lobby's high regard for Clinton is not merely because of her total and complete identification with Israel—as stated at the March 2007 AIPAC Convention—but by the family's notorious track record. Former CIA Director George Tenet, in his latest book, *At the Center of the Storm*, devotes an entire chapter to then President Bill Clinton's proposal to free American-Israeli master-spy, Jonathan Pollard, from federal prison. Under prodding from Israel's far right-wing president, Benyamin Netanyahu, the Zion-lib Sandy Berger, his National Security Advisor, Dennis Ross, Zion-Con envoy to the Middle East and a substantial sector of the Lobby, Clinton proposed to release the convicted spy Pollard. According to his book, Tenet told Clinton that he would resign because he would lose all his moral capital with the entire intelligence apparatus, which would argue that an American traitor was being rewarded. More likely, the entire military and intelligence community was outraged that Clinton would follow the policies laid out by the Israeli spymasters and their US lobbyists over American national security concerns.

Clinton later broke precedent in granting a pardon to a fugitive criminal, the billionaire swindler Marc Rich, now a citizen of Israel and close friend of the Lobby and Israeli leaders. Hillary Clinton has demonstrated that she and Bill not only speak, but also act, for the primacy of Israeli interests even when it involves going against the entire US security community and its legal system. That sordid history must count a lot in securing guarantees that the Clintons are bona fide 100% Israel camp followers, something none of the other candidates can boast.

In early May 2007, the Bush Administration proposed an 8-month timetable of steps meant to bolster prospects for peace between Israel and Palestine. The proposal simply asked Israel to allow Palestinians normal but urgent bus and truck travel between Gaza and the West Bank in exchange for Palestinians curbing the homemade cross border rocket firings. As was predictable, the Israelis objected to even the slightest breach in the oppressive ghettoization of the Palestinians.[23] Israeli leaders rejected a timetable because it prevented them from procrastinating: Israeli military officers opposed any loosening of their stranglehold on Gaza for "security reasons".[24] They maintained that Hamas might increase its influence in the West Bank through persuasion. Once the Israeli military rejected the Bush initiative, the Zionist Power Configuration went to work. The Democrats, including all their leading Presidential candidates and Congressional leaders, refused to back Bush's anemic effort to open the Gaza ghetto. The mass media followed suit. The pro-Israel lobby buried the entire proposal before it even entered into public debate.

The Lobby Versus Federal Prosecutors: The AIPAC Spy Trial

On August 4, 2005 two AIPAC leaders and a Pentagon analyst, Larry Franklin, were indicted by a federal grand jury and charged with spying for Israel. The indictment lists numerous acts of espionage dating back to 1999 in which the two AIPAC leaders acted as conduits for classified information flowing from Washington to Tel Aviv. Franklin has confessed and cooperated with the FBI in recording his meeting with Rosen and Weissman regarding the passing of a high security White House document related to US policy on Iran to Israeli Embassy agents. Faced with overwhelming evidence, AIPAC 'fired' Rosen and Weiss, stopped paying for their legal expenses and initially denied any responsibility for the pair.

Subsequently, however, AIPAC and numerous satellite and auxiliary organizations decided to turn the spy trial into a campaign over 'free speech'. Accordingly the liberal and conservative members of the pro-Israel lobby succeeded in rounding up a 'Who's Who' of otherwise leftist journalists, progressive news broadcasters and academics in defense of Rosen and Weissman. Speaking in defense of the two AIPAC functionaries, Pulitzer Prize winning journalist, Dorothy Rabinowitz, argued in the editorial pages of the *Wall Street Journal* that handing high security government documents to Israeli Embassy security agents are "activities that go on every day in Washington and that are clearly protected under the First Amendment".[25] Major pro-Israel organizations, billionaire Hollywood producers and most, if not all, of the Jewish press in the US have taken the defense of Rosen and Weissman. Except for a few internet bloggers, not a single political party, social or political movement has dared to criticize acts of handing over classified documents to Israel or to raise eyebrows over the equation of 'free speech' with spying for a foreign power. Because of the pervasive pressure of the Lobby, the Federal Judge, T.S. Ellis, has made several procedural rulings weakening the case of the prosecution. Once again the Zionist Power Configuration seems to have successfully out-muscled US institutions, in this case, federal prosecutors and the FBI.

AIPAC Trial Inadvertently "Outs" Israel's Strategic Informant in the White House

The spy trial of two top officials of AIPAC, who admitted to handing over strategic documents to Israeli diplomats, (and who have been defended on the basis of 'free speech' by a host of American progressive left Zionists) has turned up further evidence of their deep penetration of the highest echelons of the White House. In the preliminary hearings of the spy trial, defense attorney Abby Lowell, in an attempt to exonerate the Zionist spy suspects, announced that the accused received 'explosive' and even more volatile information from then National Security Adviser Condoleezza Rice.[26] There is little doubt that Rice's transmission of confidential security information to AIPAC was also handed over to the Israeli embassy and its undercover Mossad agents operating in Washington.

The Lobby spy network extends beyond confessed Pentagon spy, Laurence Franklin, who handed confidential documents to the accused AIPAC officials. According to the *Jewish Telegraph Agency* quoting Attorney Abby Lowell, "Rice had not merely been Rosen's interlocutor but had leaked information identical to and at times more sensitive than examples cited in the indictment." Lowell claimed that 'three other current and former Middle East policy officials, in addition to Rice" were providing information to the AIPAC accused Israeli spies.

In an unusual ruling, Rice and other administration officials were called to testify in the AIPAC trial.

> The ruling threatens to expose how officials used calculated leaks to the American Israel public affairs committee (AIPAC) to influence ideological infighting about the Middle East within the Bush administration ...
>
> Steve Rosen, the former foreign policy chief, and Keith Weissman, the organization's senior Iran analyst, argue that their conversations were in line with the administration's unofficial practice of using the lobby as a diplomatic back channel.
>
> Judge TS Ellis III granted lawyers for the two men wide latitude to question Ms Rice, the former national security adviser, Stephen Hadley, the deputy national security adviser and leading official on the Middle East, Elliot Abrams and other key officials.

"Defendants are entitled to show that, to them, there was simply no difference between the meetings for which they are not charged and those for which they are charged," Mr Ellis wrote.

"They believed that the meetings charged in the indictment were simply further examples of the government's use of AIPAC as a diplomatic back channel."[27]

In other words, the neo-cons in government (left arm) routinely used AIPAC (right arm) to help whip administration opponents to their Middle East policies into line. Hence AIPAC's indicted officials might escape spying charges because figures in the administration were actually giving them the information. Because they were doing so *all the time*, there was now no cause for concern...

Israel Pushes Islamo-Fascism Rhetoric

Racist rabble-rousing against Muslims runs rife among zealous Zionists inside the US Government and outside among mainstream pro-Israel organizations with no apparent reprimands. The Conference of Presidents of the Major Jewish Organizations (CPMJO) backed efforts by co-thinker and Israeli-US dual citizen Michael Chertoff (head of the Department of Homeland Security) to curtail Muslim visits to the US, including British citizens of what *The New York Times* diplomatically refers to as "of Pakistani origin".[28] In a follow-up lead article in the CPMJO news bulletin, the *Daily Alert* featured a xenophobic article by Josh Meyer and Erika Hayasaki titled, "Six Foreign-born 'Radical Islamists' Charged in Plot to Strike Fort Dix Army Base."[29] When pro-Israel zealots in high government positions engage in blatant racist witch-hunts against Muslims and respectable mainstream Zionist umbrella organizations publish inflammatory, xenophobic rhetoric, no Congress members or Justice Department officials call for public hearings or inquiries. Blatant and repeated hate rhetoric committed by prominent Jewish leaders and ideologues is neither investigated nor prosecuted, in contrast to the painting of a single swastika on a tombstone, which becomes the basis for a national hue and cry

Re-arming Clients: The Washington/ZPC War Machine Rolls On

The political-military setbacks inflicted on US-Israeli policy in the Middle East in 2006-2007 has not led to any moves toward serious diplomacy or negotiations. On the contrary, the solution proposed by Washington and Tel Aviv is to escalate the militarization of client groups and prepare for destructive civil and ethnic wars.

In Lebanon

In response to the failure of the US-backed Israeli attack on Lebanon to destroy Hezbollah, Washington has been engaged in a large-scale rearming of right-wing Christian, Druze and Sunni militias in Beirut and throughout North-Central Lebanon.[30] The purpose is to provoke an armed conflict with Hezbollah which will force it to move its resistance fighters northward and weaken its defense of the Southern Lebanese border. A US/Israeli-induced 'civil war' will, it is presumed, divide the Lebanese army and weaken any auxiliary role it might play in defending the country from Israeli cross border attacks or invasions. Given the widespread violence which could be presumed to result from a conflict, Israeli aircraft, now engaged in illegal daily over-flights and reconnaissance, would then be free to bomb and destroy any and all reconstruction and Hezbollah defenses.

In May 2008, the Washington- and Zionist-backed Siniora regime attempted to undermine Hezbollah security by closing its communication networks and purging a neutral general in charge of Beirut airport. Hezbollah's massive and prompt counter response—taking over the center of Beirut and major highways—forced the regime to retreat .The US-backed move backfired, increasing Hezbollah's power and undermining any new plans for another Israeli invasion.

In the Occupied Territories

Israeli-backed American arming of a Palestinian military force led by senior Fatah leader and longtime CIA collaborator, Mohammed Dahlen, working with 'President' Abbas, entailed the training of hundreds of officers in Jordan, pre-selected for political loyalty by Israeli and US officials. A heavily-armed force of 12,000 US-paid Palestinian mercenaries was prepared to oust Hamas from power, destroy its police and defense forces, hunt down its leaders, and intimidate its electoral supporters.

The Zionist lobby succeeded in inserting an extraordinary clause in Bush's military aid to the Abbas faction in the Palestinian government. Thereby, the lobby secured Israeli as well as US political screening of all Palestinian trainees before they were allowed to travel to Jordan for the US-funded training. In defense of the Jewish state's right to oversee the administration of US military aid, the Lobby argued that the clause was necessary because of Israeli 'fears'—in other words, Israeli interests in retaining Palestine as a colony policed by Israeli-screened Palestinian mercenaries.[31]

A Palestine destroyed by US-Israeli induced 'civil strife' would be in no position to negotiate any peace agreement that returns Israel to its pre-1967 borders. The idea was to establish a pro-US Palestinian-run police state within the territorial limits dictated by Israel. Washington's subsequent effort to prop up the failed puppet Abbas regime within the West Bank via the

Annapolis "peace talks" while forcing the Palestinians in Gaza to starve in the dark has been a total failure.

Israel keeps expanding settlements, and dispossessing Palestinians. Several hundred noncombatant Palestinians have been killed in the seven months that followed. In contrast, Hamas' support increases in the West Bank despite savage repression by Abbas police and Israeli military forces. During Bush's speech to the Israeli Knesset celebrating the destruction of Palestine and the "founding" of Israel, he made no mention of Palestine, treating Abbas like a used condom.

In Iraq

The third area of militarization involves Northern Iraq where the US and Israel have financed the Kurdish military build-up. They politically support Kurdish separatists who for all intents and purposes operate as an independent state. According to Laura Rozen's article, "Kurdistan: Covert Back Channels",[32] the US and Israel support a willing Kurdish client in the plot to break up Iraq, impoverish Baghdad as its capital and set up Irbil as their capital. In June 2004, US top official Paul Bremer transferred $1.4 billion US dollars from Iraq's oil for food funds to the Kurds. Israeli 'counter-terrorist' training given to Kurdish security forces is used by Kurdish death squads under US direction in Northern Iraq and elsewhere. Seymour Hersh, writing in *The New Yorker* (June 2004), stated that Israeli-trained Kurdish commandos infiltrate Iran and Syria. According to Rozen, Eliezer Geizi Tsafrir, the Mossad station chief in Irbil, the 'capital' of Iraqi Kurdistan, set up a Kurdish intelligence service for the warlord Mustafa Barzani. He is better known as the 'rent-a-Kurd' mercenary leader, who has served the US CIA, the former Shah of Iran and whoever else could pay him. The Kurds provide the bulk of what General David Petraeus has called 'reliable Iraqi troops' collaborating with the US colonial occupation forces. They have been active in infiltrating Iraqi resistance groups and fomenting ethnic-religious strife. They are responsible for the massive forced eviction of Iraqi Arabs, Turkomen and Assyrian Christians from Kirkuk and other multi-ethnic towns and cities in the north, and repopulating them with Kurds. The Kurdish leaders in Northern Iraq have provided bases and arms for pro-US armed groups operating in Iran, Syria and Turkey, although the latter is without formal US approval. The Kurds serve as commandos and guides for US Special Forces engaged in assassination missions in Iran. The Kurds based in Northern Iraq are instructed to incite 'separatist' regional movements in Iran. With strong backing from the US, the Kurds seized control of the rich oil wells in Kirkuk and surrounding areas, signed oil contracts with European and US oil companies, de facto privatizing Iraqi public enterprises, though in January 2008 the Iraqi Oil Ministry rolled that back:

> An official spokesman for the Iraqi Ministry of oil, Aasem Jihad, said in statements to VOI on Friday that the ministry had invited foreign corporations to invest in the oil field in all Iraqi provinces, including those in the Kurdistan region and in Kirkuk, but excluded the companies that have signed contracts with the region without a prior approval from the ministry.
>
> The region had signed 15 contracts with 20 foreign oil corporations despite the central government's objection and ahead of the Iraqi parliament's final endorsement of a new draft law on oil.[33]

Insofar as the Iraqi parliament has not yet signed off on the privatization of Iraqi oil, the issue is still pending.

The Kurds are scheduled to play a vital role in the US-Israeli strategy of breaking up Iraq into a multiplicity of mini-client entities divided by sectarian ethnic-religious identities with no influence in the region and incapable of ousting long-term US military bases in the country.

The consensus in both Sunni and Shia circles appears to be that attempts to emphasize Sunni-Shia rivalries are intended to deflect attention from both the US occupation of Iraq and continuing Israeli aggression. That the US is working to fuel such tensions is almost an article of faith for Muslims on both sides. In its attempt to create an anti-Iran alliance, they say, the US is resorting to a strategy which aims to raise the spectre of sectarianism across the Muslim world.

Even before Seymour Hersh blew the whistle in *The New Yorker* on Washington's role in fuelling Sunni-Shia tensions, leading Shia and Sunni figures had warned that the US was behind much of the sectarian violence in Iraq and Lebanon.

When, in an Al-Jazeera interview, prominent Shia leader Sayed Mohamed Hussein Fadlullah was asked who it was that is threatened by the Shia, he answered, simply, "Israel".[33]

In Somalia

In the Horn of Africa, the US armed and directed the Ethiopian client regime to restore the totally discredited 'Transitional Regime' to power in Mogadishu, killing over one thousand Somali civilians and displacing over 300,000 civilians during April-May 2007. With the advice of US Special Forces officers and Israeli counterinsurgency advisers, the Ethiopian mercenary armed forces caused over $1.5 billion dollars in destruction. Once again, US policy is directed at destroying an Islamic country as much as it is defeating a potential political adversary—the Islamic Court Councils. Certainly the policy of relying on the military might of a hated Ethiopian dictator to invade and occupy Somalia has no possibility of creating a viable client regime. Washington's quick resort to military escalation follows recent defeats and is preparatory to any forthcoming large-scale air war supplemented by mercenary ground attacks against Iran.

While one can debate whether the latest wave of US military escalation is the 'dying gasp' of a desperate empire, an irrational miscalculation by civilian militarists pursuing a military victory to bolster flagging domestic support or a continuation of long-standing imperial policies in the region, the fact remains that the principle domestic backer of the re-escalation strategy is the ZPC. No other organized political-economic force *consistently* supports *all* US military efforts in *each* of the zones of conflict. No other group backs US military action in countries where there is little or no oil. No other group totally ignores the 'overstretch' of the US military—the over-extension of US military forces in the Middle East and the Horn of Africa at the expense of providing military defense of other strategic imperial regions. Only the ZPC, of all theoretically possible influential 'interest groups' has put all countries—Islamic or secular—critical of Israel on the US's military hit-list.

Judeo-Centrism: From Ghetto Defense to Imperial Ambitions

One of the driving forces of the Zionist Power Configuration's accumulation of political power has been its ability to totally displace pre-existing non-Zionist and anti-Zionist organizations from influence in the Jewish community over the past 60 years. The formation of the ZPC resulted from the unification and centralization of a vast array of disparate groups and local community organizations around a single dominant political issue: unconditional and total support for a foreign power, Israel, with a kind of intolerant religious fervor which in the past burnt dissenters in public displays of piety and today hounds them from public office. In the past and in the recent period, there was a popular Yiddish saying in evaluating public policy: 'Is it good for the Jews?' This narrow, parochial viewpoint had special meaning at a time when Jews were a persecuted minority trying to maximize their security and minimize risks in relatively closed societies. In recent times, in certain New York intellectual circles, it became part of a jocular repertoire designed at one and the same time to recall an earlier identity, and to mock some of the overweening pretensions of new rich upstarts, especially real estate billionaires who displace and exploit low-income and minority tenants while making generous contributions to Israel.

But what was defensive and perhaps justified in an earlier era has become a deadly practice in the context of affluence, political power, and organizational cohesion. A Judeo-centric view of the world, which sees the embodiment of 'what's good for the Jews' as providing unconditional support to an aggressive colonial state (Israel), has become a formula for global disaster. In the new context where Jews represent almost a quarter of US billionaires and occupy high positions of government decision-making, the dominant Zionist discourse and practice has resulted not in defensive measures protecting a persecuted minority but offensive actions prejudicial to the American majority. In the case of Iraq, it has led to the deaths of over a million Iraqi civilians[25] and the displacement of many millions more. In the US it has resulted in milking the US taxpayers annually for well over $3 billion dollars to subsidize a Jewish-Israeli population with an annual per capita income of $30,000 and universal health care. In the US, the Judeo-centric narrative has led to the denial of Americans' democratic rights, our freedom to publicly and rationally discuss debate our Zionist problem: the ZPC's support for Israel's pursuit of Middle East dominance through American military power.

Judeo-centrism is not the ideology or practice of the great majority of US Jews, even less of a rising number of young, better-educated Jews who have no deep ideological ties to Israel. But Judeo-centrism is the perspective which guides the *organized, active minority driving the major Zionist organizations* and their billionaire camp followers. And it is always the organized, zealous and well-financed minority, which *assumes* that it has a 'legitimate' claim to speak 'for the community'—despite the protests of numerous unorganized Jewish intellectual critics, or those Jewish anti-Zionist organizations that the Jewish elite then disempowers.[26]

From 9/11 to the present, the pro-Israel power configuration has broadened its definition of 'the areas of interest for Israel', and thus the issues on which it will intervene, thus narrowing the parameters for discussion and policymaking in the US. By defining the *limits of action* that the US President and Congress can take on issues *relating to Israel*, the ZPC now influences US policies toward the entire Middle East. Today issues of war and peace, trade and investment agreements by US, European and Asian oil companies and banks in the Middle East, multi-billion dollar arms sales to Saudi Arabia are all subject to ZPC scrutiny and veto. The new 'broad definition' of what affects Israel includes Lobby backing for Bush's shredding of Constitutional restraints on his war powers. According to Zionist ideologues, unleashing presidential authoritarianism at the service of Israeli extremism is no vice.

The Lobby's concept of what 'relates to Israel'—its guiding light for intervening in US politics—has been stretched, along with Israel's expanding interests. During the 1940s to '50s, the main focus of the Lobby was to secure US diplomatic support for Israel's ethnic cleansing of Palestine. The Lobby's focus on areas of 'interest to Israel' extended to Israel's wars with Egypt and Syria in the 1960s and 1970s; to Lebanon and Iraq during the 1980s and 1990s; and to Iraq and Iran during the current decade. The extension of the Lobby's intervention in US Middle East politics mirrors

Israel's growing regional aspirations. But according to both Israel and its bucket carriers in the Lobby, it is not merely regional expansion which 'interests Israel' but economic and military aid and sales—namely who determines what military goods the US can sell to Arab states as well as what high end military technology the US should provide to the world's fourth biggest arms merchant—Israel (which is also the US's arms export competitor).

What 'relates to Israel' involves the Lobby in intervening and determining the US votes in the United Nations, what pressures it will exert on the European Union in the Security Council, and how the White House should react to peace proposals from its clients in the Gulf states. As Jeff Blankfort correctly points out: every US President starting with Richard Nixon[35] has attempted to pressure Israel to withdraw from land it occupied in 1967. And except for Jimmy Carter forcing Israel out of Sinai, Israel has successfully pressured the Israeli Lobby to mobilize the US Congress to end these presidential efforts. Today the 'Israel Firsters' do not have to 'mobilize the Democratic Congress' nor will they when the new administration takes over in 2009. They are all automatically pre-programmed to work for Israel; it's one of the conditions for running.

Where will it take us? When will it end?

ENDNOTES

[1]   See UN Doc CERD/C/ISR/CO/13, dated 9 March, 2007.

[2]   *Daily Alert*, March 26-30, 2007.

[3]   "US War in Iraq—The Sharon War", *Haaretz*, April 4, 2007).

[4]   First proposed by Crown Prince Abdullah in 2002, the initiative was put forward again most lately after endorsement at the Arab League Summit in 2007.

[5]   According to Pinchas Bicharis, Director-General of Israel's Defense Ministry, "Israel is in fourth place (in the world) in defense exports, above Britain." "UPI, "Analysis: Israel's Defense Exports Strong.", December 13, 2007.

[6]   Almost a quarter (24%) of *Forbes'* richest 400 are Jews.

[7]   See Uri Avnery, "The Lion and the Gazelle," transmitted to listserv on April 19, 2008. He writes: "Right from the beginning, when the "Jews" came back from Babylon, the Jewish community in this country was a minority among the Jews as a whole. Throughout the period of the "Second Temple", the majority of Jews lived abroad, in the areas known today as Iraq, Egypt, Libya, Syria, Cyprus, Italy, Spain and so on...The modern Jewish myth has it that almost all the Jews are descendents of the Jewish community that lived in Palestine 2000 years ago and was driven out by the Romans in the year 70 AD. That is, of course, baseless..."

[8]   The World Bank Report put unemployment in the occupied West Bank at 23%, and as high as 33% in the Gaza Strip, which has been under a punishing Israeli embargo since the Islamist Hamas movement seized power in June. See World Bank Report, December 17, 2007.

[9]   AP, March 13, 2007.

[10]   Cited by Rabbi Arthur Waskow, "AIPAC, Iran and Presidential War-making," *Huffington Post*, March 19, 2007.<http://www.huffingtonpost.com/rabbi-arthur-waskow/aipac-iran-presidenti_b_43814.html>

[11]   *Associated Press*, March 13, 2007.

12   *Ibid.*
13   *Haaretz,* March 12, 2007.
14   *Ibid.*
15   Conducted between Oct. 8 and 16, 2003 by Taylor Nelson Sofres/EOS Gallup of Europe, the poll found 59 percent of Europeans believe Israel represents the biggest obstacle to Mideast and world peace.
16   See *The Nation,* April 23, 2007, on the AIPAC Alternative.
17   *The New York Times*, April 5, 2007.
18   *Supra* endnote 5.
19   "Gates said he made clear that the United States would help Israel maintain its military advantage over its Arab neighbors, and urged Israel not to oppose the proposed sale, which the Bush administration sees as a way to counter Iran's growing strength" David S. Cloud, "Gates Reassures Israel about Arms Sale to Saudi Arabia," *International Herald Tribune*, April 29, 2007.
20   Due, perhaps, to the fact that, the foregoing and talk of a "booming Israeli economy" aside, the Israeli economy remains shaky and dependent on US and/or external support. The following article appeared in *Haaretz* on April 6, 2008: "*The Economist*, arguably the most important economic magazine in the world, has devoted a special section in this week's edition to the Israeli economy in honor of Israel's upcoming 60th birthday—and what is has to say is not all good, to put it mildly. Israel may have an astonishing economy despite having so many wars, writes the *Economist* in classic British understatement, but then continues to draw much less complimentary conclusions: The economic miracle and high growth is mostly based on a one-time opportunity in high tech, and the country is not prepared for the future... It further says "Israel's ability to capitalize on the internet boom was a lucky one-off." *Haaretz* Staff, "*Economist*: Israeli Economy Stable but has Shaky Foundation," April 6, 2008.
21   *Jerusalem Post*, April 26, 2007.
22   See Robert Kagan, "Obama the Interventionist", *Washington Post*, April 29, 2007.
23   *Daily Alert*, May 2, 2007.
24   *Daily Alert*, May 8, 2007.
25   *Wall Street Journal*, April 2, 2007.
26   *Jewish Telegraph Agency*, April 10, 2007.
27   Suzanne Goldberg, "Condoleezza Rice Forced to Testify in AIPAC's Lobbyist's Spy Trial," *Guardian*, November 3, 2007.
28   *The New York Times*, May 2, 2007.
29   *Daily Alert*, May 9, 2007.
30   *Guardian*, April 11, 2007.
31   Adam Entous, *Reuters News Service* quoted in the *Daily Alert*, March 29, 2007.
32   *Mother Jones*, April 12, 2007.
33   "The Shia-Sunni Divide: Myths and Reality by Omayma Abdel-Latif, *Al Ahram Weekly*, March 1-7, 2007, carried on Carnegie Endowment for International Peace website. These same lines appear in updated same-titled article by Abdel-Latif on Saturday, 02.23.2008, 12:32pm, <http://www.arabamericannews.com/news/index.php?mod=article&cat=ArabWorld&article=69>
34   "MP: Ministry's stance on Kurdistan's oil contracts politically motivated", Iraq Updates, <http://www.iraqupdates.com/p_articles.php/article/26070>
35   "Chomsky ignores or misinterprets the efforts made by every US president beginning with Richard Nixon to curb Israel's expansionism, halt its settlement building and to obtain its withdrawal from the Occupied Territories." Jeff Blankfort, "The Israel Lobby and the Left: Uneasy Questions," carried on numerous websites, including that of Russian-Israeli intellectual, Israel Shamir <http://www.israelshamir.net/friends/blankfort.html>

Part V

CHALLENGING THE LOBBY

CHAPTER 9

AMERICAN JEWS ON WAR AND PEACE
WHAT THE POLLS DO AND DON'T TELL US

*"It's no great secret why the Jewish agencies
continue to trumpet support for the discredited policies
of this failed administration. They see defense of Israel
as their number-one goal, trumping all other items
on the agenda. That single-mindedness binds them
ever closer to a White House that has made combating
Islamic terrorism its signature campaign. The campaign's
effects on the world have been catastrophic.
But that is no concern of the Jewish agencies."*
J.J. Goldberg, Editor
***Forward* (the leading Jewish weekly in the United States)**
December 8, 2006

Introduction

Once again, a poll recently released by the American Jewish Committee (AJC)[1] has confirmed that on *some* questions of major significance there are vast differences between the opinion of the Conference of Presidents of Major American Jewish Organizations and the mass of American Jews. On questions of the Iraq war, the escalation of US military forces in Iraq (the 'Surge') and military action against Iran, most Jewish Americans differ from the leaders of the major American Jewish organizations.

Most liberal, progressive or radical Jewish commentators have emphasized these differences to argue, *"most American Jews resoundingly reject the Middle East militarism and GOP foreign policy championed by right-wing Jewish factions."*[2] This progressive interpretation, however, avoids an even more fundamental question: How is it that a majority of US Jews who, according to the AJC poll (and several others going back over two decades) differ with the principal American Jewish organizations, have not or *do not* challenge the position of the dominant Jewish organizations, have virtually no impact on the US Congress, the Executive and the mass media in comparison to the Conference of Presidents of Major American Jewish Organizations?

The issue of the 'silent majority' is questionable since all Jewish and non-Jewish commentators point to the highly vocal and disproportionate rates of participation of American Jews in the political process, from electoral campaigns to civil society movements. Nor is it clear that the progressive majority lacks the high incomes of the reactionary 'minority'. There are some Jewish millionaires and even a few billionaires who hold views opposing the leadership of the major Jewish organizations. There are several probable explanations that account for the *power* of Jewish leaders in shaping US Middle East policy and the relative *impotence* of the majority of American Jews.

The Poll: A Re-Analysis

The poll results highlighted by progressive Jewish analysts point to the 59% to 31% majority of Jews disapproving the way the US is handling the 'campaign against terror." The problem with using the answers to this question to indicate progressive opinion is that a number of Zionist ideologues and their followers also oppose the 'handling of the campaign' because it is not sufficiently brutal, authoritarian and arbitrary, or—indeed—successful. Other findings cited include a 67% to 27% majority currently believing that the US should have stayed out of Iraq, and a 76% to 23% majority who believe the war is going 'somewhat' or 'very badly' in Iraq, which at this point is only common sense, and no indicator of approval or disapproval of the war itself, any more than the poll where a 68% to 30% majority believed that the 'surge' has either made things worse or has no impact.

However, perhaps more significantly, a large majority (57% to 35%) of American Jews oppose the United States launching a pre-emptive military attack against Iran, even if it were taken 'to prevent (Iran) from developing nuclear weapons." The progressive analysts then cite the polls finding that most American Jews are 'some shade of liberal' rather than 'conservative' (42% to 25%) and overwhelmingly identified as Democrats rather than Republicans by 58% to 15%. Most Jews believe that Democrats will make the 'right decisions' on the war in Iraq (61% to 21%). Finally, the progressives had very favorable views of the top three Democratic presidential candidates who seem to want to take the United States out of Iraq—despite their openness to attacking—even obliterating?—Iran.

On the surface, these polling results would suggest that American Jews would be at the cutting edge of the congressional anti-war movements, arousing their fellow Jews to join and resurrect the moribund peace movement in a manner reminiscent of '60s Jewish activism. Nothing of the sort has occurred.

One reason for the gap between the 'progressive' polling results and the actual pro-war behavior of the major American Jewish Organizations is found in several of the opinions *not* cited by progressive analysts but emphasized by the 52 leaders of the major communal organizations.[3] Over eighty percent (82%) of American Jews agree that 'the goal of the Arabs is not the return of occupied territories but rather the destruction of Israel'. Only 12% of Jews disagree. And 55% to 37% do not believe Israel and its Arab neighbors will settle their differences and live in peace. As it concerns a compromise on the key issue of Jerusalem, American Jews reject by 58% to 36% an Israeli compromise to insure a framework for permanent peace.

Given the high salience of being pro-Israel for the majority of American Jews and the fact that the source of their identity stems more from their loyalty to Israel than to the Talmud or religious beliefs, myths and rituals, then it is clear that both the 'progressive majority' of Jews and the reactionary minority who head up all the major American Jewish organizations have a fundamental point of *agreement* and *convergence*: support for and identity with Israel and its anti-Arab prejudices, its expansion, and the dispossession of Palestine. This overriding convergence allows the reactionary Presidents of the Major Jewish Organizations in America to speak for the Jewish community with virtually *no opposition* from the progressive majority either within or outside their organizations.

The Failure of Jewish Anti-Zionist Resistance

The following communication received by my editor from another Clarity Press author and dedicated anti-Zionist activist, Abraham (eibie) Weizfeld (*The End of Zionism and the Liberation of the Jewish People*), gives a clear indication of the difficulties faced by anti-Zionist Jewish activists. Reprinted here with permission, Weizfeld writes:

> Petras denounces the "progressive Jews" for subordinating themselves to the reactionary Jewish organizational leadership, as if this was wilful. Someone like Petras who is supposed to be researching his well-read articles should ask around at least as to what is happening in Jewish civil society. Does he not realize that the Likud right-wing Zionist faction is slowly but surely taking over all the Jewish communal institutions? Perhaps he did not read that the

Canadian Jewish Congress refused to accept the affiliation of the Alliance of Concerned Jewish Canadians? When I tried to speak at the CJC Plenary for the ACJC, the CEO threatened to have me thrown out, in front of all. This is what one normally calls a dictatorship. Petras considers it consensus! To break through into the public agenda, the Jewish opposition must be recognized for what it is, and not more; a major body of opinion now organized since a number of years that is blocked from the media, in academia and from the Jewish community organizations exclusively controlled by Zionists. This blockade is perpetuated not only by the Zionist activists and the Christian fundamentalists, together with the public that disguises its Judaeophobia with loyalty to Israel, but also by a number of Palestinian supporters who resort to Jewish bashing as if it were their personal test of loyalty... The March Alliance of Concerned Jewish conference in Toronto saw 23 groups attend in addition to ACJC members. With their subsequent affiliation, we are now 2000 organized activists...

Sadly, it nonetheless remains the case that the majority of Jews can be *objectively regarded* as having failed to mount a resistance challenging the elites as their spokespeople—however diligently individuals among them may have tried—and likely mostly for the reasons cited above. Rather, by raising the Israeli flag, repeating clichés about the 'existential threat' to Israel at each and every convenient moment, they have bowed their heads and acquiesced or, worse, subordinated their *other 'progressive' opinions* to actively backing their leaders' 'identity' with Israel. Pro-Zionists' seizure of the role of recognized Jewish spokespeople intimidates and/or forces progressive Jews to publicly abide to the line that 'Israel [*sic*] knows what is best for Israel' and by extension, for all American Jews who identify with Israel.

Israeli Anti-Arab/Muslim Racism

A second important factor in undermining progressive American Jewish activity against US-Israeli war policy in the Middle East (Lebanon, Iran, Iraq and Palestine) is the influence of Israeli public opinion. A *Haaretz* report documents a civil rights poll showing that *'Israel has reached new heights of racism...'*,[4] citing a 26% rise in anti-Arab incidents.[5] The report cites the *doubling* of the number of Jews expressing feelings of hatred to Arabs. Fifty percent of Israeli Jews oppose equal rights for their Arab compatriots. According to a Haifa University study, 74% of Jewish youth in Israel think that Arabs are *'unclean'*.[6]

Progressive American Jews, identifying with a racist colonial state, face a dilemma: whether to act against their primary identity in favor of their progressive opinions, or to back Israel and submit to its American franchise holders and recognized leaders in the Israel Lobby.

Given these issues, a serious analyst clearly must distinguish between 'opinions' and 'commitment'. While a majority of American Jews may voice private progressive opinions, their commitments (and indeed, in all likelihood, their circles of family and friends, and even employment or professional relationships) are based on their identity as Jews, which in turn has been successfully linked to the State of Israel and from there, back to its principal mouthpieces in the US.

This probably explains the unwillingness of progressive Jews to *criticize* the principal reactionary Jewish leaders and their mass organizations, and even worse, their willingness to attack and slander any critics of the pro-Israel power configuration. Progressive Jews have subordinated their progressive opinions to their loyalty and identity with Israel. Organizationally this has meant that the majority of major American Jewish organizations are still led and controlled by pro-war, pro-Israel leaders. Progressive Jewish organizations are on the fringe of the organizational map, with virtually no influence in the Congress or Presidency and are backers of a pro-war Democratic Party and Congress.

Progressive analysts who cite overwhelming Jewish support for the Democratic Party, its top three Presidential candidates and their preference for the liberal label as differentiating them from the leaders of the major organizations, commit an elementary logical and substantive fallacy. Liberals, like the Clintons, supported the wars against Iraq and are among the driving forces promoting a military attack on Iran. The Democratic majority in Congress has backed every military appropriation demanded by the Republicans and the White House. Being Democrat and 'liberal' is no indicator of being 'progressive' using any foreign policy indicator, from the Middle East wars to destabilizations efforts in Venezuela, let alone in relation to Israel. The apparent paradox of progressive anti-war Jews contributing big bucks to pro-war Democrats is based on the latter's unconditional support for Israel which trumps any 'dissonance' that might exist in the head of progressive Jewish political activists.

As the American Pro-Israel Power Configuration led the way to savaging the National Intelligence Estimate study released in December 2007 on the absence of an Iranian nuclear weapons program, Jewish opinion was silent or complicit.

The Role of American Jews in the Peace Movement

Worse still, progressive liberal and radical Jewish peace activists have acted as gate-keepers in the anti-war movement—prohibiting any criticism of Israel and labeling individuals or citizen activists critical of the pro-war Zionist lobby as 'anti-Semites'.

As a November 1, 2005 op-ed in *The Jerusalem Post* put it:

> A great amount of nonsense has recently been written about the efforts of some Jews in the US to establish a parallel organization to AIPAC. These "unrepresentative left-wing American Jewish groups" have been accused of being anti-Zionist, of undermining the State of Israel, even of treason. Nonsense.
>
> I had a chance of meeting some of these so-called traitors during a visit I made last week to the US. They are imbued with a feeling of concern for what is happening in Israel. As one of the most vocal and active members of the group put it, "Our uppermost worry is for the security of Israel. If we do establish a new organization, it will be by definition pro-Israel, conscious of Israel's security above all else. It will be bipartisan, centrist."
>
> They do not see a new organization as being a rival to AIPAC. On the contrary, they see it as a broadening of Israel's message. "We need another organization to broaden the political debate," I was told, "to broaden what can be said and what can't be said, to broaden the scope of being a friend of Israel."[7]

ENDNOTES

[1] See <http://www.ajc.org/site/c.1J1TSPHKoG/b.36428551>

[2] Glen Greenwald, "New Poll Reveals How Unrepresentative Neo-Con Jewish Groups Are", on salon.com, December 12, 2007.

[3] *Daily Alert*, December 13, 2007.

[4] *Haaretz*, December 9, 2007.

[5] Association for Civil Rights in Israel Annual Report for 2007.

[6] See http://www.israel-academia-monitor.com/index.php?type=large_advic &advice_id=4668&page_data%5Bid%5D=172&cookie_lang=en&the_session_id= 443a80a463e8f6b665e3856d53ea129f&PHPSESSID=c03dc9db85b29df61a 211f37f5544b3f

[7] See David Kimche, "Soros a Zionist? That would be Great", *Jerusalem Post*, November 1, 2006. Interestingly, the *Jerusalem Post* now has menu tabs immediately under the masthead which include "Iranian Threat":

Home Headlines Iranian Threat Jewish World Opinion Business Real Estate Local

CHAPTER 10

WHY CONDEMNING ISRAEL AND THE ZIONIST LOBBY IS SO IMPORTANT

Introduction

Many writers, including those who are somewhat critical of Israel, have raised pointed questions about our critique of the Zionist power configuration (ZPC) in the United States and what they wrongly claim to be our harsh singling out of the state of Israel. Some of these accusers claim to see signs of 'latent anti-Semitism' in the critique; others, of a more 'leftist' coloration, deny the influential role of the ZPC, arguing that US foreign policy is a product of 'geo-politics or the interests of big oil'. With the recent publication of several widely circulated texts highly critical of the power of the Zionist 'lobby', several liberal pro-Israel publicists have conceded that it is a topic that should be debated (and not automatically stigmatized and dismissed), and should perhaps even be 'taken into account.'

ZPC Deniers: Phony Arguments for Fake Claims

The main claims of ZPC deniers take several tacks:

1.   *The ZPC is just 'another lobby'* like the Chamber of Commerce, the Sierra Club or the Society for the Protection of Goldfish.

2.   *There are equally violent abuses by rulers, regimes and states elsewhere.* By focusing mainly on Israel and by inference on the 'Lobby', the critics of Zionism and of the power of its supporters in the United States discriminate against both Israel

and Jews. In contradistinction, they propose that human rights advocates should condemn all human rights abusers everywhere.

3.   *'Exclusive focus' on Israel reveals a latent or overt anti-Semitism.*

4.   *Israel is a democracy*—at least outside of the Occupied Territories (OT)— *"the only democracy in the region"*, and therefore not as condemnable as other human rights violators and should be 'credited' for its civic virtues along with its human rights failings.

5.   *Because of the Holocaust and the history of persecution suffered by Jews*, criticism of Jewish-funded and led pro-Israel lobbies should be handled with great sensitivity.

6.   *Any discussion of Israel/Palestine should be "balanced"*. Only specific abuses should be addressed, after investigating all charges—especially those from Arab/Palestinian/United Nations/European/Human Rights sources—and in the framework of recognizing that Israeli public opinion, the press and even the Courts or sectors of them may also be critical of regime policies.

These objections to treating the Israeli-Palestinian-Arab conflict and the activities of Zionist Lobbies as *central to peace and war in our time* serve to dilute, dissipate and deflate criticism and organized political activity directed at the ZPC and its directors in Israel. But in point of fact, as will be elaborated further, below:

1.   There is no lobby in America remotely equal to the Israel Lobby in its influence over a gamut of US policy decisions.

2.   The reason for primary concern with Israel over other human rights abusers has to do with the centrality, through its influence on the policies of the world's sole superpower, of its impact on global issues of war and peace, as well as its impact on the well-being of the United States, itself.

3.   The accusation of anti-Semitism is an adhominem argument, seeking to deflect reasoned discussion by the application of a feared epithet.

4.   Israel's democratic credentials are tarnished by its refusal to permit Palestinian democracy. And other states in the region

do hold democratic elections, or would do, if puppet regimes were not held in place by the US to ensure state support of Israel.

5.   Many populations have suffered dreadful calamities and ongoing discrimination, not least American Indians, who endured genocide and continental dispossession. The Jewish tragedy in Germany has been exploited to excuse the victimization of another people who did not cause it.[1]

6.   The issue of imbalance in representation should be viewed within the wider framework of balance in representation overall, where coverage of the Israel-Palestine issue is in fact overwhelmingly favorable to Israel, as internet websites and listservs of pro-Palestinian activists face off against pro-Israeli major wire service, print and television networks.

The Careful Crafting of Critiques of Israel /ZPC

The response of the critics of Israel and the ZPC to these attacks has been weak at best and circuitous and circumscribed at worst. Critiques are couched in such provisos as:

- their criticism is only directed toward a specific policy or leader, or to Israeli policies in the OT and that they recognize Israel is a democracy, that it requires secure borders, and that it is in the interests of the Israeli 'people' to lower their security barriers;

- their criticism is directed at securing Israeli interests, influencing the Zionist Lobby or to opening a debate;

- the views of 'most' Jews' in the US are not represented by the 52 organizations that make up the Conference of Presidents of the Major Jewish Organizations of America, or the thousands of PACs, local federations, professional associations and weekly publications which *speak with one voice as unconditional supporters* of every twist and turn in the policy of the Zionist State.

The fact that those who offer even the mildest criticism of Israel/ZPC feel compelled to couch their criticism in protestations of loyalty to the interests of Israel is in itself an indication of the power of the ZPC and the dangers posed by making even the mildest criticism—which caution has availed them nothing, as has been borne out by the vitriolic response to the very measured criticism of the Lobby's most prominent critics, Mearsheimer and Walt, and former president, Jimmy Carter—as is the notion that this mild criticism merited, as Chomsky put it before going on to attack Mearsheimer and Walt, recognition as "a courageous stand, which merits praise".[2] What other special interests/issues are there, in the United States at least, where the courage it takes to address them has been so widely (and deservedly) recognized? What M/W did, did take courage. They were not, after all, revolutionaries who had already placed themselves in certain alignments. They were right in the center, with a lot to lose.

That critics of Israel or domestic Zionist influence also seek to absolve American Jews as a whole by placing the blame on their elites in the US and in Israel reflects a natural, correct, and indeed legally normative human aversion to placing collective blame on masses of people rather than on specific perpetrators. However, it remains the case that the masses of American Jews will not be spared a stigmatism related to actions by their elites, any more than were white South Africans—or indeed Americans in relation to Iraq—*if it cannot be seen* that they have made substantial efforts to try to change the policies of their elites.

There are numerous similarly circumscribed lines of criticism of Israel, which basically avoid the fundamental issues raised by the Israeli state and the ZPC. But these fundamental issues cannot be avoided. The primary reason that criticism and action directed against Israel and the ZPC are of central importance today in any discussion of US foreign policy— especially (but not exclusively) of Middle East policy and US domestic policymaking—is that *they play a decisive role and have a world-historic impact on the present and future of world peace and social justice*. We turn now to examine the 'big questions' facing Americans as a result of the power of Israel in the United States.

The ZPC Lobbies For War

Critical study of the lead up to the US invasion of Iraq; US involvement in providing arms to Israel (cluster bombs, two-ton bunker buster bombs and satellite surveillance intelligence) prior to, during and after Israel's abortive invasion of Lebanon; Washington's backing of the starvation blockade of the Palestinian people; and the White House and Congress' demands for sanctions and war against Iran reveals that they are all directly linked to Israeli state policy and its Zionist policymakers in the Executive branch and US Congress. One needs to look no further than the documents, testimony and reports of AIPAC and the Conference of Presidents of Major American Jewish Organizations proclaiming their success in authoring legislation, providing (falsified) intelligence, engaging in espionage (AIPAC) and turning documents over to Israeli intelligence (an act now dubbed 'free speech' by liberal Zionist apologists in an effort to exonerate the AIPAC officials concerned).

If, as the overwhelming evidence indicates,[3] the ZPC has played a major role in the major wars of the early 21st century that are capable of igniting new armed conflicts, then it ill behooves us to dilute the role of the Zionist/Jewish Lobby in promoting future US wars. Given Israel's militarist-theocratic approach to territorial aggrandizement and its announced plans for future wars with Iran and Syria, and given the fact that the ZPC acts as an unquestioning and highly disciplined transmission belt for the Israeli state, then US citizens opposed to present and future US engagement in Middle East wars must confront the ZPC and its Israeli mentors. Moreover, given the extended links among the Islamic nations, the Israel/ZPC proposed 'new wars' with Iran will result, not just in the alienation of one quarter of the world's population (Muslims), but also in the increased possibility of global wars. Hence what is at stake in confronting the ZPC are questions which go beyond the Israeli-Palestinian peace process, or even regional Middle East conflicts: it involves the big question of World Peace or War.

"Democratic" Israel Diminishes Democracy in the United States

Without the bluster and public hearings of former Senator Joseph McCarthy, the Jewish Lobby has systematically undermined the principal pillars of our fragile democracy. While the US Congress, media, academics, retired military and public figures are free to criticize the President, any criticism of Israel, much less the Jewish Lobby, is met with vicious attacks in all the op-ed pages of major newspapers by an army of pro-Israeli 'expert' propagandists, with accompanying demands for firings, purges and expulsions of the critics from their positions or denial of promotions or new appointments. In the face of any prominent critic calling into question the Lobby's role in shaping US policy to suit Israel's interests, the entire apparatus (from local Jewish federations, AIPAC, the Conference of Presidents of Major American Jewish Organizations, etc) goes into action—smearing, insulting and stigmatizing the critics as 'anti-Semites'. By denying free speech and public debate through campaigns of calumny and real and threatened repercussions, the Jewish Lobby has denied Americans one of their more basic freedoms and constitutional rights.

The massive, sustained and well-financed hate campaigns directed at any Congressional candidate critical of Israel effectively eliminates free speech among the political elite.[4] The overwhelming influence of wealthy Jewish contributors to both parties—but especially the Democrats—results in the effective screening out of any candidate who might question any part of the Lobby's Israel agenda. The takeover of Democratic campaign finance by two ultra-Zionist zealots, Senator Charles Schumer and Israeli-American Congressman Rahm Emanuel ensured that every candidate was totally subordinated to the Lobby's unconditional support of Israel. The result is that there is no Congressional debate over, let alone investigation of, the key role of prominent Zionists in the Pentagon involved in fabricating reports on Iraq's 'weapons of mass destruction', and in designing and executing the war and the disastrous occupation policy.

The Lobby's ideologues posing as Middle East 'experts' dominate the op-ed and editorial pages of all the major newspapers (*Wall Street Journal, New York Times, Los Angeles Times, Washington Post*). In their pose as Middle East experts, they propagandize the Israeli line on the major television networks (CBS, NBC,ABC, Fox, and CNN) and their radio affiliates. The Lobby has played a prominent role in supporting and implementing highly repressive legislation like the Patriot Act and the Military Commissions Act as well as modifying anti-corruption legislation to allow the Lobby to finance Congressional 'educational' junkets to Israel. The head of Homeland Security with its over 150,000 functionaries and multi-billion dollar budget is none other than Zionist fanatic, Michael Chertoff, head persecutor of Islamic charity organizations, Palestinian relief organizations and other ethnic Middle Eastern or Muslim constituencies in the US, which potentially might challenge the Lobby's pro-Israel agenda.

The biggest threat to democracy in its fullest sense of the word—the right to debate, to elect, to legislate free of coercion—is found in the organized efforts of the Zionist lobby to repress public debate, control candidate selection and campaigning, and direct repressive legislation and security agencies against electoral constituencies opposing the Lobby's agenda for Israel. No other lobby or political action group has as much sustained and direct influence over the political process—including the media, Congressional debate and voting, candidate selection and financing, Congressional allocation of foreign aid and Middle East agendas as do the organized Zionist Power Configuration (ZPC) and its indirect spokespeople heading key Congressional positions.

A first step toward reversing the erosion of our democratic freedoms is recognizing and publicly exposing the ZPC's nefarious organizational and financial activities and moving forward toward neutralizing their efforts.

Israeli Interests Trump US Interests

Intimately and directly related to the loss of democratic freedoms and a direct consequence of the Jewish Lobby's influence over the political process is the making of US Middle East policy and who benefits from it—or indeed, who suffers from it. The entire political effort of the Lobby (its spending, ethnic baiting, censorship and travel junkets) is directed toward controlling US foreign policy, and through US power, to influencing the policy of US allies, clients and adversaries in Europe, Asia and the Middle East.

The Lobby's systematic curtailment of our democratic freedoms is intimately related to our own inability to influence our nation's foreign policy. Our majoritarian position against the Iraq War, the repudiation of the main executioner of the War (the White House) and our horror in the face of the Israeli invasion of Lebanon and destruction of Gaza are totally neutralized by Zionist influence over Congressional and White House policymakers. The recently victorious Congressional Democrats repudiate their electorate to follow the advice and dictates of the pro-Zionist leadership (Nancy Pelosi, Harry Reid, Rahm Emmanuel, Stephan Israel and others) by backing an escalation of troops and an increase in military spending for the war in Iraq. Bush follows the war policy against Iran proposed by the zealous Zionist fanatics in the American Enterprise Institute, repudiating the diplomatic proposals of the bi-partisan Baker Commission. Congress quadruples US arms stored in Israel (supposedly for dual use) in the aftermath of Israel's bombing of Southern Lebanon with one million anti-personnel bomblets from cluster bombs in direct defiance of US electoral opinion. While hundreds of millions of undernourished women and children suffer and die in Africa, Latin America and Asia, the Lobby ensures that over half of US foreign aid goes to Israeli Jews with per capita incomes of over $30,000 USD.

No other organized political action group or public relations firm acting on behalf of the Cuban and Venezuelan exiles or Arab, African, Chinese or European Union states comes remotely near the influence of the Zionist lobby in shaping US policy to serve the interest of Israel.

While the Lobby speaks for less than 2% of the US electorate, its influence on foreign policy far exceeds the great majority who have neither comparable organizational or financial muscle to impose their views.

Never in the history of the US republic or empire has a powerful but tiny minority been able to wield so much influence by using our nation's military and economic power and diplomatic arm-twisting in the service of a foreign government. Neither the Francophiles during the American Revolution, the Anglophiles in the Civil War, nor the German Bund in the run-up to World War Two, nor the (anti-China) Nationalist Taiwan Lobby possessed the organizational power and sustained political influence that the ZPC exerts on US foreign and domestic policy at the service of the State of Israel.

And what have been the ramifications for the US of subservience to Israeli interests?

1. The US has become engaged in wars in which nearly 1.5 million Iraqis and 4100 US soldiers have been killed, with 300,000 injured

2. This has cost US taxpayers US$1 trillion plus $US120 billion up to now plus 30 billion over the next 10 years.

3. It has led to the alienation of nearly 2 billion Arabs and Muslims.

4. It has destabilized the Middle East and the world oil market resulting in record prices, in turn undermining the US economy and further impoverishing hundreds of millions of the world's poor.

5. By supporting Israel, we have strengthened and encouraged the Zionists to tighten their stranglehold over US political and economic institutions.

6. Our support for a colonial militaristic Israel reinforces militaristic and authoritarian political leaders in the US— leading to the loss of our constitutional freedoms.

7. Supporting Israel can lead to the equivalent of 11 holocausts, as reflected in Hillary Clinton's willingness *to obliterate* 70 million-Iranians to defend Israel.

8. Supporting Israel encourages racist doctrines of chosen peoples and superior races—and breeds racial dispossession. This tends to create caste enclaves and the maintenance of class privileges.

9. Supporting Israel creates diasporas who act as fifth columns within their respective countries militating for its interests over national citizen needs, impacting in turn their domestic and foreign policies in a manner similar to that which has occurred in the United States.

Social Opposition and Political Impotence

Everywhere I visit from Copenhagen to Istanbul, Patagonia to Mexico City, journalists and academics, trade unionists and businesspeople, as well as ordinary citizens, inevitably ask me why the US public has tolerated the killing of over a million Iraqis over the last two decades, and thousands of Afghans since 2001?

Why, they ask, is a public, which opinion polls reveal as over sixty percent in favor of withdrawing US troops from Iraq, so politically impotent?

A journalist from a leading business journal in India asked me what is preventing the US government from ending its aggression against Iran, if almost all of the world's major oil companies, including US multinationals, are eager to strike oil deals with Teheran? Anti-war advocates in Europe, Asia and Latin America ask me at large public forums: what has happened to the US peace movement in the face of the consensus between the Republican White House and the Democratic Party-dominated Congress to continue funding the slaughter of Iraqis, and supporting Israeli starvation, killing and occupation of Palestine and destruction of Lebanon?

What Happened to the Peace Movement?

Just prior to the US invasion of Iraq in March 2003, over one million US citizens demonstrated against the war. Since then there have been few and smaller protests even as the slaughter of Iraqis escalates, US casualties mount and a new war with Iran looms on the horizon. The demise of the peace movement is largely the result of the major peace organizations' decision to shift from independent social mobilizations to electoral politics, namely channeling activists into working for the election of Democratic candidates—most of whom have supported the war. The rationale offered by these 'peace leaders' was that, once elected, the Democrats would respond to the anti-war voters who put them in office. Of course practical experience and history should have taught the peace movement otherwise: the Democrats in Congress have voted in favor of every military budget since the US invaded Iraq and Afghanistan. The total capitulation of the newly elected Democratic majority has had a major demoralizing effect on the disoriented peace activists and has discredited many of its leaders.

Absence of a National Movement

As David Brooks correctly reported at the US Social Forum,[5] there is no coherent national social movement in the US. Instead we have a collection of fragmented 'identity groups,' each embedded in narrow sets of (identity) interests, and totally incapable of building a national movement against the war. The proliferation of these sectarian 'non-governmental' 'identity' 'groups' is based on their structure, financing and leadership. Many depend on private foundations and public agencies for their financing, which precludes them from taking overtly political positions. At best they operate as 'lobbies' simply pressuring the elite politicians of both parties. Their leaders depend on their organization's maintaining a separate existence in order to ensure their salaries and secure future advances in government agencies.

The US trade unions are virtually non-existent in more than half of the United States: they represent less than 9% of the private sector and 12% of the total labor force. Most national, regional and citywide trade union officials receive salaries comparable to senior business executives: between $300,000 to $500,000 dollars a year. Almost 90% of the top trade union bureaucrats finance and support pro-war Democrats and have supported Bush and the Congressional war budgets, bought Israel Bonds ($25 billion dollars) and the slaughter of Palestinians and the Israeli bombing of Lebanon.

No Naming and Shaming for the Israel War Lobby

The US is the only country in the world where the peace movement is unwilling to recognize and publicly condemn or oppose the major influential political and social institutions consistently supporting and promoting the US wars in the Middle East. The political power of the pro-Israel power configuration, led by the American Israel Political Affairs Committee (AIPAC), supported within the government by highly placed pro-Israel Congressional leaders and White House and Pentagon officials, has been well documented in books and articles by leading journalists, scholars and former President Jimmy Carter—as has its role in applying the use of American military power against Iraq and calling for its use against Iran.

Despite the massive and sustained pro-war activity of the leading Zionist organizations inside and outside of the government and despite the absence of any overt or covert pro-war campaign by 'Big Oil', the leaders of the US peace movement have refused to attack the pro-Israel war lobby and continue to mouth unfounded clichés about the role of 'Big Oil' in the Middle East conflicts.

The apparently 'radical' slogans against the oil industry by some leading intellectual critics of the war has served as a 'cover' to avoid the much more challenging task of taking on the powerful, Zionist lobby. There are several reasons for the failure of the leaders of the peace movement to confront the militant Zionist lobby. One is fear of the powerful propaganda and smear campaign which the pro-Israel lobby is expert at mounting, with its aggressive accusations of 'anti-Semitism' and its capacity to blacklist critics, leading to job loss, career destruction, public abuse and death threats. The second reason that peace leaders fail to criticize the leading pro-war lobby is because of the influence pro-Israel 'progressives' still hold in the movement. These progressives condition their support of 'peace in Iraq' only if the movement does not criticize the pro-war Israel lobby in and outside the US government, the role of Israel as a belligerent partner to the US in Lebanon, Palestine and Kurdish Northern Iraq. A peace movement claiming to be in favor of peace, which refuses to name and confront the main proponents of war, and cannot squarely face the root cause of the US's wars in the Middle East—the Israeli dispossession and oppression of the Palestinian people—cannot get a firm grip on its own issue. Rather, deflecting attention from the role of Israel, and the pro-Israel high officials in the government and the lobbyists in Congress who back the war and set the White House's Middle East agenda is among its central concerns. By focusing attention exclusively on President Bush (and indeed, on his impeachment), the peace leaders diverted public attention from the complicity of the mid-term newly-elected majority pro-Israel Democratic congress people who fund Bush's war, back his escalation of troops and give unconditional support to Israel's military option for Iran—to say nothing of the Presidential candidates who are uniformly bellicose on Iran, and are never challenged on it.

The collapse of the US peace movement, the lack of credibility of many of its leaders and the demoralization of many activists can be traced to strategic political failures: the unwillingness to identify and confront the real pro-war movements and the inability to create a political alternative to the bellicose Democratic Party. The political failure of the leaders of the peace movement is all the more dramatic in the face of the large majority of passive Americans who oppose the war, most of whom did not display their flags this Fourth of July and are not led in tow by either the pro-Israel lobby or their intellectual apologists within progressive circles.

The word to anti-war critics of the world is that over sixty percent of the US public opposes the war but our streets are empty because our peace movement leaders succumbed to the Democratic primaries frenzy, and increasingly failed to hold candidates to account not just for Iraq, but for their views on Iran.

Why Confronting the Lobby Matters

The question of the power of the Lobby over US policies of war or peace, internal authoritarianism or democracy and over who defines the interests served by US foreign policy obviously go far beyond the politics of the Middle East, the Israeli-colonial land grabs in Palestine and even the savage occupation of Iraq. The playing out of Zionist influence over the greatest military power in the world, with the most far-reaching set of client states, military bases, deadly weapons and decisive voice in international bodies (IMF/World Bank/United Nations Security Council) means that the Lobby has a means to leverage its reach in most regions of the world. This leverage power extends over a range of issues, from defending the fortunes of murderous Russian-Jewish gangster oligarchs, to bludgeoning European allies of the US, to complicity with Israel's ethnic cleansing of Palestine.

The ZPC represents a basic threat to our existence as a sovereign state and our ability to influence whom we elect and what agendas and interests our representatives will pursue. Even worse, by serving Israeli interests, we are becoming not just complicit with but imitative of a State whose Supreme Court legalizes political assassinations across national boundaries, torture, systematic violations of international law including collective punishment,[6] and a regime which repudiates United Nations resolutions and unilaterally invades and bombs its neighbors and practices military colonist expansionism. In a word Israel resonates with and feeds into the most retrograde tendencies and brutal practices of contemporary American politics. In this sense the Lobby through its media, Congressional influence and think tanks is creating an Israeli look-alike. Like Israel, the US has established its own Pentagon assassination teams; like Israel, it invades and colonizes Iraq; like Israel, it violates and rejects any constitutional or international legal restraints and systematically tortures accused but untried prisoners.

Because of these fundamental considerations, we cannot oblige our Jewish 'progressive' colleagues and compatriots by refraining from confronting the Zionist Lobby with force and urgency. Too many of our freedoms are at stake; too little time is left before the ZPC/Israel succeed in securing a greater military escalation; too little of American sovereignty remains in the face of the concerted effort by the Lobby and its Middle Eastern 'expert-ideologues' to push and shove us into a new and more devastating war with Iran at the behest of Israel's pursuit of Middle East dominance.

No other country, abuser of human rights or not, with or without electoral systems, has the influence over our domestic and foreign policy as does the state of Israel. No other Lobby has the kind of financial power and organizational reach as the Jewish Lobby in eroding our domestic political freedoms or our war-making powers. For those primary reasons, Americans need to put our fight against Israel and its Lobby at the very top of our political agenda. It is not because Israel has the worst human rights record in the world—other states have even worse democratic credentials and have directly unleashed mayhem on larger numbers of people. We must fight the Israel Lobby *not only* because of its role in degrading our democratic principles, robbing us of our freedom to debate and our sovereignty to decide our own interests, *not only* because it pushes the United States into actions which threaten its own physical, economic and military infrastructure, but because, when the Lobby puts the military and budgetary resources of the Empire at the service of Greater Israel— *that* results in uncontainable humanitarian calamities whose ramifications impact the entire world.

Democratic, just and peaceful responses to the Big Questions that face Americans, Europeans, Muslims, Jews and other peoples of the world passes through the defeat and dismantlement of the Israeli-directed Zionist Power Configuration in America. Nothing less will allow us to engage in an open debate on the alternatives to repression at home and imperialism abroad.

ENDNOTES

[1]   See Norman G. Finkelstein, *The Holocaust Industry: Reflections on the Exploitation of Jewish Suffering*, Verso, 2003.

2   Noam Chomsky, "The Israel Lobby?" ZNet, March 28, 2006.

3   See Chapter 1 hereto, as well as James Petras, *The Power of Israel in the United States*, and *Rulers and Ruled in the US Empire: Bankers, Zionists, Militants*, both published by Clarity Press, Inc. in 2006 and 2007 respectively.

4   Witness, inter alia, AIPAC's capacity to unseat Congressman Earl Hilliard, Congresswoman Cynthia McKinney, and Congressman Paul Findley.

5   *La Jornada* July 2, 2007.

6   See, most lately, Israeli High Court decision authorizing fuel and electricity cuts to Gaza (HCJ 9132/07, issued January 30, 2008.

INDEX